THE HEALTHY MEAL PREP COOKBOOK

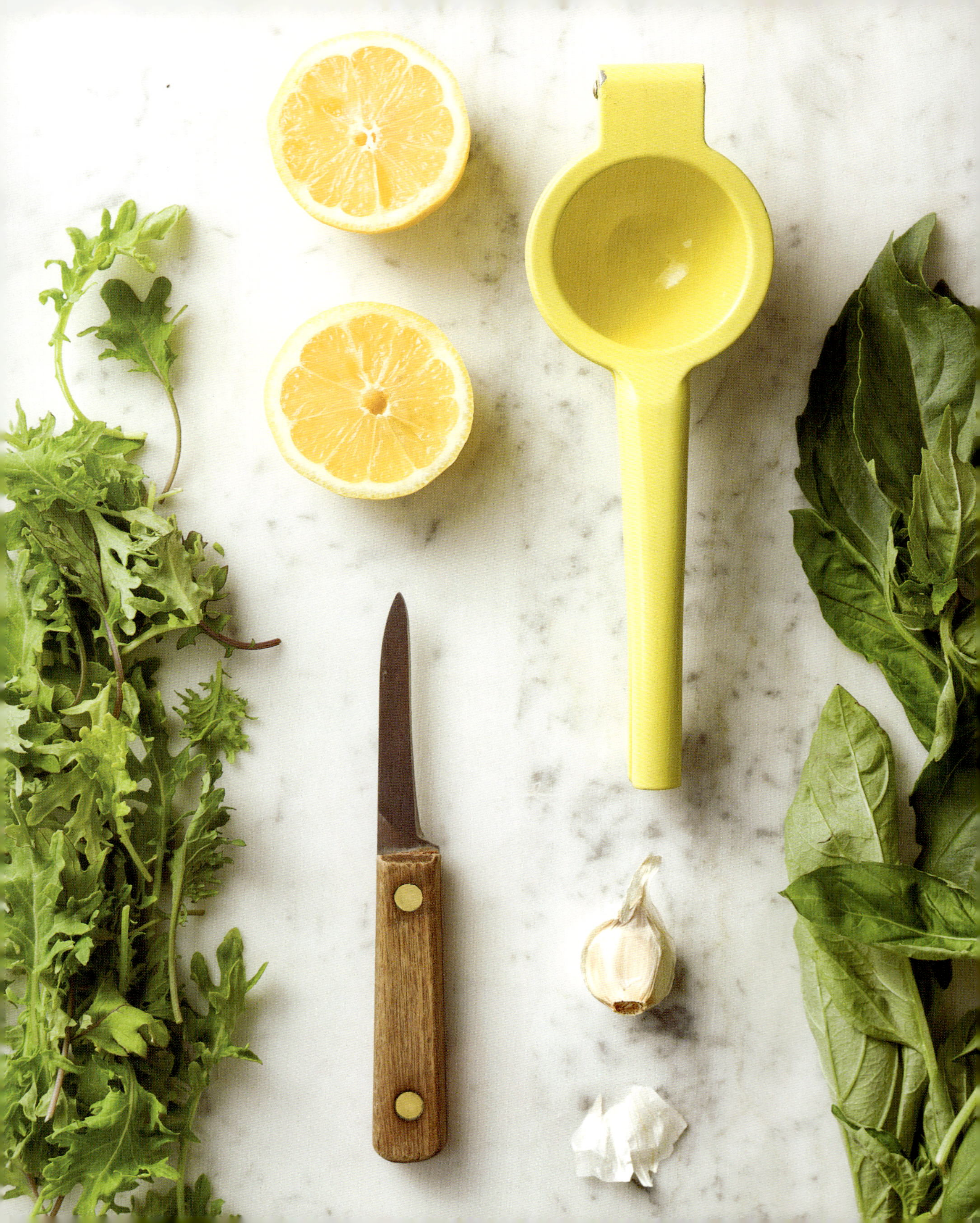

The Healthy MEAL PREP Cookbook

EASY AND WHOLESOME MEALS
TO COOK, PREP, GRAB, AND GO

Toby Amidor, RD, CDN

R
ROCKRIDGE
PRESS

Copyright © 2017 by Toby Amidor

No part of this publication may be reproduced, stored in a retrieval system or transmitted in any form or by any means, electronic, mechanical, photocopying, recording, scanning or otherwise, except as permitted under Sections 107 or 108 of the 1976 United States Copyright Act, without the prior written permission of the Publisher. Requests to the Publisher for permission should be addressed to the Permissions Department, Rockridge Press, 918 Parker St, Suite A-12, Berkeley, CA 94710.

Limit of Liability/Disclaimer of Warranty: The Publisher and the author make no representations or warranties with respect to the accuracy or completeness of the contents of this work and specifically disclaim all warranties, including without limitation warranties of fitness for a particular purpose. No warranty may be created or extended by sales or promotional materials. The advice and strategies contained herein may not be suitable for every situation. This work is sold with the understanding that the publisher is not engaged in rendering medical, legal or other professional advice or services. If professional assistance is required, the services of a competent professional person should be sought. Neither the Publisher nor the author shall be liable for damages arising herefrom. The fact that an individual, organization or website is referred to in this work as a citation and/or potential source of further information does not mean that the author or the Publisher endorses the information the individual, organization or website may provide or recommendations they/it may make. Further, readers should be aware that Internet websites listed in this work may have changed or disappeared between when this work was written and when it is read.

For general information on our other products and services or to obtain technical support, please contact our Customer Care Department within the U.S. at (866) 744-2665, or outside the U.S. at (510) 253-0500.

Rockridge Press publishes its books in a variety of electronic and print formats. Some content that appears in print may not be available in electronic books, and vice versa.

All photography © Nat & Cody Gantz except page 29: © Lumina/Stocksy

TRADEMARKS: Rockridge Press and the Rockridge Press logo are trademarks or registered trademarks of Callisto Media Inc. and/or its affiliates, in the United States and other countries, and may not be used without written permission. All other trademarks are the property of their respective owners. Rockridge Press is not associated with any product or vendor mentioned in this book.

ISBN: Print 978-1-64152-432-2 | eBook 978-1-62315-945-0
Printed in China

To my children,
Schoen, Ellena,
and Micah.

Thank you for bringing
laughter, happiness, and
love into my life.

I love you.

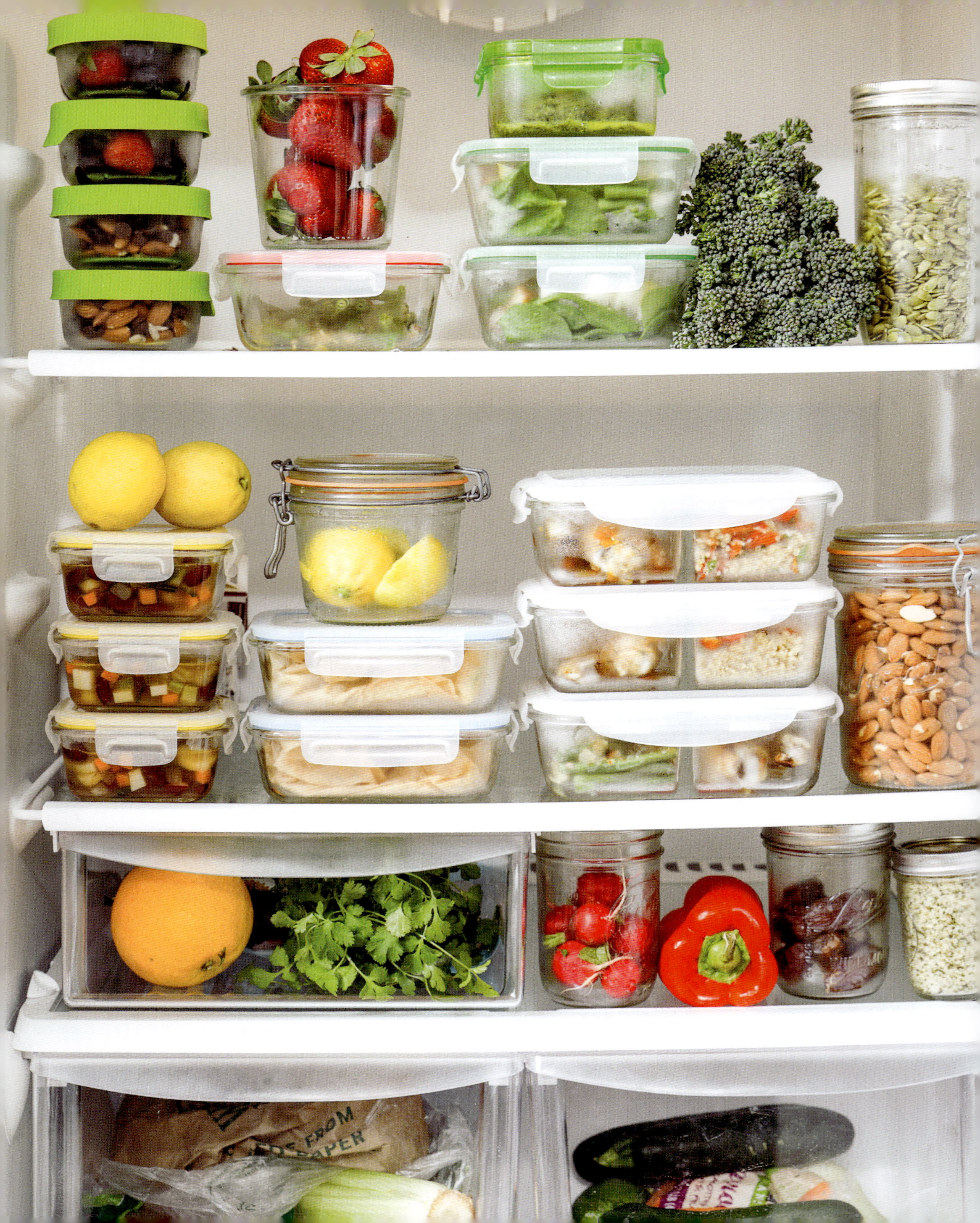

Contents

Introduction 8

1. MEAL PREP 101 11
2. MEAL PLANS 33
3. BREAKFAST 69
4. GRAINS & BEANS 95
5. SALADS & VEGETABLES 109
6. FISH & SEAFOOD 131
7. POULTRY 145
8. MEAT 167
9. READY-TO-GO SNACKS 187
10. SAUCES, DRESSINGS & STAPLES 205

Conversion Tables 219

Recipe Index 220   Index 222

Introduction

When I was about 16, I visited my grandmother just before she left for Israel to see her sisters. Every time she traveled, she enlisted me to help care for my grandfather. Over their 50 years of marriage, she cooked every meal for him. So when she traveled, she did what any loving wife would do—she prepared a month's worth of meals, packaged them in individual containers, and froze them. When my grandmother opened the freezer to show me the results of her cooking labor, she explained what was in the stacks of the individual containers all ready to be reheated. That's the first time I realized that, with proper planning and a little organization, delicious recipes can be prepared ahead of time.

Now as a single, working mom of three, I want to make sure my kids have healthy, delicious food for every meal. Even as a registered dietitian specializing in culinary nutrition, it's no easy feat!

One of the healthy habits I am most proud of is that my family eats a homemade breakfast each morning. How is that possible? I organize myself every week so I have all the necessary ingredients stocked. I prep as much in advance as possible. For meals I plan to make in the morning, I set pantry ingredients on the counter the night before. Whether I've made overnight oats or muffins in advance, or whip up a quick scrambled egg wrap to be eaten on the go, my kids never skip breakfast, which tells me that I've instilled in them the healthy habit of being lifelong breakfast eaters.

In this cookbook, I share with you all my tips—labeled Toby's Tip—for getting your meal prep done so that you can eat healthy each day. These are tricks that have worked for me over the years, and I share them in the hopes that they work for you. One of my favorite tips is to hang a shopping list so anyone in the house can add a needed item. Some weeks I do get "CHOCOLATE" or "ICE CREAM" written in all caps on the list, but as a mom I make the call as to when it's appropriate to bring sweets and treats into the house. Overall, however, the ongoing shopping list helps keep tabs on everything I need so I don't have to remember everything right before heading to the market or, even worse, when I am at the market.

Throughout the first two chapters you'll find my tips on keeping your kitchen stocked with essentials and planning for weekly meals. You probably know that prepping involves storing food before you eat it, so I also provide the proper guidelines on freezing, thawing, and reheating recipes to keep the food tasty and safe to eat. I am a huge food-safety geek and I'll provide you with all the recommendations to follow in your kitchen so you can help prevent foodborne illnesses. Fortunately, they are all common sense activities.

The recipes I include in this book were carefully selected so they are easy to prepare, contain easy-to-find ingredients, keep nutrition in mind, and are delicious. Each recipe provides exact measurements (or portions) for a serving size to help keep calories in check. A nutrition breakdown is also available for each recipe so you can make the healthiest decision for your individual needs. Preparation and cooking time is also listed, to help you plan accordingly.

I hope the recommendations and tips in this cookbook help you create healthier meal-planning habits. I truly believe it can be done if you put your mind to it, while still enjoying healthy, delicious food whether you're eating at your kitchen table, your desk, or while leaving the gym after a great workout.

Happy, healthy cooking!

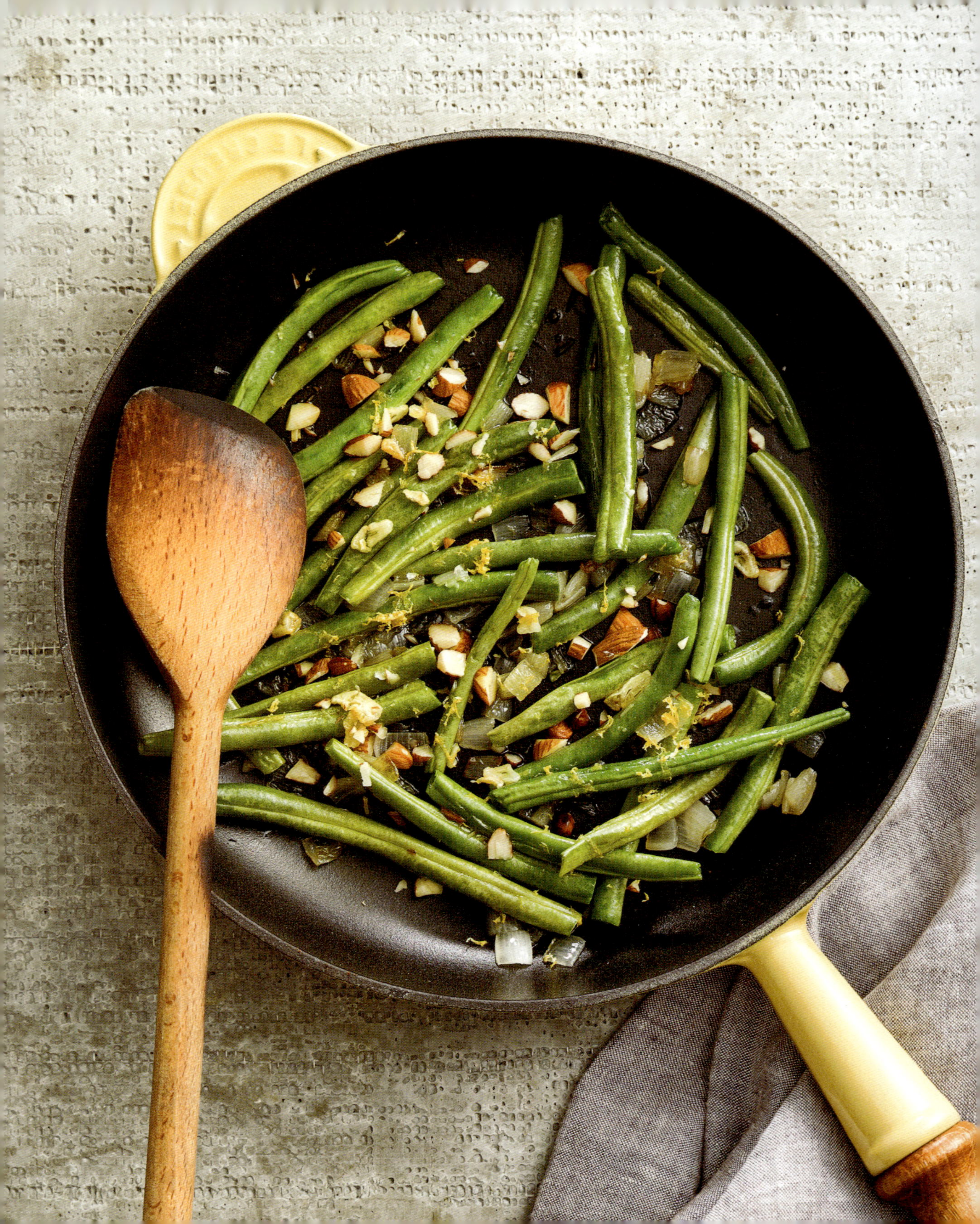

1 MEAL PREP 101

SAY GOODBYE TO YOUR OVERSIZED, CARB-FILLED morning muffin from the corner deli and artery-clogging fast-food lunch. Meal prepping is about to change all your daily unhealthy grab-and-go choices.

What exactly is meal prepping? It means scheduling and planning time to prepare and cook several meals at a time and packing them so they're ready for you to grab and go. Meal prepping also means that you plan in advance for super-quick meals during the week, so you have all the necessary ingredients on hand. You can even plan a little prep before bed, so breakfast is ready in a flash, or to cut back on dinnertime prep. There are many shortcuts, or "Toby's Tips," that will make your life easier, while still enjoying meals that are healthy, delicious, balanced, quick, and portable.

« Lemony Green Beans with Almonds (page 124)

Why Meal Prep?

Meal prepping is the number one reason I am able to feed myself and my kids healthy, delicious meals each day. The benefits of meal prepping include:

Saving money: If you know what you are going to cook, you can purchase accordingly. You can purchase meat and other ingredients in bulk, divide them into meal portions, and place them in resealable plastic bags in the refrigerator or freezer. This stretches your food dollar.

Saving time: Although you will spend some time in the kitchen on a set day of your choosing, during the week you won't be slaving for hours over a hot stove. Plus, you won't have much cleanup to do during those busy weeknights. That extra 30 to 60 minutes can be spent as quality time with loved ones instead!

Controlling portions: In order to make a meal last, you need to divide the food and account for portions. Each of my recipes provides exact measurements for portions to help make your life easier. By controlling portions, you not only save money, but also keep meal and snack calories in check.

Getting more done with less effort: Some nights it just feels like you are cooking nonstop while your to-do list gets longer and longer. It takes less effort to prepare a double batch of chili or burgers in advance than it does to cook a new meal every night; even on busy weeknights you'll be able to sit down, breathe, and enjoy a healthy meal.

Eating healthier: A stop at a fast-food joint or hitting up the vending machine will be a thing of the past. These unhealthy choices are where many high-calorie, high-fat, and high-sugar foods are eaten. When you're armed with prepared meals and snacks, these unhealthy eating habits start to disappear.

Improving multitasking skills: Meal prepping will hone your multitasking skills and even improve them. You'll learn to set a timer for the oven (a good use of your iPhone) while preparing the dressing for your lunch salad. Multitasking allows you to save time and become more efficient at meal prepping.

Clean Eating

All the recipes and meal plans in this book follow clean eating guidelines. Eating clean means choosing wholesome foods that do not contain a laundry list of unpronounceable ingredients nor are not overly processed. Many of the foods you eat every day are processed to some degree. Think about yogurt and shelled pistachios: Those have both undergone some type of processing from their original forms. The same goes for frozen vegetables or canned beans. However, these foods also contain important nutrients that you should be eating daily. When choosing foods like canned beans, I'll specify to look for "reduced sodium" or "no added sodium" on the label. When buying frozen vegetables, you want the only ingredient on the bag to be the name of the vegetable itself. Avoid buying frozen vegetables with added butter or calorie-laden sauces.

A major problem with processed foods is that they lose their nutritional value—this includes foods like ground or canned pork, potato chips, cookies, and cakes. The easiest way to minimize processed foods is by learning how to replace store-bought items with homemade ones.

Here is a list of foods to enjoy and those to minimize on a clean eating plan:

FOODS TO ENJOY

The bulk of your clean eating diet should come from the following foods:

- Fresh fruits and vegetables
- Whole grains like brown rice, whole-wheat pasta, quinoa, and barley
- Raw or dry-roasted nuts (without salt) and nut butters (e.g., peanut butter and almond butter)
- Dry or canned beans, peas, lentils (reduced-sodium or no-added sodium, if canned)
- Lean proteins (e.g., skinless chicken breasts or thighs, 90% lean ground beef, lamb, pork, eggs, fish, and seafood)
- Low-fat and nonfat dairy like milk, traditional or Greek yogurt, cottage cheese, and part-skim mozzarella and ricotta cheeses
- Oils like olive, peanut, safflower, canola, and coconut
- Seeds like sesame

MIX AND MATCH HEALTHY MEALS

According to the 2015 USDA Dietary Guidelines for Americans, you want to eat a well-balanced diet consisting of fruits, vegetables, grains, low- and nonfat dairy, lean protein, and healthy oils. Below is a list of the recommended servings of each group, based on a 2,000-calorie diet.

LEAN PROTEIN

RECOMMENDED AMOUNT: Five ½-ounce equivalents per day

EXAMPLES of 1-ounce equivalent:

- 1 ounce skinless chicken breast, fish, or lean beef
- 1 large egg
- 1 tablespoon peanut butter
- ½ ounce of nuts, such as almonds, pistachios, or cashews
- ½ ounce of seeds, such as sunflower or sesame

GRAINS

RECOMMENDED AMOUNT: 6-ounce equivalent per day, with at least half your daily grains being whole

EXAMPLES of 1-ounce equivalent:

- 1 slice bread
- 1 cup ready-to-eat cereal
- ½ cup cooked rice, pasta, or cooked cereal
- 3 cups popped popcorn
- 1 small (6-inch) flour tortilla
- 1 (6-inch) corn tortilla

FRUIT

RECOMMENDED AMOUNT: 2-cup equivalent per day

EXAMPLES of 1-cup equivalent:

- 1 cup sliced fruit, such as apples, bananas, grapes, or peaches
- 1 cup 100% fruit juice, such as orange or apple
- ½ cup dried fruit
- 1 medium (4-inch) grapefruit
- 32 seedless grapes
- 1 large peach
- 3 medium plums
- 8 large strawberries

VEGETABLES

RECOMMENDED AMOUNT: Two ½-cup equivalents per day. This includes dark green vegetables (such as lettuce, kale, and spinach), red and orange vegetables (such as carrots, beets, and summer squash), and starchy vegetables (such as corn and potatoes).

EXAMPLES of 1-cup equivalent:

- 1 cup raw or cooked vegetables, such as broccoli, cooked spinach, or red bell peppers
- 1 cup 100% vegetable juice
- 2 cups raw leafy greens (spinach, kale, lettuce)
- 1 large baked sweet potato
- 1 large ear of corn
- 1 medium baked potato

LOW- AND NONFAT DAIRY

RECOMMENDED AMOUNT: 3-cup equivalent per day

EXAMPLES of 1-cup equivalent:

- 1 cup low-fat or nonfat milk
- 1 cup low-fat or nonfat yogurt (traditional or Greek)
- 1 cup soy beverage
- 1½ ounces natural cheese, such as Swiss or Cheddar
- ½ cup part-skim ricotta cheese
- 2 cups reduced-fat or nonfat cottage cheese
- ⅓ cup shredded cheese, such as part-skim mozzarella

OILS

RECOMMENDED AMOUNT: about 2 tablespoons per day

EXAMPLES:

- Vegetable oils like canola, corn, cottonseed, olive, peanut, safflower, soybean, and sunflower

Although there is much hype about coconut oil, it is still considered a solid fat at room temperature and may contribute to heart disease. However, you can still make coconut oil part of your healthy eating plan by using it in your oil repertoire. This means rotating between several oils, and not focusing on only one.

FOODS TO MINIMIZE

Foods that are high in added sugar, saturated fat, and sodium should be minimized in your everyday diet. On some occasions, you will add small amounts of natural sweeteners (like 100% maple syrup or agave), but keep these to a minimum. Some of the baking recipes will contain all-purpose flour, but it is combined with whole-grain flour and many good-for-you ingredients (like nuts and fruit). Again, look at the entire picture and not only one ingredient in situations like these. Where possible, use the following foods minimally:

- Added sugars, like 100% maple syrup, agave, honey, brown sugar, and granulated sugar
- Butter and lard
- Dark chocolate
- Alcohol
- Fried foods
- Whole milk, full-fat cheese, ice cream
- Processed meats like hot dogs and sausage (if eating, choose nitrite-free)
- 100% fruit juice

FOODS TO AVOID

Highly processed foods or foods that provide zero nutrients should be avoided completely, including:

- Store-bought cakes, cookies, doughnuts, and other highly processed baked goods
- Sweets like candy and processed chocolate (like bars with caramel and nougat)
- Canned ground pork
- Processed soups, boxed macaroni and cheese, or other processed meals that are high in sodium, saturated fat, and added sugar
- Fruits canned in heavy syrup
- Frozen vegetables in butter or sauces
- Energy drinks
- Sodas and other sugar-filled beverages like bottled lemonade and iced tea

Healthy Meal Prep Principles

There are different ways you can prep meals so they are ready in a flash. I tend to use a combination of these five methods. I recommend trying each one to see which best suits your lifestyle based on your work hours, family engagements, and the types of meals and snacks you like to eat.

SIMPLE MEALS FIRST, VARIETY SECOND

Start slow and simple. Begin with simple meals that are easy to pull off and enjoy. The recipes you'll find in this cookbook usually contain 7 to 10 easy-to-find ingredients. The last chapter contains sauces, dressings, and other staples to prepare in advance, so you have them on hand for your weekly meals. Start with staples like hamburgers or quinoa and add one or two new ingredients. For example, I include a recipe for Baked Turkey Meatballs (page 148), which swaps ground turkey for beef, and Onion-Parsley Quinoa (page 102), which uses only two ingredients to add flavor (onions and parsley). Over time, you'll start to master the recipes and can add more ingredients or switch them up from week to week. For example, you may eventually choose to add chopped mango to the Onion-Parsley Quinoa.

BATCH COOK

Batch cooking means to cook a large amount or double the quantity of a recipe so you can enjoy half during the week and freeze the rest for later. Although it may seem overwhelming to cook several large dishes in one day, you'll reap the benefits—especially when you don't have to cook over a hot stove on a busy weeknight. Batch cooking works well for meals like meatballs and chicken with sauces (like my Lemony Chicken Breasts on page 159). Furthermore, batch cooking doesn't have to be for just dinner. Think about the meals that take the longest or give you the most trouble to prepare during the week. For me, that's breakfast muffins or a healthy vegetable quiche. These breakfast meals can also be prepped in batches and frozen. Other recipes I like to prepare in batches are dressings, which can last two weeks in the refrigerator and automatically slash 10 minutes off my weeknight meal prep time.

CREATIVE REUSE

I have included many recipes in the book because you can use them in a variety of ways to create different meals. This helps eliminate the boredom of eating the same few meals throughout the week. The same dish can oftentimes be used for a sandwich or wrap or topped over a green salad. Some can even go far beyond those two meals. For example, the Slow-Cooker Barbecue Chicken (page 164) can be eaten as a sandwich or wrap, or served over a baked potato, inside a salad, or on a homemade whole-wheat pizza. The Balsamic Onion and Mango Quinoa (page 99) can be served over a green salad, put in a wrap, or eaten as a side dish. The possibilities of reuse are endless—it's just a matter of a little thinking outside of the box.

VEGETABLES AND SALADS

Eating enough vegetables is a key component of a healthy diet. According to the 2015 USDA Dietary Guidelines, 90 percent of Americans don't eat the recommended daily amount of vegetables. A major part of meal prep is to make sure you organize your time so you can prep salads and cooked vegetable dishes to include with lunches and dinners throughout the week. You'll also see that many of my recipes add vegetables, not only for flavor but also to up your veggie intake. For example, the Beef-Mushroom Meatballs (page 170) use equal amounts of lean beef and mushrooms and are one of my favorites to make. To keep vegetables at their freshest, you may want to split your vegetable prep into twice a week.

EASY RECIPES WITH INGREDIENTS YOU ALWAYS HAVE

The recipes included in this book are for beginner home cooks and are easy to follow. I have read thousands of recipes, and it frustrates me when ingredient amounts are not included or ingredients are virtually impossible to find at my local market. Meal prepping should make your life as easy as possible—and using common, easy-to-find ingredients is just another way of accomplishing that. Each recipe in this book includes the exact amount of each ingredient you will need, even down to the amount of salt you should use! From my years teaching at culinary schools and universities, I have learned to explain concepts and cooking methods in a simple way. My recipes are written in that same manner—they're easy to understand and follow.

WRITE IT DOWN

You've heard it a million times before. If you write down your goals and plans, you're more likely to accomplish them. To help you organize your meal plans, I recommend you write them down. Purchase a notebook, create a meal prep doc on your computer or on the notes app of your smartphone, and write down each meal you will prepare for the week. That will help you generate a shopping list (which should also be written down). I have too much going on in my busy life to remember every food item, so writing it down helps a tremendous amount. On the occasions I try winging it without a shopping list, I always end up forgetting several items and have to make a second trip to the market. Learn from my time-wasting mistakes, and write it down!

GRAB-AND-GO CONTAINERS

Containers are everything to meal preppers. Having the right storage container helps protect the flavor, color, and texture of the food. The right container reduces the food's exposure to air, which helps maintain the quality of the meal. Below is a list of what to look for when purchasing your storage containers, and even a few of my favorite brands.

Stackable/Nestable: Your freezer and refrigerator have limited space, so you need to use it wisely. Stackable containers help maximize space and keep your food storage organized. Many containers can also fold or stack nicely when not in use, which means less mess in your storage cabinets.

BPA-free: The industrial chemical bisphenol A (BPA) has been around since the 1960s. Although the Food and Drug Administration (FDA) concluded that BPA found in canned goods and storage containers is safe in small amounts, with frequent use I recommend you look for only BPA-free storage containers. To ensure containers are BPA-free, read the package label. Avoid using plastic containers that contain the recycle codes 3 or 7, which indicate the items may contain BPA. Glass containers do not contain BPA.

FOODS THAT DO NOT FREEZE WELL

If you meal prep week by week, you might think you don't need the freezer, only the refrigerator. However, if you batch cook any food—from egg muffins to beef stew to rice dishes—you're not necessarily going to eat it all in one week. Your freezer can help jumpstart meals for the next week. Many folks never seem to know which foods do and do not freeze well. Here is a list of foods that do not tend to freeze well.

- Certain raw vegetables (such as cabbage, celery, watercress, cucumber, lettuce, and radishes)
- Plain cooked pasta
- Cooked egg whites
- Meringues
- Milk-based sauces (like for gravies and casseroles)
- Cheese or crumb toppings in casseroles
- Mayonnaise
- Salad dressing
- Fried foods

Leakproof: Nothing is worse than opening your bag when you get to work and finding that your grab-and-go container has leaked all over the place. Do a little research before purchasing your storage containers, and even do your own test by shaking the container for several minutes and checking if it leaks. If you commute to work by train, bus, or car, this will simulate the everyday conditions your container will have to endure.

Microwave-, Dishwasher-, and Freezer-safe: Some of the meals you'll tote to work will need to be reheated. As such, I recommend finding containers that can go from freezer to microwave. Also, if you're looking to shave off even more time from cleanup, purchase containers that go right in the dishwasher (many will recommend using the top rack only).

A few brands I recommend include:

Ball jars: Glass mason jars can be frozen, refrigerated, and tossed in the dishwasher. Ball makes different-size jars and sells a small storage unit for 12 (1-quart) jars.

Cook Pro: This inexpensive brand has click-and-lock airtight lids that nest for easy storage. They're freezer-, microwave-, and dishwasher-safe and come in a variety of shapes and sizes. They're also sold at stores like Walmart and Amazon.com and are less expensive than other similar brands.

Snapware by Pyrex: You can cook, store, and reheat (in the microwave or oven) all in the same glass container. The airtight lid snaps in place, is leak-proof, and is easy to open and close. The containers are easily stackable and BPA-free.

OXO LockTop containers: One of my longtime favorite brands, these won't let you down when it comes to meal prepping. The LockTop containers are leakproof, airtight, stackable, and BPA-free. They also resist warping and staining and are safe for freezers, microwaves, and dishwashers. They cost a little more than other brands, but will stay around for a long time.

Kitchen Equipment

To be ready for meal prepping, you need to be armed with the right supplies. Start with the "must-have" list and move on to the "nice-to-have" supplies once you get started. It won't take long to figure out what works best for you.

MUST-HAVE SUPPLIES

Baking sheet: From roasting vegetables to toasting granola to baking whole-grain pizza, baking sheets will serve as an all-purpose cooking vessel in your kitchen. They're lightweight, inexpensive, and durable. Make sure your kitchen is stocked with at least two.

Cast iron pan: Although it takes a bit longer to heat, a cast iron pan is very versatile and can be used to cook an array of dishes like steak and grain-based dishes. It's great to use on the stove and in the oven. Cast iron is reliable, long-lasting, ruggedly handsome, and easy to maintain.

Sauté pan: A 12-inch, straight-sided sauté pan has a larger bottom surface area and better protects against splattering. There's also lots of room for making double batches, and it can easily be transferred to the oven.

Muffin tins: Muffin tins aren't just for muffins. I like to use them to cook other dishes like mini quiches and meatballs. I recommend getting one regular and one mini tray. It's always nice to mix and match the sizes for meals and snacks.

Blender: You don't need to invest hundreds of dollars in a fancy blender. You'll get a lot of use out of your blender when making smoothies, sauces, and dips (like hummus). When cleaning your blender, make sure to take it apart entirely so you can clean the blender blades properly.

Measuring cups and spoons: Portion control is essential when eating healthy. If you overpour oil, for example, it can add hundreds of unnecessary calories to a recipe, as 1 tablespoon of any oil contains 120 calories. The same goes for baked goods—if a recipe calls for ¼ cup of chopped nuts, measure it out so you don't end up adding hundreds of extra calories to the dish.

NICE-TO-HAVE SUPPLIES

Slow cooker: A slow cooker will change your life! Purchase a larger-size one (8-quart, or bigger) that can be used for double (or even triple) batches of chili, soup, and chicken or beef dishes, which can be frozen for later. I recently purchased an inexpensive slow cooker (no bells or whistles on this one) and can't believe how little work is involved to make a tasty meal.

Mixing bowls: Many recipes call for mixing batters or ingredients. I recommend a set of mixing bowls that have nonslip bottoms, solid construction, and nontoxic lids. Dishwasher- and freezer-safe is a plus. Although many mixing bowl sets can be expensive, shop around and you can find a good set for a good price.

Good utensils: If your cooking utensils need an update, once you get into the swing of things with meal prepping, you'll want to update these kitchen tool essentials. Purchase a spatula, a few wooden spoons (they're usually sold in packs), and a ladle. If you have a nonstick pan, opt for a plastic or silicon-coated spatula to avoid damaging the pan's surface.

Cutting board: Plastic cutting boards are inexpensive and are dishwasher-safe. Bamboo and wooden cutting boards must be washed by hand and tend to warp a little quicker. If any cutting board ends up with nicks and grooves from lots of use, it should be replaced immediately. The grooves can harbor microorganisms, which can end up in your food.

Good set of knives: You don't need to spend hundreds of dollars on a new set of knives, but a good chef's knife and paring knife can make meal prepping go that much more smoothly. The chef's knife is perfect for slicing meat, cutting vegetables, and chopping herbs and nuts. A paring knife is perfect for smaller tasks like peeling potatoes, seeding peppers, or segmenting orange slices.

Meal Prep Sunday

For many, Sunday makes the most sense as a meal prep day. If you can get your meal planning done on Saturday or even Sunday morning, you'll have the rest of the day to organize a week's worth of meals. If your time on a particular weekend is limited, that's where the slow cooker comes in handy. Pop the ingredients in the slow cooker before heading out, and voilà, your meal will be done when you walk in the door. If Sunday's aren't your ideal prep day, then figure out which day works best for you. When I used to work the weekend shift as a clinical dietitian, Tuesdays were my day off and the days I used to go food shopping and prep my meals.

Meal prepping will take about 4 or 5 hours, depending on how efficient you are. To save time, organize your meals on Saturday (and write them down!) and go food shopping. That should shave off at least an hour from the actual time you spend preparing your meals.

For the first few weeks, start slowly. Perhaps only make lunches or dinners for the week so you can get a feel of the timing and work involved. I started with lunches because I found myself dropping at least $10 a day at work and wanted to save money. If you tend to order pizza or go to the drive-through on certain nights of the week, then meal prep for those nights during the first few weeks. If a certain dish eats up your busy weeknight time, that's the dish to prepare ahead of time.

Here is what a sample meal prep day looks like, but what you do depends on the dishes being made. As always, adjust the following to make it your own:

Meal planning: Every week, select the meal you will prep for. Write down the variations of the meals and when you'll be eating them. For example, if you plan on making the Spicy Tuna with Edamame (page 132), write down if you'll be eating it over a bed of greens or stuffed into a whole-wheat pita.

You'll need to add the salad greens, pita, or both to your shopping list. I do my meal planning on Friday or Saturday.
APPROXIMATE TIME: 30 MINUTES

Go shopping: Once you select and organize your meals, create a shopping list. Review the ingredients needed for each recipe and compare them to what you already have in your pantry or refrigerator. Make sure to write out measurements of expensive ingredients, like beef or chicken. It's sometimes cheaper to order the exact amount from the butcher counter as opposed to picking it up prepackaged. If you do purchase your meat in bulk, you can divide it as needed for each recipe, which is also more cost efficient.
APPROXIMATE TIME: 1 HOUR

Store ingredients: If you go shopping on a day or two before your meal prep day, make sure to immediately store your food in the refrigerator or freezer. Meats, fish, or chicken that will be used within the next 48 hours should be portioned and stored in the refrigerator. The remaining raw proteins should be properly labelled and stored in the freezer. If you're shopping the same day you're prepping food, place cold items in the refrigerator to maintain their temperature until you start your meal prep.
APPROXIMATE TIME: 15 MINUTES

Prep ingredients: The trick is to have all the ingredients prepped and measured, so when the recipe calls for it there isn't much to do except add it in. That's exactly what you're trying to accomplish here—to make cooking go as smoothly as possible. Take out all the ingredients you'll need based on the recipe's ingredient list. Read each recipe thoroughly, including the instructions, so you understand each step you need to take. Wash, chop, dice, mince, zest, or juice any vegetable, fruit, herb, seed, or nut needed. Marinate any meats, fish, or poultry. Prepare any other ingredients you'll need for each recipe so they're ready to be used.
APPROXIMATE TIME: 30 MINUTES, DEPENDING ON THE RECIPES

Slow cook: The first recipe to prepare is one in the slow cooker. This is because the slow cooker takes between 4 and 6 hours to cook the dish. There isn't much to do except prep and toss the ingredients inside (okay, and press the "cook" button), and after that you can move onto another task.
APPROXIMATE TIME: 15 MINUTES

Prep sauces, dips, and dressings: Hopefully you have a salad or two on your meal prep list for the week. Salads typically have dressings that are quick and easy (5 minutes, tops) to whisk together. Salad dressings can last 2 weeks, so make them as 1-cup portions so they last a while. The same goes for salsa, hummus, chimichurri, and other sauces and dips. These are easy-to-make recipes that are ready within 10 to 15 minutes and require no or minimal cooking.
APPROXIMATE TIME: 30 MINUTES

Cook ingredients: Another step in meal prep is cooking the separate ingredients needed for a recipe. This could be roasting or steaming vegetables, cooking starches like brown rice or quinoa, or toasting nuts or seeds. You want all parts of the dish to be ready before the dish is put together.
APPROXIMATE TIME: 1 HOUR (DEPENDING ON HOW MUCH COOKING NEEDS TO BE DONE)

Put it together: Once you have all the components of the dish prepped and cooked, it's time to put it all together. Toss them together to make the dish, or put the meal together by cooking the components together to make it, like a stir-fry. What you combine depends on the recipe you're making.
APPROXIMATE TIME: 1 HOUR (DEPENDING ON HOW MUCH COOKING NEEDS TO BE DONE)

Box it up: Once the dish is complete, divide it into portions for the refrigerator or freezer. For a dish like meatballs, you may decide to divide it into two large containers, one for the refrigerator and one for the freezer. If you're planning on bringing a 4-ounce serving of Lemony Chicken Breasts (page 159) with a side of quinoa to work, then pack those two items together in a single container. If you made muffins or quiches, wrap them individually so you can grab and go. Portion out spiced nuts or popcorn for easy-to-grab snack packs for work. Sometimes you won't be cooking the dish until right before you eat it, like an egg scramble or smoothie, but you can still package the ingredients together so they're ready to go.
APPROXIMATE TIME: 30 MINUTES

The Art of Storage

One of the most common questions I get is: How long can certain foods be stored in the refrigerator, freezer, or pantry? Here are the guidelines to follow to make sure your food maintains the highest quality possible.

ORGANIZE YOUR REFRIGERATOR, FREEZER, AND PANTRY

I recommend organizing your refrigerator at least weekly. Clean any spills immediately and read the recommended use-by dates so you can use those ingredients before they spoil.

Organize your freezer at least every few weeks so you know what's inside. Stack the meals in an organized way so you can easily grab what you need.

Once a month, organize your pantry. If you have a few packages or cans of the same item, place the one with the soonest use-by date in front so you use it first. This can help ensure that the foods don't spoil.

SMART LABELLING

It's tough to always tell what's in a container or to remember when you froze it. Labelling takes away the guesswork. Label each container with the food item and the date you should eat it by. The chart on page 30 can help you label your foods with the correct use-by dates.

REFRIGERATOR AND FREEZER BASICS

There are basic guidelines to follow for storing food in your refrigerator and freezer. Food lasts longer in the freezer, but it can still spoil if it's left in there for too long.

Place perishable foods in the refrigerator and freezer as soon as you get home: Follow the "2-hour rule," which says that perishable foods should not be left outside the refrigerator or freezer for over 2 hours. If the temperature in your kitchen is above 90°F, food should not be left out at room temperature for over 1 hour.

Don't crowd the refrigerator and freezer: Air needs to circulate in the refrigerator and freezer units in order to maintain the proper temperature. Do not line shelves with aluminum or anything else that will cut off proper air circulation.

Maintain proper temperatures: Your refrigerator should be set at a maximum of 41°F and the freezer should keep everything frozen and be set around 0°F. You can purchase affordable thermometers to double check if your units are set at the correct temperatures.

When in doubt, toss it out: Be on the lookout for foods that spoil. Be aware of signs of spoilage like bad odors and slimy foods. Mold isn't necessarily a health threat, but it can cause the food's flavors to be off.

Store foods properly in the refrigerator: Raw foods like raw chicken and fish should be stored on the bottom of the refrigerator, wrapped to catch any juices. Ready-to-eat foods like cooked dishes and fresh food like produce and yogurt should be stored above the raw food. This will help prevent cross-contamination and potential foodborne illnesses.

THAWING AND REHEATING

When the food you prep and cook moves into the refrigerator or freezer before your mouth, it's important to know how to thaw and properly reheat food. Below are the guidelines for thawing and reheating properly.

How to Thaw Safely

You can thaw raw proteins like meat, poultry, and fish in several ways. First, you can place it in the refrigerator the night before. For a whole turkey or chicken you will need 2 to 3 days in the refrigerator for proper thawing. Smaller items, like frozen shrimp, can be run under cool water for 1 to 2 hours. Make sure there are no dishes in the sink when thawing food in this manner. You can also thaw frozen raw proteins in the microwave. However, because you get an uneven distribution of heat, some of the meats or fish may start to cook. If you do use the microwave to thaw, it is recommended to cook the food right away.

For cooked meals, you can use the same methods mentioned above. Thawing in the refrigerator is best since the food is at a safe temperature the entire time. After the food is thawed completely, it can be stored in the refrigerator for 3 to 4 days. The internal temperature of any reheated food should reach 165°F and should be measured with a thermometer placed in the thickest part of the dish.

FREEZER STAPLES FOR YOUR BUSIEST WEEKS

Sometimes you won't have time to prep on Sunday (or any days of the week). For these unavoidable situations, I recommend having these five staples previously prepped and frozen. Once thawed, they can be used to prepare a quick meal.

QUINOA
This whole grain contains a whopping 8 grams of protein and 5 grams of fiber per cooked cup. It's also brimming with numerous B vitamins, zinc, potassium, folate, and selenium, along with 15 percent of the recommended daily amount of iron. It can be enjoyed hot or cold. Pair with:
- Beans and sautéed greens (such as spinach) in a "power bowl"
- A green salad—spoon over the greens

BEANS
Beans are an excellent source of fiber, providing about 7.5 grams per ½ cup. Fiber helps keep you feeling full for longer so you won't be hungry right after you eat. Pair with:
- Shredded mozzarella cheese in a whole-wheat quesadilla
- A Mexican burrito filled with scrambled eggs, cheese, and salsa

FROZEN BERRIES
Strawberries, blueberries, and raspberries are brimming with anthocyanins, one of the most powerful anti-inflammatory antioxidants. Purchase packaged frozen berries with no added sugar. You can use them frozen or thawed in many dishes including:
- Frozen in a Greek yogurt smoothie
- Thawed in parfaits or a bowl of oatmeal

FROZEN VEGETABLES

Some weeks you just can't make it to the market to buy fresh vegetables. That's when frozen veggies come in handy. Purchase frozen vegetables without added butter or sauces. The only ingredient on the package should be the name of the vegetables. My favorites include string beans, broccoli, and spinach. Pair with (thaw the vegetables first):
- A vegetable omelet
- A chicken or beef stir-fry

FISH FILLET

Small fillets of fish like cod and tuna can be cooked from frozen packages. Package frozen fish into 5-ounce portions and store so you can easily remove them from the freezer. You can bake or sauté these fillets with a touch of olive oil, lemon juice, salt, and pepper for a quick meal. Pair with:
- A tossed salad
- Sautéed spinach and quinoa

	FRIDGE	FREEZER
Salads: egg salad, tuna salad, chicken salad, pasta salad	3 TO 5 DAYS	DOES NOT FREEZE WELL
Hamburger, meatloaf, and other dishes made with ground meat (raw)	1 TO 2 DAYS	3 TO 4 MONTHS
Steaks: beef, pork, lamb (raw)	3 TO 5 DAYS	3 TO 4 MONTHS
Chops: beef, pork, lamb (raw)	3 TO 5 DAYS	4 TO 6 MONTHS
Roasts: beef, pork, lamb (raw)	3 TO 5 DAYS	4 TO 12 MONTHS
Whole chicken or turkey (raw)	1 TO 2 DAYS	1 YEAR
Pieces: chicken or turkey (raw)	1 TO 2 DAYS	9 MONTHS
Soups and stews with vegetables and meat	3 TO 4 DAYS	2 TO 3 MONTHS
Pizza	3 TO 4 DAYS	1 TO 2 MONTHS
Beef, lamb, pork, or chicken (cooked)	3 TO 4 DAYS	2 TO 6 MONTHS

*CHART BASED ON FOODSAFETY.GOV

WHAT NOT TO DO

When I was a teenager, I remember my mom leaving raw meat on the counter overnight to thaw. The next morning, it was gone. Our German shepherd ate like a king that night (ironically, his name was King). If you have pets, the last thing you want to do is thaw on the countertop overnight. Also, thawing at room temperature allows bacteria to grow and thrive and is mighty messy to clean up.

About the Meal Plans and Recipes

While the desire to consistently eat healthy food is common with those who want to meal prep, there are often other specific goals that accompany it. This book offers three different meal plans to support different goals.

Clean Eating: This meal plan is for folks looking to eat more wholesome and less processed food. Included here are a variety of whole grains, fruits, vegetables, lean protein, dairy, and healthy fats. Items like tomato sauce, dressings, and muffins are made from scratch so you can better control the ingredients.

Weight Loss: For those looking to lose weight, the meal plan emphasizes calorie-controlled meals, with recipes that include a measurable portion size. This plan also emphasizes regular physical activity. (Note: Always speak to your physician before starting any exercise program.)

Muscle Building: This meal plan is for anyone looking to build muscle and get lean. The plan includes a combination of fat and carbs for energy and protein to help maintain and repair muscles.

These meal plans do not correspond to breakfast, lunch, and dinner. Rather they focus on making a variety of meals over the course of a day so you can choose when to eat. The recipes are all prepared with fresh, minimally processed ingredients that you can find at your local grocery store. All recipes include detailed nutrition information and measurable portion sizes.

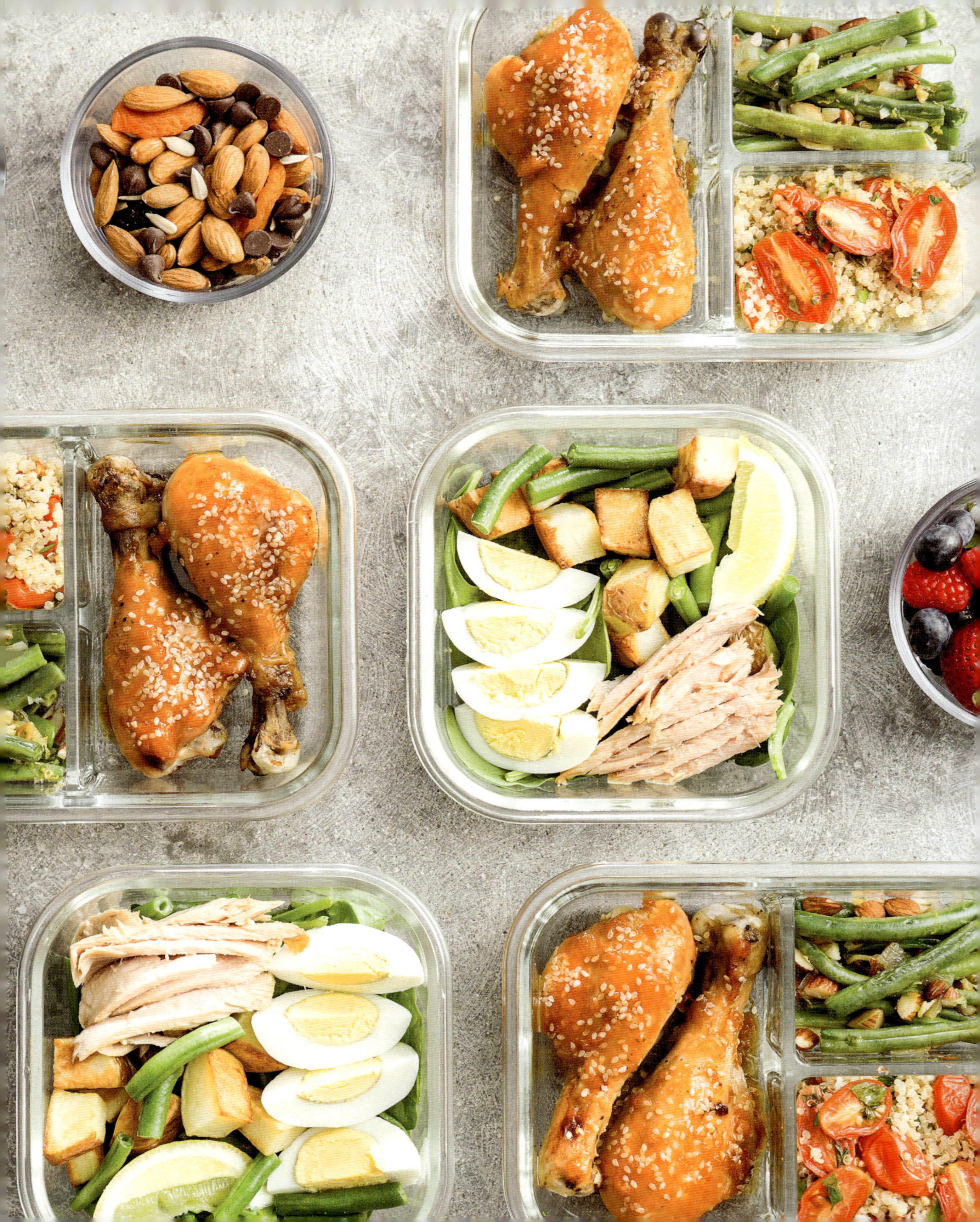

2 MEAL PLANS

MEAL PREPPING IS A GREAT STRATEGY to support your meal goals for clean eating, weight loss, and muscle building. The meal plans in this chapter are not intended to dictate what you should eat for every meal during every day of the week. Rather, they provide guidance on how to kickstart your meal prep for your specific goals.

Each meal plan will have its own shopping list of perishable foods for both weeks. Nonperishable items (those stored in your pantry), will be provided before the weekly meal plans.

Each meal plan will offer two different Sunday prep days. Each Sunday prep day should generate five to six meals plus one prepared snack. For example, your prep may result in two breakfasts, four lunches/dinners, and one prepared snack. The meal plans will also include prep for no-cook snacks for the week, like hummus, fruit salad, or trail mix. Happy Prepping!

CLEAN EATING

Clean eating is about eating wholesome foods that don't contain a long list of unpronounceable ingredients, additives, and preservatives. Clean eating means choosing fresh foods whenever possible or in season, but some canned and frozen foods are absolutely fine, too. Many foods are processed to some degree, like cheese and whole-grain bread, but they come with a boatload of good-for-you nutrients your body needs to stay healthy. It's the overly processed foods where most nutrients are destroyed—think of potato chips compared to a baked potato where, during processing, much of the potassium and vitamin C are destroyed. The good news is that most of the highly processed packaged foods you want to avoid are also those you can easily make at home. Why buy salad dressing when you can easily whip up a batch in a matter of minutes with full control over the ingredients? The same goes for granola, trail mix, salsa, hummus, and sauces.

On this clean eating plan, you'll be eating well-balanced meals from a variety of food groups, including fruits, vegetables, lean protein (lean meat, eggs, fish, chicken, beans, lentils), low- and nonfat dairy, whole grains, and healthy fats (oils, avocado). You will find minimally processed canned and frozen foods—like canned black beans that have reduced or no-added salt, or frozen fruit with no added sugar. These types of foods can fit into your clean eating plan, and to help your selections I will always note what to look for on the package ingredient list when purchasing them.

If you're following a clean eating plan and want to maintain your current weight, aim for 2,000 calories per day if you're male and 1,800 calories per day if you're female. Plan for about two snacks per day—thinking of them as mini-meals and an opportunity to take in nutrients you may not be getting enough of, or that you missed during regular meals. Clean snacks should be around 150 to 200 calories each and include foods with fiber (whole grains, fruits, and vegetables), calcium (milk, yogurt, and cheese), or potassium (fruits and vegetables). If your snacks don't contain much fiber, then adding a lean protein (like an egg or a little nut butter) helps keep you satisfied for longer. A good time to add a snack into your diet is when you go for a 5-hour or longer stretch without food. You may need to up your number of snacks to three per day, if you have particularly long stretches between meals, or go down to one snack if you feel you're eating too much food, and you're not hungry enough for a snack.

CLEAN EATING PANTRY

- 100% maple syrup
- Applesauce (unsweetened)
- Baking powder
- Baking soda
- Beef broth, low-sodium
- Black pepper, freshly ground
- Chicken broth, low-sodium
- Chili powder
- Chocolate chips, dark
- Cinnamon, ground
- Cocoa powder, unsweetened
- Cooking spray
- Cornstarch
- Cumin, ground
- Garlic powder
- Flour, unbleached all-purpose
- Flour, whole-wheat
- Honey
- Mustard, Dijon
- Nutmeg, ground
- Oil, canola or safflower
- Oil, toasted sesame seed
- Olive oil
- Olive oil, extra-virgin
- Onion powder
- Peanut butter, natural
- Rice vinegar, unseasoned
- Rosemary, dried
- Salt, table
- Sea salt
- Soy sauce, reduced-sodium
- Sriracha
- Sugar, brown
- Sugar, granulated
- Vanilla extract
- Vegetable broth, low-sodium
- Vinegar, white balsamic
- Worcestershire sauce

CLEAN EATING MEAL PLAN # 1

RECIPE 1: SLOW-COOKER WHITE CHICKEN CHILI
Page 162   **Makes** 4 servings   **Prep time:** 15 minutes   **Store:** Allow the chili to cool for 1 to 2 hours. Once cooled, store in resealable containers for up to 1 week.

RECIPE 2: TART CHERRY–ALMOND BREAKFAST COOKIES
Page 79   **Makes** 16 cookies   **Prep time:** 15 minutes   **Store:** Store half the cookies in a resealable glass or plastic container for up to 5 days at room temperature. Individually package each remaining cookie in separate resealable plastic bags labeled with the use-by date of up to 2 months, and freeze. Alternatively, wrap each cookie in plastic wrap.

RECIPE 3: BLACKBERRY-LEMON OVERNIGHT OATS
Page 77   **Makes** 1 serving   **Prep time:** 10 minutes   **Store:** Store sealed in a glass jar in the refrigerator for up to 3 days. Eat cold or warm.

RECIPE 4: GRILLED ASIAN STEAK SALAD
Page 114   **Makes** 4 servings   **Prep time:** 15 minutes   **Store:** Store the four individual salad containers in the refrigerator for up to 5 days. When ready to eat, top each with 1½ tablespoons of dressing. Alternatively, the dressing can be placed at the bottom of a Mason jar and then topped with the steak salad. Refrigerate for up to 5 days and shake the jar to evenly coat the salad before eating.

RECIPE 5: SOY-SESAME DRESSING
Page 210   **Makes** 6 servings   **Prep time:** 5 minutes   **Store:** Store the dressing in a resealable container in the refrigerator for up to 2 weeks.

RECIPE 6: ROASTED TROUT WITH GREEN OLIVE TAPENADE
Page 134   **Makes** 4 servings   **Prep time:** 5 minutes   **Store:** Place cooled fish in a resealable container in the refrigerator for up to 5 days.

RECIPE 7: GREEN OLIVE TAPENADE
Page 216   **Makes** 1½ cups   **Prep time:** 10 minutes   **Store:** Place the tapenade in a resealable container in the refrigerator for up to 5 days.

RECIPE 8: HONEY RICOTTA WITH STRAWBERRIES
Page 192   **Makes** 4 servings   **Prep time:** 10 minutes   **Store:** Place the honey ricotta and strawberries in separate resealable containers in the refrigerator for up to 5 days.

RECIPE 9: HOMEMADE TRAIL MIX
Page 193   **Makes** 4 servings   **Prep time:** 5 minutes   **Store:** Store the trail mix in a resealable container at room temperature for up to 1 month.

RECIPE 10: WHITE CHICKEN CHILI AND SPINACH QUESADILLAS
Page 163   **Makes** 4 servings   **Prep time:** 15 minutes   **Store:** Place cooled quesadillas in a resealable container, or individually wrapped with plastic or foil, in the refrigerator for up to 1 week.

CLEAN EATING MEAL PLAN # 1

SHOPPING LIST

PANTRY
- See page 35

FRUIT
- ½ cup blackberries
- 3 lemons
- 3 cups strawberries
- 10 dried apricots
- 1¼ cups dried tart cherries

VEGETABLES, HERBS, AND SPICES
- 1 carrot
- 1 (14-ounce) bag frozen corn kernels
- 1 medium cucumber
- 1 (9-ounce) package spring mixed greens, or other mixed greens
- 3 garlic cloves
- 1 large yellow onion
- 1 cup fresh parsley
- 1 bunch fresh rosemary
- 2 cups baby spinach leaves
- 1 cup cherry tomatoes

PROTEIN
- 2 eggs
- 1 pound flank or skirt steak
- 4 (5-ounce) fillets rainbow trout
- 1 pound skinless, boneless chicken tenders

GRAINS
- 1 cup old-fashioned oats
- ½ cup rolled oats
- 4 (10-inch) whole-wheat tortillas

DAIRY
- 1 cup shredded low-salt Cheddar cheese
- ½ cup nonfat plain Greek yogurt
- ⅔ cup nonfat milk
- 1 cup low-fat milk
- 1 cup part-skim ricotta cheese
- ¼ cup reduced-fat sour cream

LEGUMES
- 2 (15-ounce) cans low-sodium Northern beans

NUTS AND SEEDS
- 1½ cups raw unsalted almonds
- ¼ cup unsalted cashews
- 2 tablespoons unsalted sunflower seeds

OTHER
- ¼ cup capers
- 2 (8-ounce) cans chile peppers
- 1 (6-ounce) can pitted green olives

CLEAN EATING MEAL PLAN # 1

MEAL PREP DAY

Start with the **Slow-Cooker White Chicken Chili**. Add the first nine ingredients into the slow cooker and cook on high for 4 hours.

Next, prepare the **Tart Cherry–Almond Breakfast Cookies**. Preheat the oven to 350°F. Line two baking sheets with parchment paper, and coat the paper with cooking spray. Mix the dry mixture in one bowl and the wet mixture in another. Add the dry mixture to the wet and stir to combine. Fold in the cherries and almonds, making sure to evenly distribute them throughout the batter. For each cookie, drop 2 tablespoons of batter onto the prepared sheet pans. Bake for 15 to 20 minutes and allow 5 minutes for the cookies to cool. Store half the cookies in a resealable container at room temperature. Individually wrap the remaining half of the breakfast cookies and freeze.

While the cookies are baking, prepare the **Blackberry-Lemon Overnight Oats**. Combine the first three ingredients in a Mason jar, seal, and store overnight in the refrigerator. Zest the lemon and measure the blackberries. Store in the refrigerator until the oats are ready to be eaten.

Next prepare the **Grilled Asian Steak Salad**. Prepare the **Soy-Sesame Dressing**. Marinate the steak in ¼ cup of the dressing in the refrigerator for at least 30 minutes. Prep the vegetables for the salad while the steak marinates and preheat the grill. Grill the steak for 3 to 5 minutes on each side. Allow to rest for 10 minutes and then thinly slice and separate into 4 (4-ounce) portions. Store the salad and dressing in separate containers in the refrigerator.

Prepare the **Roasted Trout with Green Olive Tapenade**. Preheat the oven to 400°F. Coat a baking sheet with cooking spray. Evenly spread the rosemary across the pan. Place the fish, skin-side down, on the rosemary. Coat the top of the fish with cooking spray. Roast the fish for 10 minutes. Let the fish cool before dividing and storing it in four resealable containers in the refrigerator. While the fish is roasting, prepare the **Green Olive Tapenade** by blending the ingredients in a food processor or blender. Store the tapenade in the refrigerator.

Next, work on the **Honey Ricotta with Strawberries**. In a small bowl, combine the honey and ricotta. Slice the strawberries and chop the nuts. Assemble each snack in four resealable containers and store in the refrigerator.

Prepare the **Homemade Trail Mix**. Measure out the ingredients in a resealable container or plastic bag and store at room temperature.

When the slow cooker chili is done, whisk the milk and cornstarch in a small bowl and stir into the chili until thoroughly combined. Let sit until the chili has thickened, 2 to 3 minutes. Once the chili is cooled, store in four single-serve containers in the refrigerator.

Prepare the **White Chicken Chili and Spinach Quesadillas**. In a medium skillet, heat 3 cups of the **Slow-Cooker White Chicken Chili**. Cook until the chili is bubbling, then lower the heat and add the spinach. Cook until the spinach is wilted, about 2 minutes. Place 1 tortilla on a flat surface and top it with ¼ cup of shredded cheese. Top with half of the chili mixture and followed by another ¼ cup of shredded cheese. Top with another tortilla.

Coat a large skillet with cooking spray and place over medium heat. Carefully add the quesadilla to the pan and cook for about 3 minutes on each side, until the tortillas are crisp and golden brown. Create and cook the second quesadilla. Cut each quesadilla into four quarters. Once cooled, store two quarters in each of four resealable containers or in aluminum foil in the refrigerator.

CLEAN EATING MEAL PLAN # 2

RECIPE 1: SLOW-COOKER THREE-BEAN CHILI
Page 107   **Makes** 6 servings   **Prep time:** 15 minutes   **Store:** Allow the chili to cool for 1 to 2 hours. Once cooled, store in resealable containers for up to 1 week.

RECIPE 2: EASY TRICOLORED PEPPER STEAK
Page 181   **Makes** 4 servings   **Prep time:** 15 minutes   **Store:** Place the cooled pepper steak with the sauce in four resealable containers for up to 1 week.

RECIPE 3: FRUIT SALAD WITH MINT
Page 198   **Makes** 4 servings   **Prep time:** 15 minutes   **Store:** Store the fruit salad in resealable containers in the refrigerator for up to 5 days.

RECIPE 4: HAWAIIAN CHICKEN SKEWERS
Page 155   **Makes** 6 servings   **Prep time:** 30 minutes   **Store:** Cool the skewers to room temperature. Take 2 skewers, remove the pieces using a fork, put in a resealable container, and top with 4 teaspoons of the coconut mixture. Store in the refrigerator for up to 1 week.

RECIPE 5: CHOCOLATE ENERGY BALLS
Page 190   **Makes** 12 balls   **Prep time:** 15 minutes   **Store:** Store the balls in a resealable container in the refrigerator for up to 1 week.

RECIPE 6: WHITE BALSAMIC VINAIGRETTE
Page 207   **Makes** 4 servings   **Prep time:** 5 minutes   **Store:** Store the dressing in a resealable container in the refrigerator for up to 1 month.

RECIPE 7: WHOLE-GRAIN PANCAKES WITH SPICED GREEK YOGURT SAUCE
Page 74   **Makes** 4 servings   **Prep time:** 15 minutes   **Store:** Store the pancakes and yogurt sauce in separate sealed containers in the refrigerator for up to 1 week.

RECIPE 8: LIGHTER PANZANELLA SALAD
Page 117   **Makes** 4 servings   **Prep time:** 30 minutes   **Store:** Store the salad in one large resealable container or four individual resealable containers in the refrigerator for up to 5 days. Store the dressing in a separate resealable container.

RECIPE 9: ZIPPY'S SHAKSHUKA
Page 72   **Makes** 6 servings   **Prep time:** 15 minutes   **Store:** Divide the shakshuka into six individual resealable containers, including one egg per container and topped with sauce. Store in the refrigerator for up to 5 days.

CLEAN EATING MEAL PLAN # 2

SHOPPING LIST

PANTRY
- See page 35

FRUIT
- 1 cup blueberries, blackberries, or raspberries
- ½ cantaloupe
- 8 pitted dates
- 2 limes
- ¼ cup freshly squeezed orange juice
- 1 pineapple
- 2 cups strawberries

VEGETABLES, HERBS, AND SPICES
- ¼ cup fresh basil leaves
- 2 green bell peppers
- 1 red bell pepper
- 1 yellow or orange bell pepper
- 2 tablespoons chopped fresh chives
- 1 tablespoon chopped fresh cilantro
- 1 medium cucumber
- 1 (2-inch) piece fresh ginger
- 4 garlic cloves
- 2 tablespoons chopped fresh mint
- 1 small red onion
- 3 medium yellow onions
- 4 cups shredded romaine lettuce
- 4 cups cherry tomatoes

PROTEIN
- 1½ pounds skinless, boneless chicken breast
- 8 large eggs
- 1 pound beef sirloin steak

GRAINS
- ½ cup rolled oats
- 4 slices 100% whole-wheat bread

DAIRY
- 2½ cups nonfat plain Greek yogurt
- 1 cup low-fat milk
- 4 ounces part-skim mozzarella cheese

NUTS AND SEEDS
- ½ cup unsalted sunflower seeds

OTHER
- 2 (15-ounce) cans reduced-sodium black beans, drained and rinsed
- 1 (15-ounce) can reduced-sodium cannellini beans, drained and rinsed
- 1 (13.5-ounce) can light coconut milk
- 1 (15-ounce) can reduced-sodium kidney beans, drained and rinsed
- 2 (28-ounce) cans crushed tomatoes

CLEAN EATING MEAL PLAN # 2

MEAL PREP DAY

Start with the **Slow-Cooker Three-Bean Chili**. Add all the ingredients to the slow cooker. Cover and cook on low for 8 hours.

Next make the **Easy Tricolored Pepper Steak**. Prepare the vegetables and slice the steak. In a medium bowl, add the marinade and steak and toss to evenly coat. Heat the oil in a medium skillet over medium heat. Add the steak strips and brown, about 6 minutes per side. Add 1¼ cups beef broth to the skillet and bring it to a boil. Lower the heat and simmer, covered, until the meat is softened and cooked through, about 30 minutes. Add the onion and peppers and continue simmering, covered, for an additional 5 minutes.

While the steak is cooking, prepare the **Fruit Salad with Mint**. Slice all the fruit and put in a large bowl. Chop the mint. In a small bowl, whisk together the dressing. Pour the dressing over the fruit and toss to combine. Store the fruit salad in four resealable containers in the refrigerator for up to 5 days.

Check on the steak. When it is several minutes from being done, in a small bowl, whisk together the remaining ¼ cup of beef broth with the cornstarch. Stir this into the beef mixture until the broth thickens. Store the cooled pepper steak with the sauce in four resealable containers for up to 1 week.

Next make the marinade for the **Hawaiian Chicken Skewers**. Grate the ginger, chop the chives, slice the pineapple, and cut the chicken. In a medium bowl, whisk together the ingredients for the marinade. Add 1 cup of the marinade and the chicken to a bowl and toss to evenly coat. Cover and refrigerate for at least 30 minutes.

While the chicken marinates, make the **Chocolate Energy Balls**. Line a medium container with parchment paper. Pulse the ingredients in a blender. Using clean hands, form the batter into 12 (2-inch) balls and place them in the prepared container. Cover and refrigerate.

Next prepare the **White Balsamic Vinaigrette**. In a small bowl, whisk together all the ingredients except the olive oil. Slowly drizzle in the olive oil while whisking vigorously to emulsify the dressing. Store in a resealable container in the refrigerator.

Preheat the oven to 375°F and coat a baking sheet with cooking spray. To assemble the **Hawaiian Chicken Skewers**, thread a piece of chicken, followed by a cherry tomato, and then a pineapple chunk. Repeat the sequence on the same skewer. Continue threading the remaining skewers in the same order. Discard the used chicken marinade. Place the skewers on the prepared baking sheet in a single layer. Bake for 20 minutes.

While the chicken skewers are baking, heat the remaining marinade in a small saucepan over medium-low heat until bubbling, about 5 minutes. Turn off the heat.

While the marinade is heating, prepare the yogurt sauce for the **Whole-Grain Pancakes with Spiced Greek Yogurt Sauce**. Place the yogurt sauce ingredients in a small bowl and stir to combine. Store in a resealable container in the refrigerator.

Allow the chicken skewers to cool to room temperature. Take 2 skewers, remove the pieces using a fork, and put in a resealable container. Top the chicken, tomatoes, and pineapple with 1⅓ tablespoons of the thickened marinade.

Next prepare the **Whole-Grain Pancakes**. In a medium bowl, sift together the dry ingredients. In a separate medium bowl, combine the wet ingredients. Add the flour mixture to the wet ingredients and stir gently to combine. Coat a griddle or large skillet with cooking spray and place over medium heat. When hot, scoop ¼ cup of batter onto the griddle, leaving room between the pancakes. Cook until the top is bubbly and the edges are set, about 2 minutes. Flip the pancakes over and cook for another 2 minutes until golden and crisp. Repeat with the remaining batter. Store the pancakes and yogurt sauce in separate resealable containers in the refrigerator.

Make the homemade croutons for the **Lighter Panzanella Salad**. Preheat the oven to 325°F. Coat a baking sheet with cooking spray. Put the cubed bread in a medium bowl. In a small bowl, whisk together the oil mixture. Drizzle the oil mixture over the bread and toss to combine. Place bread cubes on the baking sheet in a single layer. Bake for 8 to 10 minutes.

CLEAN EATING MEAL PLAN # 2

While the croutons are baking, prepare the salad. Slice the vegetables, basil, and cheese. When the croutons are done, remove the baking sheet from the oven and set aside to cool for 10 minutes. Toss the croutons with the salad. Divide into four resealable containers and store in the refrigerator.

Finally, make **Zippy's Shakshuka**. Slice the vegetables and chop the cilantro. In a large sauté pan over medium heat, heat the olive oil until shimmering. Add the onions and bell pepper and sauté for about 5 minutes. Add the garlic and sauté 1 minute more. Add the canned tomatoes, cilantro, salt, black pepper, and sriracha, and stir to combine. Raise the heat to medium-high and bring the mixture to a boil, then reduce the heat to medium-low. Cover the pan and cook for an additional 10 minutes to allow the flavors to blend.

Break 1 egg into a wine glass. Gently pour the egg into the outer edge of the sauté pan. Repeat with the remaining 5 eggs until a circle is formed with the eggs in the outer edge of the pan. Reduce the heat to low, cover the pan, and cook until the eggs are poached, about 6 minutes. Divide the shakshuka into six individual resealable containers, including one egg per container topped with sauce. Refrigerate.

Once the chili is cooled, store in six individual resealable containers in the refrigerator.

WEIGHT LOSS

Meal prepping can play a huge role in a successful weight-loss plan. You want to be prepared for lunch and dinner every day so you don't run to the corner pizzeria on your way home from work and so you can avoid the oversized muffins when you're hungry in the morning. When you're armed with healthy, low-calorie tasty foods, it makes losing weight much easier. Meal prepping allows for portion-controlled meals that focus on fruits, vegetables, grains, lean proteins, low-fat and nonfat dairy, and healthy fats.

According to the National Institutes of Health (NIH), a safe rate of weight loss is 1 to 2 pounds per week. This allows for weight loss at a steady pace so your body can adjust to the changes and keep the weight off. In addition to keeping calories low, starting or increasing a regular exercise program is highly encouraged. Always consult your doctor before starting a new exercise program. A minimum of 30 minutes most days of the week is encouraged, and if you can get it up to 45 minutes, that's even better! Walking is always a great place to start. I started playing tennis eight years ago and now I am ranked a 3.5 in the US Tennis Association (USTA) and play on numerous competitive leagues!

The calories recommended for weight loss do vary from person to person, but start with 1,600 calories for a woman and 1,800 calories for a man. If you feel you're not losing weight after a few weeks, you can cut back on calories by 100 or 200 a day. Do not go lower than 1,000 calories per day as it is not a safe amount. Eating too few calories won't provide your body with enough food to get the nutrients it needs to stay healthy and feeling good.

During the day you should eat three small meals (about 350 to 500 calories each) and include one snack of about 125 to 150 calories. The snack should be added when you go for a 5-hour or longer stretch during the day without food. You should not feel hungry on this weight-loss plan, and if you do, make sure you're including plenty of fruits, vegetables, whole grains, and lean protein to meet the calories listed. Those foods contain either fiber and/or protein that will help keep you feeling satisfied, so don't skimp on them!

WEIGHT LOSS PANTRY

- 100% maple syrup
- Baking powder
- Baking soda
- Basil, dried
- Bay leaves
- Beef broth, low-sodium
- Black pepper, freshly ground
- Chicken broth, low-sodium
- Chili powder
- Chocolate chips, mini dark
- Cinnamon, ground
- Cooking spray
- Cumin, ground
- Flour, pastry, whole-wheat
- Flour, unbleached all-purpose
- Garlic powder
- Olive oil
- Olive oil, extra-virgin
- Oregano, dried
- Paprika
- Peanut butter, natural
- Salt
- Sriracha
- Sugar, brown
- Thyme, dried
- Turmeric, ground
- Vegetable broth, low-sodium
- Worcestershire sauce

WEIGHT LOSS MEAL PLAN # 1

RECIPE 1: PEAR-CINNAMON OAT MUFFINS
Page 85   **Makes** 12 muffins   **Prep time:** 15 minutes   **Store:** Once completely cooled, individually wrap the muffins in plastic wrap or in separate freezer-safe containers.

RECIPE 2: LENTIL-BEEF MEATLOAF
Page 171   **Makes** 8 servings   **Prep time:** 15 minutes   **Store:** Store meatloaf slices in the refrigerator for up to 1 week.

RECIPE 3: SPEEDY TOMATO SAUCE
Page 213   **Makes** 7 cups   **Prep time:** 15 minutes   **Store:** Store cooled tomato sauce in a resealable container in the refrigerator for up to 1 week.

RECIPE 4: CRUDITÉ WITH HERBED YOGURT DIP
Page 194   **Makes** 4 servings   **Prep time:** 15 minutes   **Store:** Store in individual resealable containers in the refrigerator for up to 5 days.

RECIPE 5: FARRO, SARDINES, AND GREENS
Page 138   **Makes** 4 servings   **Prep time:** 15 minutes   **Store:** Store in a covered container in the refrigerator for up to 3 days.

RECIPE 6: MINI VEGETABLE QUICHES
Page 71   **Makes** 12 mini quiches   **Prep time:** 15 minutes   **Store:** Refrigerate the quiches in a resealable container for up to 5 days.

RECIPE 7: TO-GO SNACK BOXES
Page 200   **Makes** 3 boxes (each box serves 1)   **Prep time:** 15 minutes   **Store:** Store boxes in the refrigerator for up to 3 days.

RECIPE 8: LIGHTER CREAMED SPINACH
Page 129   **Makes** 4 servings   **Prep time:** 10 minutes   **Store:** Place the creamed spinach in a large resealable container in the refrigerator for up to 5 days.

RECIPE 9: TUNA NIÇOISE SALAD
Page 115   **Makes** 4 servings   **Prep time:** 30 minutes   **Store:** Place each Mason jar serving in the refrigerator for up to 5 days.

WEIGHT LOSS MEAL PLAN # 1

SHOPPING LIST

PANTRY

- See page 46

FRUIT

- 1 apple
- 1 cup seedless grapes
- 1½ lemons
- 1 medium pear

VEGETABLES, HERBS, AND SPICES

- ¼ cup chopped fresh basil
- 1 red or yellow bell pepper
- 2 cups baby carrots
- 4 celery stalks
- ½ cup chopped cilantro
- 1 cucumber
- 8 garlic cloves
- 1 cup fresh green beans
- 14 ounces button mushrooms
- 2½ medium yellow onions
- ½ medium red onion
- ¼ cup chopped fresh parsley
- 2 small red potatoes
- 1 tablespoon fresh rosemary
- 2 ounces fresh baby spinach
- 1 pound + 5 ounces fresh spinach
- 1 (10-ounce) package frozen chopped spinach
- 1 cup grape tomatoes

PROTEIN

- 1 pound lean (at least 90%) ground beef
- 18 eggs
- 2 (4.5-ounce) cans sardines packed in extra-virgin olive oil (at least 12 sardines)
- 2 (4-ounce) cans of tuna packed in olive oil

GRAINS

- 6 whole-grain crackers
- ¼ cup oat bran
- 2 tablespoons rolled oats
- 1 cup farro
- 1 cup whole-wheat panko bread crumbs

DAIRY

- 1 ounce Cheddar cheese, cubed
- 3 tablespoons low-fat plain Greek yogurt
- 2 cups nonfat plain Greek yogurt
- 1 part-skim mozzarella cheese stick
- ¾ cup + 1 teaspoon grated Parmesan cheese

OTHER

- 1 (15-ounce) can low-sodium lentils, drained and rinsed
- 1 (6-ounce) can tomato paste
- 2 (28-ounce) cans crushed tomatoes

WEIGHT LOSS MEAL PLAN # 1

MEAL PREP DAY

Start with the **Pear-Cinnamon Oat Muffins**. Preheat the oven to 375°F and coat a muffin tin with cooking spray. Chop the pear. In a medium bowl, sift together the dry ingredients. In a large bowl, combine the wet ingredients. Add the dry ingredients to the wet ones and stir to combine. Fold in the pear. Using a ¼ cup scoop, scoop the batter into the prepared muffin tin. Evenly sprinkle each muffin with the rolled oats. Bake for 20 minutes.

While muffins are baking, prepare the **Lentil-Beef Meatloaf**. Coat a 9-by-5-inch loaf pan with cooking spray. Chop the mushrooms and cilantro and beat the egg. In a large bowl, combine the ingredients for the meatloaf. Place the meat mixture into the loaf pan, making sure the top is even.

Remove the muffins from the oven and allow them to cool in the tin for 5 minutes, then transfer the muffins to a wire rack to finish cooling for another 10 minutes. Lower the oven temperature to 350°F. Wash the muffin tins.

Next make the **Speedy Tomato Sauce**. Chop the onions and mince the garlic. In a medium pot over medium heat, heat the olive oil until it shimmers. Cook the onions for 3 minutes. Add the garlic and cook an additional 30 seconds. Add the remaining ingredients and stir to combine. Increase the heat to high and bring the mixture to a boil, then reduce the heat to medium-low. Cover the pot and simmer until the flavors combine, about 15 minutes. Remove the bay leaves.

Top the meatloaf with ¾ cup of tomato sauce. Store the remaining tomato sauce in a resealable container in the refrigerator. Bake the meatloaf for 1 hour to 1 hour, 10 minutes.

While the meatloaf is in the oven, make the **Crudité with Herbed Yogurt Dip**. Slice the vegetables and chop the herbs. In a small bowl, mix together the ingredients for the yogurt dip. Spoon ¼ cup of the yogurt dip into mini resealable containers with 1¼ cups of the vegetables on the side. Store in the refrigerator.

Next make the farro for the **Farro, Sardines, and Greens**. In a medium pot over high heat, bring the broth to a boil. Stir in the farro, then reduce the heat to

WEIGHT LOSS MEAL PLAN # 1

medium-low and simmer for about 30 minutes. Drain off any excess liquid. Cool the farro for about 10 minutes.

Meanwhile, open the sardine cans halfway and pour the oil from the cans into a medium-size pot placed over medium heat. Add the garlic and sauté for 1 minute. Add the spinach and cook, stirring occasionally, for about 10 minutes. Cover the pot with a lid between stirring the spinach. In each of four resealable containers, place ½ cup of farro, 3 sardines, and ¾ cup of spinach. Store in the refrigerator.

Remove the meatloaf from the oven and allow it to cool for 10 minutes. Keep the oven on 350°F. Slice the meatloaf into 8 (1-inch) slices and store in the refrigerator.

Next make the **Mini Vegetable Quiches**. Coat a muffin tin with cooking spray and place liners in each cup. In a medium bowl, whisk together the eggs and egg whites. Add the Parmesan cheese, rosemary, salt, and black pepper. In a medium sauté pan, heat the olive oil over medium heat, and sauté the red onion and garlic for 1 minute. Add the chopped mushrooms and continue sautéing for about 5 minutes. Remove the pan from the heat and allow it to cool, slightly.

Place 1 heaping tablespoon of the mushroom mixture into each of the muffin cups, and cover with a pinch of chopped spinach. Evenly pour the egg mixture over each muffin, filling the cup to the rim. Bake until set, about 25 minutes.

While the quiches are baking, prepare the **To-Go Snack Boxes**. Hard boil 5 eggs (4 will be for the **Tuna Niçoise Salad**). Place the eggs in a medium pot and cover with water. Place the pot over high heat and bring the water to a boil; boil the eggs for 3 minutes. Remove the pot from the heat, cover it, and allow the eggs to stand for 15 minutes. Drain, then run cold water over the eggs until completely cool, about 10 minutes.

In one snack box add cheese, grapes, and crackers. In a second box add 1 sliced hardboiled egg, 1 mozzarella cheese stick, and 1 sliced cucumber. In a third box add 2 celery stalks, cut into 3-inch sticks, 1 sliced apple (with a few drops of freshly squeezed lemon juice on top to prevent them from browning), and 1 tablespoon of peanut butter. Cover each box and store in the refrigerator. Set the remaining 4 hardboiled eggs aside.

WEIGHT LOSS MEAL PLAN # 1

Next prepare the **Lighter Creamed Spinach**. Place the thawed spinach and ¼ cup of water in a medium saucepan over high heat. Bring it to a boil, then reduce the heat to medium-low. Cook for about 5 minutes and let the spinach cool for 5 minutes.

Place spinach on a clean dish towel or in cheesecloth and squeeze over the sink to remove any excess liquid. Transfer the spinach to a medium bowl. Add the remaining ingredients and stir to combine. Allow the spinach to cool slightly, then store in a resealable container in the refrigerator.

Remove the mini quiches from the oven, and set aside to cool for 10 minutes. Keep the oven at 350°F. Remove the quiches from the tin and place in a resealable container for up to 5 days.

Next make the **Tuna Niçoise Salad**. Coat a baking sheet with cooking spray. Slice the potatoes. In a small bowl, add the potatoes, olive oil, and salt and toss to evenly coat. Spread the potatoes in a single layer on the baking sheet. Roast the potatoes for 20 to 25 minutes. Chop and slice the salad vegetables. Let the roasted potatoes cool for 10 minutes.

To layer the salad in Mason jars, place 1 cup of spinach in each of four jars. Top each with ¼ cup of potatoes, 1 quartered hardboiled egg, ¼ cup each of the green beans and tomatoes, and ½ can of tuna (with the oil). Sprinkle each with black pepper and add the lemon wedge. Cover the jars and store them in the refrigerator.

WEIGHT LOSS MEAL PLAN # 2

RECIPE 1: SLOW-COOKER BEEF STEW
Page 177   **Makes** 4 servings   **Prep time:** 15 minutes   **Store:** Store the cooled stew in resealable containers in the refrigerator for up to 1 week.

RECIPE 2: ONE-POT MEDITERRANEAN CHICKEN AND QUINOA
Page 152   **Makes** 6 servings   **Prep time:** 20 minutes   **Store:** Store in a resealable container in the refrigerator for up to 1 week.

RECIPE 3: KALE PESTO
Page 206   **Makes** 6 servings   **Prep time:** 10 minutes   **Store:** Store the pesto in a resealable plastic container in the refrigerator for up to 1 week.

RECIPE 4: PESTO CHICKEN
Page 150   **Makes** 4 servings   **Prep time:** 5 minutes   **Store:** Store the chicken in a resealable container in the refrigerator for up to 1 week.

RECIPE 5: CACAO-DATE OATMEAL
Page 78   **Makes** 4 servings   **Prep time:** 5 minutes   **Store:** Place 1 cup of oatmeal into each of 4 individual containers, cover, and store in the refrigerator for up to 3 days.

RECIPE 6: TURMERIC WILD RICE AND BLACK BEANS
Page 97   **Makes** 6 servings   **Prep time:** 15 minutes   **Store:** Store the rice and bean mixture in a resealable container in the refrigerator for up to 5 days.

RECIPE 7: HOMEMADE GRANOLA
Page 84   **Makes** 12 servings   **Prep time:** 15 minutes   **Store:** Once completely cooled, store at room temperature in a resealable container for up to 1 month.

RECIPE 8: SRIRACHA HUMMUS
Page 201   **Makes** 6 servings   **Prep time:** 10 minutes   **Store:** Place the hummus in a resealable container in the refrigerator for up to 5 days.

RECIPE 9: MASON JAR KEY LIME PARFAITS
Page 199   **Makes** 2 servings   **Prep time:** 10 minutes   **Store:** Place the sealed jars in the refrigerator for up to 5 days.

WEIGHT LOSS MEAL PLAN # 2

SHOPPING LIST

PANTRY
- See page 46

FRUIT
- 6 dates
- ½ cup unsweetened dried apples
- 1 lemon
- 1 lime

VEGETABLES, HERBS, AND SPICES
- 1 cup baby carrots (about 20)
- 1 celery stalk
- 4 cups fresh basil leaves
- 7 garlic cloves
- 2 cups baby kale
- 1 (10-ounce) container button mushrooms
- 2½ medium yellow onions
- 1 cup frozen peas
- 1¼ pounds sweet potatoes

PROTEIN
- 1½ pounds beef stew meat
- 1 (3.75-pound) whole chicken, cut into 8 pieces
- 1¼ pounds boneless, skinless chicken breasts

GRAINS
- 2 cups old-fashioned oats
- 2 cups rolled oats
- 1½ cups quinoa
- 1 cup wild rice

DAIRY
- 2 cups nonfat milk
- 1¼ cups nonfat plain Greek yogurt

NUTS AND SEEDS
- ½ cup raw almonds

OTHER
- 1 (8-ounce) can reduced-sodium black beans
- 2 (15-ounce) cans low-sodium chickpeas
- ¾ cup pitted Kalamata olives
- 3 tablespoons tahini
- 2 tablespoons tomato paste
- 2 (14.5-ounce) cans low-sodium diced tomatoes

Meal Plans | 53

WEIGHT LOSS MEAL PLAN # 2

MEAL PREP DAY

Start with the **Slow-Cooker Beef Stew**. Dice the potatoes. In a small bowl, whisk together the liquid ingredients and spices. Place the vegetables and meat in the slow cooker and pour the liquid mixture over them. Cover and cook on high for 4 to 6 hours.

While the stew is cooking, prepare the **One-Pot Mediterranean Chicken and Quinoa**. Chop the onions and slice the olives. Heat the olive oil in a large skillet over medium heat. Add the chicken and cook for about 8 minutes, stirring frequently. Transfer the chicken to a plate and set aside.

In the same skillet over medium heat, add the garlic and onion and sauté for 3 minutes. Add the remaining ingredients except the quinoa, increase the heat to high, and bring the mixture to a boil. Reduce the heat to low and let simmer for about 5 minutes. Return the chicken to the skillet and toss to coat. Add the quinoa, increase the heat to high, and bring the mixture to a boil. Reduce the heat to low and simmer, covered, until the chicken and quinoa are cooked through, about 15 minutes, stirring occasionally. Allow the chicken and quinoa to cool. Transfer to a resealable container and refrigerate.

Next prepare the **Kale Pesto**. In a food processor or blender, purée the ingredients into a paste. Keep the pesto in a resealable container in the refrigerator.

Preheat the oven to 350°F for the **Pesto Chicken**. Spoon ¼ cup of the **Kale Pesto** into a small bowl. Brush the pesto on both sides of the chicken and place the breasts in a single layer in a large ovenproof baking dish. Bake until the chicken is cooked through, 60 to 75 minutes.

While the chicken is baking, make the **Cacao-Date Oatmeal**. Combine the oats and milk in a pot over medium-low heat. Bring it to a simmer, stirring frequently. Cook until the oats begin to soften, about 7 minutes. Stir in the cinnamon, chopped dates, and cacao nibs until evenly distributed and the chocolate is melted. Remove the pot from the heat and divide 1-cup portions of the oatmeal into four individual containers and allow to cool for 10 to 15 minutes. Cover and store in the refrigerator.

WEIGHT LOSS MEAL PLAN # 2

Next prepare the **Turmeric Wild Rice and Black Beans**. Bring a medium pot of water to a boil over medium-high heat. Stir in the wild rice, then reduce the heat to medium-low to bring it to a simmer. Cover the pot and let the rice cook until it gets fluffy, about 1 hour.

Remove the chicken from the oven and allow it to cool. Keep the oven at 350°F. Transfer the cooled chicken to a resealable container and refrigerate.

While the rice is cooking, prepare the **Homemade Granola**. Line a baking sheet with parchment paper or aluminum foil and coat with cooking spray. In a medium bowl, mix together the oats, almonds, and apples. Add the cinnamon and salt and stir to evenly distribute. In a small bowl, whisk together the maple syrup and water. Pour this over the oat mixture, then fold together to evenly coat. Allow the mixture to stand for 5 minutes so the oats absorb the liquid. Spread the oat mixture in a thin, even layer on the baking sheet. Bake until golden brown, about 40 minutes, stirring the granola with a wooden spoon every 10 minutes.

While the rice continues to cook and the granola is in the oven, prepare the **Sriracha Hummus**. Put all of the ingredients except the olive oil in a food processor or blender and blend to combine. With the machine running, slowly add the olive oil and water and blend until well incorporated. Transfer the hummus to six individual storage containers and place in the refrigerator.

The rice should be done and fluffy. Drain any excess water.

Continue making the **Turmeric Wild Rice and Black Beans**. Chop the mushrooms and onion and mince the garlic for the beans and rice. In a large skillet over medium-low heat, heat the oil until it shimmers. Add the onions, mushrooms, and garlic and sauté until the onions are translucent and the mushrooms are tender, about 3 minutes. Add the wild rice and beans to the skillet and stir to combine. Stir in the turmeric, cumin, and salt and continue cooking to allow the flavors to combine, about 3 minutes. Allow the rice to cool, then store in a resealable container in the refrigerator.

Remove the granola from the oven and allow it to cool for 15 minutes.

WEIGHT LOSS MEAL PLAN # 2

Finally, prepare the **Mason Jar Key Lime Parfaits**. In a small bowl, combine the Greek yogurt, lime juice and zest, and maple syrup. In each of two Mason jars, layer 5 tablespoons of the Greek yogurt and top it with 2 tablespoons of the cooled granola. Repeat for a second layer. Seal the jars and place in the refrigerator.

Once the stew is done, divide it between four resealable containers and allow to cool. Cover and store in the refrigerator, or put two of the containers in the freezer.

MUSCLE BUILDING

This muscle building meal plan is designed for those who hit the weights hard at the gym. In order to fuel intensive strength training, you need fat and carbs for energy and protein for muscle building. The meals I've included are designed to give you a balance of muscle building nutrients naturally available in grains, lean proteins, dairy, fruits, vegetables, and healthy fats. The menu focuses mostly on whole grains, with minimal added sugar (like maple syrup and agave) and controlled amounts of saturated fats and sodium. Aim for a carbs-to-protein-to-fat ratio of 45:25:30. There are many ways to dress up the meal, while still adhering to this ratio. And, of course, don't forget to stay hydrated before, during, and after workouts.

An effective muscle building meal plan will have men consuming about 2,500 calories daily, with about 600 at breakfast and 700 at both lunch and dinner. Include two 250-calorie snacks throughout the day, especially when you are hungriest or go for stretches of 5 or more hours without food. If you need fewer calories for your body size (weight and height) and amount of training, keep it to just one snack per day for a total daily calorie intake of about 2,250. If you need more calories or feel hungry with two snacks, go for three snacks per day for a total of 2,750 calories.

Women should consume about 2,000 calories daily with about 400 calories at breakfast and 600 calories at both lunch and dinner. Include two 200-calorie snacks during the day. If you need fewer calories for your body size (weight and height) and amount of training, go with one snack a day for a total of 1,800 calories daily. If you need more calories or feel hungry, increase it to three snacks per day for a total of 2,200 calories.

MUSCLE BUILDING PANTRY

- 100% maple syrup
- Almond butter
- Bay leaves
- Black pepper, freshly ground
- Black peppercorns
- Brown sugar
- Cayenne pepper
- Chicken broth, low-sodium
- Chocolate chips, dark
- Cinnamon, ground
- Cocoa powder, unsweetened
- Cooking spray
- Cumin, ground
- Dijon mustard
- Garlic powder
- Honey
- Italian seasoning
- Nutmeg, ground
- Olive oil
- Olive oil, extra-virgin
- Onion powder
- Oregano, dried
- Paprika, smoked
- Peanut butter, natural smooth
- Rosemary, dried
- Salt
- Sriracha
- Tahini
- Tarragon, dried
- Vegetable broth, low-sodium
- Vinegar, apple cider
- Vinegar, red wine
- Vinegar, rice, unseasoned
- White wine, dry

MUSCLE BUILDING MEAL PLAN # 1

RECIPE 1: SLOW-COOKER BARBECUE PULLED PORK
Page 185   **Makes** 6 servings   **Prep time:** 10 minutes   **Store:** Once cooled, place in resealable container in the refrigerator for up to 1 week.

RECIPE 2: MINI VEGETABLE QUICHES
Page 71   **Makes** 12 mini quiches   **Prep time:** 15 minutes   **Store:** Refrigerate the quiches in a resealable container for up to 5 days.

RECIPE 3: QUINOA POWER BREAKFAST JAR
Page 91   **Makes** 1 serving   **Prep time:** 10 minutes   **Store:** The sealed glass jar can be stored in the refrigerator for up to 3 days.

RECIPE 4: HONEY RICOTTA WITH STRAWBERRIES
Page 192   **Makes** 4 servings   **Prep time:** 10 minutes   **Store:** Place the honey ricotta and strawberries in separate resealable containers in the refrigerator for up to 5 days.

RECIPE 5: ARUGULA SALAD WITH SALMON
Page 111   **Makes** 4 servings   **Prep time:** 15 minutes   **Store:** Store individual salad containers in the refrigerator for up to 5 days. When ready to eat, top each serving with 1 tablespoon of the dressing. Alternatively, the dressing can be placed at the bottom of a Mason jar and then topped with the arugula and salmon. Keep in the refrigerator for up to 5 days and shake the jar to evenly coat the salad before eating.

RECIPE 6: LEMONY CHICKEN BREASTS
Page 159   **Makes** 4 servings   **Prep time:** 15 minutes   **Store:** Place one breast in each of four resealable containers in the refrigerator for up to 1 week.

RECIPE 7: CHOCOLATE ENERGY BALLS
Page 190   **Makes** 12 balls   **Prep time:** 15 minutes   **Store:** Store the balls in a resealable container in the refrigerator for up to 1 week.

RECIPE 8: CAULIFLOWER-RICE MUSHROOM RISOTTO
Page 123   **Makes** 4 servings   **Prep time:** 15 minutes   **Store:** Store the cooled risotto in a resealable container in the refrigerator for up to 5 days.

MUSCLE BUILDING MEAL PLAN # 1

SHOPPING LIST

PANTRY
- See page 58

FRUIT
- ½ banana
- ¼ cup frozen wild blueberries
- 8 pitted dates
- 2 lemons
- 3 cups strawberries

VEGETABLES, HERBS, AND SPICES
- 7 ounces arugula
- 1 (12-ounce) package frozen riced cauliflower
- 4 garlic cloves
- 1 (8-ounce) container brown mushrooms
- 6 ounces button mushrooms
- ½ medium red onion
- ½ white onion
- 3 ounces fresh baby spinach
- 1 tablespoon fresh rosemary
- 3 cups cherry tomatoes

PROTEIN
- 4 (5-ounce) skinless, boneless chicken breasts
- 11 eggs
- 6 pounds bone-in pork shoulder
- 1 pound salmon fillet

GRAINS
- ½ cup rolled oats
- ½ cup quinoa

DAIRY
- ½ cup unsweetened plain almond milk
- 1 tablespoon unsalted butter
- 1 cup grated Parmesan cheese
- 1 cup part-skim ricotta cheese

NUTS AND SEEDS
- ¼ cup unsalted cashews
- ½ cup unsalted sunflower seeds
- ¼ cup raw walnuts

MUSCLE BUILDING MEAL PLAN # 1

MEAL PREP DAY

Start with the **Slow-Cooker Barbecue Pulled Pork**. In a small bowl, combine the ingredients for the dry rub. Rub the spice mixture all over the pork. Add the cider vinegar and water to a slow cooker and then add the pork. Cover and cook on high for 6 hours.

Next prepare the **Mini Vegetable Quiches**. Preheat the oven to 350°F. Coat a muffin tin with cooking spray and place liners in each cup. In a medium bowl, whisk together the eggs and egg whites. Stir in the Parmesan cheese, rosemary, salt, and black pepper. In a medium sauté pan over medium heat, heat the olive oil until it shimmers. Add the red onion and garlic and sauté for 1 minute. Add the chopped mushrooms and continue to cook for 5 minutes. Remove the pan from the heat and allow the vegetables to cool slightly. Place 1 heaping tablespoon of the mushroom mixture into each of the muffin cups and cover with a large pinch of chopped spinach. Gently pour the egg mixture into each muffin cup, filling them to the rim. Bake for 25 minutes.

While the quiches are baking, prepare the **Quinoa Power Breakfast Jar**. In a small bowl, mix the mashed banana, almond butter, and honey until smooth and creamy. Add the almond milk and whisk to thoroughly combine. Gently fold in the quinoa and 2 tablespoons of the blueberries. Pour this mixture into a 10-ounce glass jar and top with remaining 2 tablespoons of blueberries. Seal the jar and refrigerate for at least 8 hours to allow the flavors to combine.

Next prepare the **Honey Ricotta with Strawberries**. In a small bowl, combine the ricotta, honey, and cashews. Place ¼ cup of the mixture and ¾ cup of halved strawberries in each of four resealable containers and store in the refrigerator.

Remove the quiches from the oven and let them cool for 10 minutes before removing them from the tin. Increase the oven temperature to 425°F. Store the quiches in a resealable container in the refrigerator. If desired, individually wrap and freeze the quiches for another week.

Prepare the **Arugula Salad with Salmon**. Coat a baking sheet with cooking spray. Place the salmon, skin-side down, on the sheet. Season the salmon with ⅛ teaspoon each of the salt and black pepper. Bake for 20 to 22 minutes.

MUSCLE BUILDING MEAL PLAN # 1

While the salmon is baking, prepare the salad and dressing. Wash the arugula, halve the tomatoes, mince the garlic, and chop the walnuts. In a small bowl, whisk together the rice vinegar, garlic, lemon juice, mustard, tarragon, and remaining 1/8 teaspoon each of salt and black pepper. While whisking vigorously, slowly drizzle in the olive oil until it's combined. Transfer to a resealable container and refrigerate.

Remove the salmon from the oven and reduce the oven temperature to 400°F. Once the salmon has cooled for 10 minutes, slice it into 4 even pieces. In each of four containers, add 1½ cups of arugula, ½ cup of cherry-tomato halves, 1 tablespoon of chopped walnuts, and 1 piece of salmon. Cover the containers and store in the refrigerator. When it comes time to serve the salad, top each serving with 1 tablespoon of the dressing.

Next prepare the **Lemony Chicken Breasts**. Coat an 8-by-11-inch baking dish with cooking spray. Coat the chicken breasts with cooking spray and season with the salt and black pepper. Place them in the baking dish.

In a small saucepan over medium heat, heat 1 tablespoon of olive oil until it shimmers. Add the garlic and cook until fragrant, about 30 seconds. Add the wine, chicken broth, lemon juice and zest, and rosemary and bring to a boil. Reduce the heat to low and continue cooking until flavors combine, 3 to 4 minutes. Pour the lemon sauce over the chicken and tuck the lemon slices around the breasts. Bake for 25 minutes, then cover the dish with aluminum foil and continue to bake an additional 10 minutes.

While the chicken is baking, prepare the **Chocolate Energy Balls**. Line a medium container with parchment paper. Add the ingredients to a food processor or blender and pulse until crumbly. Transfer the batter to a medium bowl. Using clean hands, roll 1 tablespoon of batter into a 2-inch ball and put it in the container. Repeat for remaining balls for a total of 12. Cover the container and put it in the refrigerator to allow the balls to set. Store in the refrigerator until ready to eat.

Remove the chicken from the oven and allow it to cool. Transfer it to four resealable containers and store in the refrigerator.

MUSCLE BUILDING MEAL PLAN # 1

Finally, prepare the **Cauliflower-Rice Mushroom Risotto**. Chop the mushrooms and onions, halve the tomatoes, and mince the garlic. In a medium skillet over medium heat, heat the butter. Add the onions, mushrooms, and garlic and sauté until the onions are translucent, about 5 minutes. Add the cauliflower rice and tomatoes and stir to combine. Add the broth and bring the liquid to a boil. Reduce the heat to low and simmer, uncovered, about 7 minutes, stirring occasionally. Remove the skillet from the heat and stir in the Parmesan cheese. Allow the risotto to cool, then put it in a resealable container and refrigerate.

When the slow-cooker pork is ready, transfer the meat to a large bowl. Add half of the juices from the cooker to the bowl, discarding the rest. Use two forks to shred the meat, discarding any fat and bones. Store the shredded pork in a resealable container in the refrigerator. If desired, put half the pork in a freezer-safe container and freeze for another week.

MUSCLE BUILDING MEAL PLAN # 2

RECIPE 1: SLOW-COOKER TUSCAN CHICKEN
Page 161   **Makes** 4 servings   **Prep time:** 15 minutes   **Store:** Once cooled, store the chicken in resealable containers in the refrigerator for up to 1 week.

RECIPE 2: CHIMICHURRI SAUCE
Page 212   **Makes** 6 servings   **Prep time:** 10 minutes   **Store:** Store sauce in a resealable container in the refrigerator for up to 5 days.

RECIPE 3: POACHED SALMON WITH CHIMICHURRI SAUCE
Page 133   **Makes** 4 servings   **Prep time:** 5 minutes   **Store:** Store the salmon in a resealable container in the refrigerator for up to 5 days.

RECIPE 4: SRIRACHA HUMMUS
Page 201   **Makes** 6 servings   **Prep time:** 10 minutes   **Store:** Store the hummus in a resealable container in the refrigerator for up to 5 days.

RECIPE 5: HOMEMADE TRAIL MIX
Page 193   **Makes** 4 servings   **Prep time:** 5 minutes   **Store:** Store the trail mix in a resealable container at room temperature for up to 1 month.

RECIPE 6: SWEET POTATO PROTEIN PANCAKES
Page 73   **Makes** 6 servings   **Prep time:** 15 minutes   **Store:** Store the pancakes in a sealed container in the refrigerator for up to 1 week.

RECIPE 7: ZIPPY'S SHAKSHUKA
Page 72   **Makes** 6 servings   **Prep time:** 15 minutes   **Store:** Divide the shakshuka among six individual containers, including 1 egg per container topped with sauce. Store in the refrigerator for up to 5 days.

MUSCLE BUILDING MEAL PLAN # 2

SHOPPING LIST

PANTRY

- See page 58

FRUIT

- 10 dried apricots
- 3 tablespoons dried tart cherries
- 1½ lemons

VEGETABLES, HERBS, AND SPICES

- 1 cup fresh basil leaves
- 1 green bell pepper
- 1 tablespoon chopped cilantro
- 5 garlic cloves
- 1 (8-ounce) container button mushrooms
- 1½ medium yellow onions
- 1 cup packed parsley
- 1 shallot
- 2 large sweet potatoes

PROTEIN

- 4 (5-ounce) boneless, skinless chicken breasts
- 15 large eggs
- 1¼ pounds salmon fillet

GRAINS

- 1½ cups rolled oats

DAIRY

- 1½ cups low-fat cottage cheese

NUTS AND SEEDS

- ½ cup raw almonds
- 2 tablespoons unsalted sunflower seeds
- 3 tablespoons tahini

OTHER

- 1 (15-ounce) can reduced-sodium chickpeas
- 2 (28-ounce) cans crushed tomatoes
- ¼ cup pitted black olives

Meal Plans | 65

MUSCLE BUILDING MEAL PLAN # 2

MEAL PREP DAY

Start with the **Slow-Cooker Tuscan Chicken**. Add the ingredients to the slow cooker and stir to combine. Cover and cook on low for 4 to 6 hours.

Make the **Chimichurri Sauce**. In a food processor or blender, combine all the ingredients except the olive oil and pulse until combined. Add the olive oil and pulse until coarsely puréed.

Next make the **Poached Salmon with Chimichurri Sauce**. In a medium saucepan over high heat, bring 8 cups of water to a boil. Add the bay leaves and peppercorns. Add the salmon, bring the water back to a boil, and poach the salmon for 1 minute. Turn off the heat and cover the pan. Let the salmon sit, covered, for 20 minutes. Carefully remove the fillets from the saucepan and allow them to cool. Discard the liquid.

While the salmon is poaching, prepare the **Sriracha Hummus**. Put all the ingredients except the olive oil in a food processor or blender and blend to combine. With the machine running, slowly pour in the olive oil and water and continue blending until well incorporated. Transfer the hummus to storage containers and place in the refrigerator.

Now prepare the **Homemade Trail Mix**. In a medium bowl, add the ingredients and toss to combine. Equally divide among four resealable containers or plastic bags and store at room temperature.

Once the salmon is cooked, slice it into four 5-ounce pieces and allow to cool. Store in a resealable container in the refrigerator.

Next begin the **Sweet Potato Protein Pancakes**. Preheat the oven to 400°F. Pierce each potato several times with a fork. Place them on a baking sheet and bake for about 50 minutes.

While the potatoes are baking, make **Zippy's Shakshuka**. Slice the vegetables and chop the cilantro. In a large sauté pan over medium-low heat, heat the oil until it shimmers. Add the onions and bell pepper and sauté for about 5 minutes. Add the garlic and sauté for 1 minute more. Add the canned tomatoes, cilantro, salt, black pepper, and sriracha and stir to combine. Raise the heat to medium-high

MUSCLE BUILDING MEAL PLAN # 2

and bring mixture to a boil, then reduce the heat to medium-low. Cover the pan and cook for an additional 10 minutes to allow flavors to blend.

Break 1 egg into a wine glass. Gently pour the egg into the outer edge of the sauté pan. Repeat with the remaining 5 eggs until a circle is formed with the eggs in the outer edge of the pan. Reduce the heat to low, cover the pan, and cook until the eggs are poached, about 6 minutes. Divide the shakshuka into six resealable individual containers, including 1 egg per container topped with sauce. Refrigerate.

Remove the sweet potatoes from the oven and carefully make a slit lengthwise on the top of each potato. Let them cool for 10 minutes. Scoop out the flesh into the blender. Add the cottage cheese, oats, eggs, egg whites, cinnamon, nutmeg, and maple syrup to a blender and blend until smooth. Spray a large skillet with nonstick cooking spray and place it over medium heat. Scoop a heaping $1/3$ cup of the batter into the skillet and cook the pancakes until golden brown and crisp along the edges, about 4 minutes per each side. Store the pancakes in a resealable container in the refrigerator.

Once the slow-cooker chicken is done, stir in the fresh basil and olives. Divide the chicken among four resealable containers and store in the refrigerator.

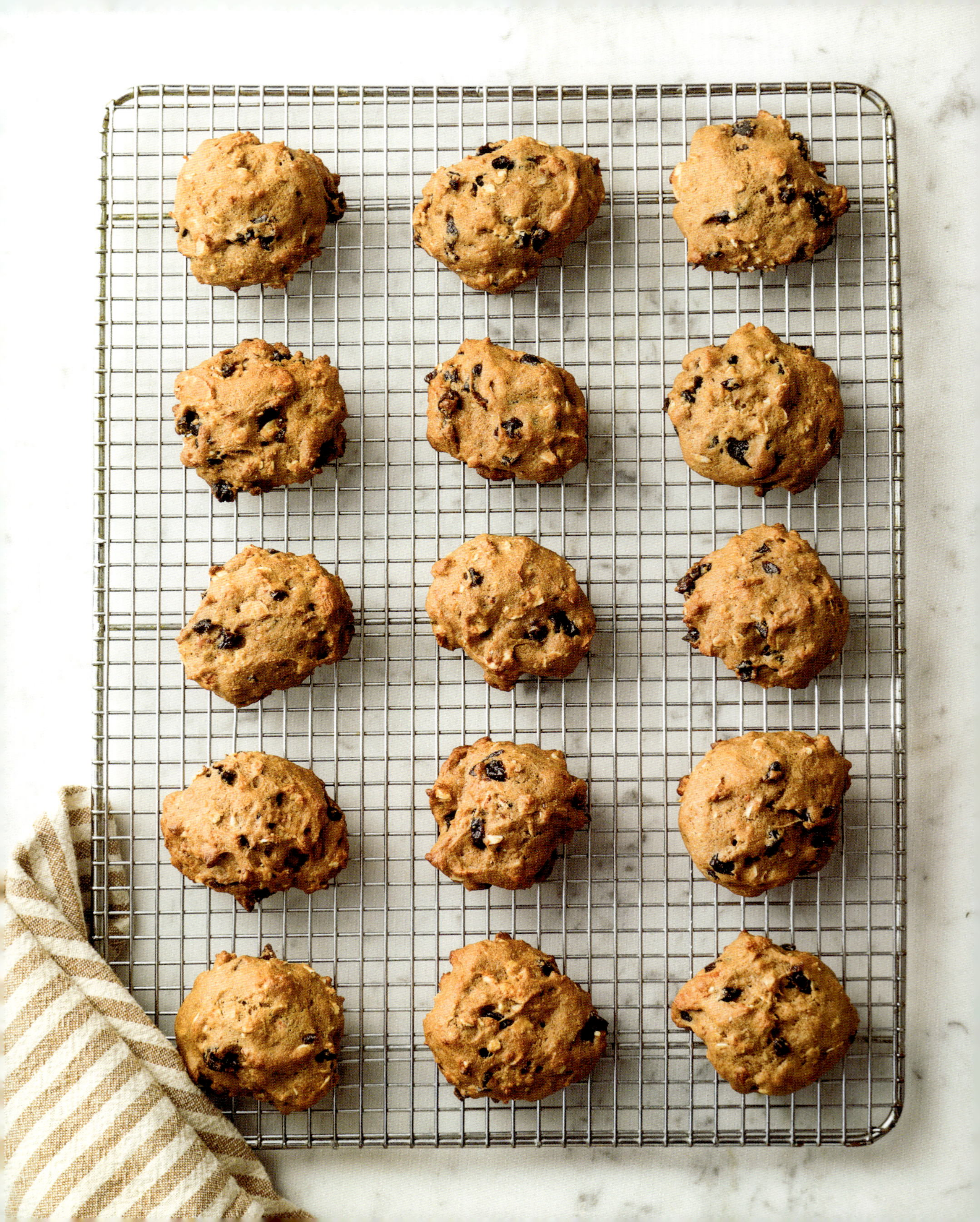

3 BREAKFAST

70 Avo-Egg Scramble Wrap
71 Mini Vegetable Quiches
72 Zippy's Shakshuka
73 Sweet Potato Protein Pancakes
74 Whole-Grain Pancakes with Spiced Greek Yogurt Sauce
76 Brooklyn Breakfast
77 Blackberry-Lemon Overnight Oats
78 Cacao-Date Oatmeal
79 Tart Cherry–Almond Breakfast Cookies
81 Apple Walnut Loaf
82 Wild Blueberry Whole-Grain Scones
84 Homemade Granola
85 Pear-Cinnamon Oat Muffins
87 Meyer Lemon Cranberry-Ricotta Muffins
89 Tropical Green Smoothie
90 Strawberry-Chocolate-Almond Smoothie Jar
91 Quinoa Power Breakfast Jar
92 Fruit Salsa and Yogurt Crêpes

« Tart Cherry–Almond Breakfast Cookies (page 79)

VEGETARIAN

AVO-EGG SCRAMBLE WRAP

MAKES 1 SERVING

PREP TIME: 10 minutes   **COOK TIME:** 10 minutes

One of my favorite breakfast foods are eggs. Their boost of protein keeps me feeling satisfied until my morning snack. I also love to pair eggs with vegetables (basically anything I have in my refrigerator), adding important vitamins and minerals into my body first thing in the morning. Rolling my egg scramble into a whole-grain wrap is the perfect grab-and-go vehicle and gives me a healthy dose of fiber, too. It's an easy recipe to double—triple, even quadruple!—for the rest of the family or to refrigerate for other mornings during the week.

1 egg

2 egg whites

⅛ teaspoon salt

⅛ teaspoon freshly ground black pepper

Cooking spray

1 (10-inch) whole-wheat tortilla

1 teaspoon olive oil

¼ small onion, chopped

1 baby bella mushroom, diced

3 cherry tomatoes, quartered

1 tablespoon crumbled feta cheese

¼ avocado, sliced

1. In a large bowl, whisk together the eggs, egg whites, salt, and black pepper. Coat a medium skillet with the cooking spray, and heat over low heat until warm. Add the tortilla and warm it for about 30 seconds, then flip and heat on the other side. Transfer the tortilla to a plate.

2. Increase the heat under the skillet to medium and add the olive oil. Add the onions and mushrooms and sauté until the onions turn translucent and the mushrooms are softened, about 3 minutes. Add the tomatoes and continue to cook until the tomatoes soften, about 2 minutes. Pour the egg mixture over the sautéed vegetables. Using a spatula, fold and invert the eggs until large, soft curds form, about 2 minutes.

3. Spoon the scrambled eggs onto the tortilla and top with the feta cheese and avocado. Roll up each tortilla, tuck in the ends, and enjoy.

TO GO: Roll the Avo-Egg Scramble Wrap in foil and slice in half. Eat within 2 hours.

> **TOBY'S TIP:** To keep sliced avocado from browning, add a few drops of citrus juice like lemon, lime, or orange and wrap it tightly with plastic wrap. Store in the refrigerator for 1 to 2 days.

Per Serving: Calories: 438; Fat: 23g; Saturated Fat: 5g; Protein: 22g; Total Carbs: 38g; Fiber: 9g; Sodium: 861mg

GLUTEN-FREE   VEGETARIAN

MINI VEGETABLE QUICHES

MAKES 12 MINI QUICHES

PREP TIME: 15 minutes   COOK TIME: 30 minutes

Quiches are an easy-to-make, portable form of eggs. Besides protein, eggs also contain the antioxidant lutein, which specifically impacts the health of your skin, eyes, and heart.

Cooking spray

5 eggs

6 egg whites

¾ cup Parmesan cheese, grated

1 tablespoon fresh rosemary, chopped, or 1 teaspoon dried rosemary

½ teaspoon salt

¼ teaspoon freshly ground black pepper

2 teaspoons olive oil

½ medium red onion, finely chopped (about ½ cup)

1 garlic clove, minced

6 ounces button mushrooms, finely chopped

3 ounces (about ¾ cup) fresh baby spinach, finely chopped

1. Preheat the oven to 350°F and coat a muffin tin with the cooking spray and place liners in each muffin cup.

2. In a medium bowl, whisk together the eggs and egg whites. Whisk in the Parmesan cheese, rosemary, salt, and black pepper.

3. In a medium skillet over medium heat, heat the olive oil. Add the onion and garlic and sauté until fragrant, about 1 minute. Add the mushrooms and continue cooking until the mushrooms are softened, about 5 minutes. Remove the pan from the heat and allow the mixture to cool slightly.

4. Place 1 heaping tablespoon of the mushroom mixture into each of the muffin cups, and add a large pinch of chopped spinach. Gently pour the egg mixture into each muffin cup, filling each to the rim.

5. Bake until the tops are golden brown, about 25 minutes. Let the quiches cool for 10 minutes before removing them from the tin.

REFRIGERATE: Store the cooled quiches in a resealable plastic or glass container for up to 5 days. Reheat in the microwave for 45 to 60 seconds and allow to cool for 2 minutes before eating.

FREEZE: Store the cooled quiches in a single row in a freezer-safe container for up to 2 months. Thaw in the refrigerator overnight and reheat in a preheated 300°F oven for 5 minutes. Alternatively, microwave for 45 to 60 seconds and allow to cool for 2 minutes before eating.

> **TOBY'S TIP**: Want to save time on cleanup? Use paper muffin liners when making quiches (and muffins).

Per Serving (1 mini quiche): Calories: 83; Fat: 5g; Saturated Fat: 2g; Protein: 8g; Total Carbs: 2g; Fiber: 0g; Sodium: 289mg

DAIRY-FREE **GLUTEN-FREE** **PALEO** **VEGETARIAN**

ZIPPY'S SHAKSHUKA

MAKES 6 SERVINGS

PREP TIME: 15 minutes   **COOK TIME:** 20 minutes

Also called Eggs in Purgatory, shakshukas are a combination of eggs and vegetables in a tomato-based sauce. As a little girl I spent my summers in Israel, where the temperatures hit close to 110°F. It was so hot, nobody wanted to spend the time cooking elaborate dinners. At least once a week, my mom (her nickname is Zippy) would whip up shakshuka and serve it over couscous or with pita bread. These days I love shakshuka for breakfast and serve it with a slice of whole-grain crusty bread to dip in the delicious sauce.

- 1 tablespoon olive oil
- 1 medium onion, cut into 1-inch-wide strips
- 1 green bell pepper, cut into 1-inch-wide strips
- 1 garlic clove, minced
- 1 (28-ounce) can crushed tomatoes
- 1 tablespoon chopped fresh cilantro, or 1 teaspoon dried cilantro
- ¼ teaspoon salt
- ¼ teaspoon freshly ground black pepper
- 1 teaspoon sriracha
- 6 large eggs

1. In a large sauté pan over medium heat, heat the olive oil until it shimmers. Add the onions and bell pepper and sauté until softened, about 5 minutes. Add the garlic and cook until fragrant, about 1 minute. Stir in the crushed tomatoes, cilantro, salt, black pepper, and sriracha. Increase the heat to medium-high and bring the mixture to a boil, then reduce the heat to medium-low. Cover the pan and simmer for about 10 minutes to let the flavors blend together.

2. Break 1 egg into a wine glass. Gently pour the egg into the pan along the outer edge. Repeat with remaining 5 eggs so a circle is formed with the eggs along the outer edge of the pan. Reduce the heat to low, cover the pan, and cook until eggs are poached, about 6 minutes.

REFRIGERATE: Place the shakshuka in six individual containers, each including one egg topped with sauce. Store for up to 5 days. Reheat in the microwave for 1 minute and let it cool for 2 minutes to allow the heat to evenly distribute.

> **TOBY'S TIP:** Have extra sauce from your shakshuka? Use it over baked or grilled chicken or fish.

Per Serving (1 egg and ½ cup sauce): Calories: 153; Fat: 7g; Saturated Fat: 2g; Protein: 9g; Total Carbs: 14g; Fiber: 4g; Sodium: 469mg

GLUTEN-FREE **VEGETARIAN**

SWEET POTATO PROTEIN PANCAKES

MAKES 6 SERVINGS

PREP TIME: 15 minutes   COOK TIME: 1 hour, 15 minutes

These power-packed pancakes provide 18 grams of protein per serving and a healthy dose of the antioxidant vitamins A and C, plus a good dose of whole grains. You really can't get a more well-balanced, delicious breakfast.

2 large sweet potatoes
1½ cups low-fat cottage cheese
1½ cups old-fashioned oats
5 large eggs
4 large egg whites
1 teaspoon ground cinnamon
¼ teaspoon ground nutmeg
1½ tablespoons 100% maple syrup
Cooking spray

1. Preheat the oven to 400°F.
2. Pierce each potato several times with a fork. Place them on a baking sheet and bake until tender, about 50 minutes. Remove from the oven and carefully make a slit lengthwise across the top of each potato. Let them cool for 10 minutes. Scoop the flesh into a blender.
3. Add the cottage cheese, oats, eggs, egg whites, cinnamon, nutmeg, and maple syrup to the blender, and blend until smooth.
4. Spray a large skillet with the cooking spray and place it over medium heat. When the pan is hot, scoop a heaping ⅓ cup of the batter into the skillet and cook pancakes until they are golden brown and crisp on the bottom, about 4 minutes per side.

REFRIGERATE: Store the pancakes in resealable containers for up to 1 week. Reheat in the microwave for 20 seconds or warm in the toaster oven.

FREEZE: Store the pancakes in a freezer-safe container for up to 3 months. Thaw in the refrigerator overnight. Reheat in the microwave for 20 seconds or warm in a toaster oven.

> **TOBY'S TIP:** Don't toss out the golden yolks! Whole eggs, with the yolk, are a perfect protein, providing all the essential amino acids. The yolks contain good-for-you nutrients like vitamins A and D, omega-3 fatty acids, and the antioxidant lutein. .

Per Serving (2 pancakes): Calories: 238; Fat: 6g; Saturated Fat: 2g; Protein: 18g; Total Carbs: 28g; Fiber: 4g; Sodium: 350mg

VEGETARIAN

WHOLE-GRAIN PANCAKES WITH SPICED GREEK YOGURT SAUCE

MAKES 6 SERVINGS

PREP TIME: 15 minutes   COOK TIME: 10 minutes

Pancakes tend to be a carb-fest and put me back to sleep 30 minutes after breakfast. Instead, I like to add both fat and protein to my morning meal to keep it well-balanced. Protein, fiber, and healthy fats also take longer to digest, keeping me satisfied throughout the morning (and without making me sleepy!). These pancakes use whole-grain flour, plus protein-rich Greek yogurt in the batter, as well as canola oil—a healthy monounsaturated fat—instead of butter.

FOR THE GREEK YOGURT SAUCE

- 2 cups nonfat plain Greek yogurt
- 2 tablespoons 100% maple syrup
- 1 teaspoon vanilla extract
- ½ teaspoon ground cinnamon
- ⅛ teaspoon ground nutmeg

FOR THE PANCAKES

- 1 cup unbleached all-purpose flour
- 1 cup white whole-wheat flour, or 100% whole-wheat flour
- 3 tablespoons granulated sugar
- 1½ teaspoons baking powder
- ½ teaspoon baking soda
- ½ teaspoon salt
- 1 cup low-fat milk
- ½ cup nonfat plain Greek yogurt
- 4 teaspoons canola oil
- 2 large eggs
- ½ teaspoon vanilla extract
- Cooking spray

TO MAKE THE GREEK YOGURT SAUCE

In a medium bowl add the Greek yogurt, maple syrup, vanilla extract, cinnamon, and nutmeg, and stir to evenly combine. Set aside.

TO MAKE THE PANCAKES

1. In a medium bowl, sift together the all-purpose flour, whole-wheat flour, sugar, baking powder, baking soda, and salt.

2. In another medium bowl, whisk together the milk, Greek yogurt, oil, eggs, and vanilla extract. Pour the flour mixture into the yogurt mixture and gently stir until combined. Do not overmix.

3. Coat a griddle or large skillet with the cooking spray and place over medium heat. Once hot, scoop ¼ cup of batter onto the griddle or skillet, leaving room between cakes. Cook until the top is bubbly and the edges are set, about 2 minutes. Flip the pancakes over and cook until golden brown and crisp along the edges, about 2 minutes. Remove and keep warm until ready to serve. Repeat with remaining batter.

4. Serve 2 pancakes on a plate and topped with ⅓ cup of the yogurt sauce.

REFRIGERATE: Store the pancakes and yogurt sauce in separate resealable containers for up to 1 week. Reheat the pancakes in the microwave for 20 seconds or warm in the toaster oven, then top with the yogurt sauce.

FREEZE: Store the pancakes in a freezer-safe container for up to 3 months. Thaw in the refrigerator overnight. Reheat in the microwave for 20 seconds or warm in a toaster oven. The yogurt sauce will not freeze well.

> **TOBY'S TIP:** There are always ways to use leftovers so food doesn't go to waste. Top extra Greek yogurt sauce with berries or homemade granola, or use in a fruit smoothie.

Per Serving (2 pancakes plus ⅓ cup yogurt sauce): Calories: 311; Fat: 6g; Saturated Fat: 1g; Protein: 17g; Total Carbs: 47g; Fiber: 3g; Sodium: 467mg

BROOKLYN BREAKFAST

MAKES 1 SERVING

PREP TIME: 5 minutes   COOK TIME: 5 minutes

I was born in Brooklyn, New York, and this was the breakfast served when family visited, for brunch, or on a special occasion. Now that I'm a mom, I serve the same breakfast to my kids. But I'm also on a budget and don't want to spend the money on a pound of smoked salmon. Fear not! The flavor of smoked salmon is very rich, which means a small amount goes a long way. A smaller 3-ounce package of smoked salmon from Trader Joe's or my local supermarket, or asking my local deli to slice a few ounces for me, keeps me in budget and lets me enjoy this delicious breakfast.

One 100% whole-wheat English muffin, sliced in half
Cooking spray
1 large pasteurized egg
⅛ teaspoon salt
⅛ teaspoon freshly ground black pepper
1 tablespoon whipped cream cheese
1 ounce smoked salmon
2 slices tomato

1. Toast the English muffin and set it on a plate.

2. Coat a medium skillet with the cooking spray and place it over medium heat. Crack the egg into a cup then gently pour it into the skillet, being careful not to break the yolk. Cook until the white solidifies around the yolk, about 2 minutes. Carefully flip over the egg and cook it for 2 minutes more. Season it with the salt and pepper.

3. While the egg cooks, top each English muffin half with half the cream cheese, smoked salmon, and tomato slices. When the egg is cooked, slide it onto one of the tomato slices. Top the sandwich with the other English muffin, cream cheese, smoked salmon, and tomato half.

TO GO: Wrap in aluminum foil and take it on the go.

> **TOBY'S TIP:** Choose whipped cream cheese whenever possible. It has fewer calories than regular cream cheese because of the air incorporated when it is whipped. This means the same volume of whipped cream cheese has fewer calories than its regular cream cheese amount.

Per Serving: Calories: 284; Fat: 11g; Saturated Fat: 4g; Protein: 18g; Total Carbs: 29g; Fiber: 4g; Sodium: 845mg

GLUTEN-FREE   VEGETARIAN

BLACKBERRY-LEMON OVERNIGHT OATS

MAKES 1 SERVING

PREP TIME: 10 minutes, plus 8 to 10 hours to chill   COOK TIME: 0 minutes

One of the easiest breakfasts to prep ahead of time is overnight oats. The 10 minutes of work is just measuring and tossing ingredients together in a jar, and then letting the oats do the rest of the work. I like to make overnight oats for my kids, and then each child will top theirs as they like with their favorite fruits.

½ cup old-fashioned oats

⅓ cup nonfat milk

1 tablespoon 100% maple syrup

½ cup blackberries

½ teaspoon freshly grated lemon zest

1. Combine the oats, milk, and maple syrup in a 12-ounce jar, and stir to combine. Cover the jar with its lid and place in the refrigerator overnight.

2. Stir to recombine the mixture. Top with the blackberries and sprinkle with the lemon zest.

REFRIGERATE: Store for up to 3 days. If you choose to warm the oats, place the jar (without the lid) in the microwave for 2 minutes, then top with the fruit and zest.

> **TOBY'S TIP:** Make several jars of these overnight oats on your prep day so you have a prepared breakfast for several days. Overnight oats are also a quick, easy, and inexpensive lunch or dinner.

Per Serving: Calories: 289; Fat: 3g; Saturated Fat: 1g; Protein: 12g; Total Carbs: 56g; Fiber: 8g; Sodium: 72mg

Breakfast

GLUTEN-FREE   VEGETARIAN

CACAO-DATE OATMEAL

MAKES 4 SERVINGS

PREP TIME: 5 minutes   COOK TIME: 10 minutes

During the bone-chilling days of winter, I want to wake up to a warm bowl of oatmeal. Luckily, this simple dish takes just 10 minutes to prepare. I can even cook up a batch on my prep day and store the oatmeal in individual containers so I can grab it when I have an early day at work. Once at work, I pop it in the microwave and enjoy a filling, healthy breakfast.

- 2 cups old-fashioned oats
- 2 cups skim milk
- 2 cups water
- 1 teaspoon ground cinnamon
- 6 dates, pitted and chopped
- ¼ cup sweetened cacao nibs, or mini dark chocolate chips

1. Combine the oats, milk, and water in a pot over medium-low heat. Bring it to a simmer, stirring frequently. Cook until the oats begin to soften and the liquid thickens, about 7 minutes. Remove the pot from the heat.

2. Stir in the cinnamon, dates, and cacao nibs until evenly distributed and the chocolate is melted.

REFRIGERATE: Store in a resealable container for up to 3 days. Reheat in the microwave for 2 minutes and then let sit for 2 minutes so the heat distributes evenly. If desired, top with a splash of milk before eating.

> **TOBY'S TIP:** Want to up your morning protein intake? Stir in 1 tablespoon of peanut or almond butter or a scoop of whey protein to your morning bowl of oatmeal.

Per Serving (1 cup): Calories: 341; Fat: 6g; Saturated Fat: 2g; Protein: 11g; Total Carbs: 65g; Fiber: 8g; Sodium: 89mg

VEGETARIAN

TART CHERRY–ALMOND BREAKFAST COOKIES

MAKES 16 COOKIES

PREP TIME: 15 minutes   COOK TIME: 20 minutes

I love cookies for breakfast, especially when they're filled with so many good-for-you ingredients. These babies are filled with whole grains, nuts, and fruit. When I know I need to get out the door in a flash, it's easy to grab one or two and enjoy them with a cup of nonfat vanilla Greek yogurt or a glass of skim milk.

Cooking spray

½ cup rolled oats

2¼ cups white whole-wheat flour, or 100% whole-wheat flour

1 teaspoon baking soda

¼ teaspoon salt

½ cup unsweetened applesauce

½ cup nonfat plain Greek yogurt

½ packed cup brown sugar

½ cup 100% maple syrup

2 eggs

1 teaspoon vanilla extract

1 cup dried tart cherries, chopped

1 cup raw almonds, sliced

1. Preheat the oven to 350°F. Line two baking sheets with parchment paper and coat the paper with the cooking spray.

2. In a medium bowl, mix together the oats, flour, baking soda, and salt.

3. In a large bowl, whisk together the applesauce and Greek yogurt until well combined. Add the brown sugar and maple syrup and continue whisking until the mixture is smooth. Add eggs and vanilla extract and continue whisking until mixture is smooth and creamy.

4. Gently fold the dry ingredients into the wet ingredients, and stir until just combined. Fold in the cherries and almonds, making sure to evenly distribute them throughout the batter.

5. For each cookie, drop 2 tablespoons of batter onto the baking sheet, leaving about 2 inches around each cookie. Using clean hands, gently press down on the top of each cookie to slightly flatten them.

6. Bake until the cookies are soft and golden brown, and a toothpick inserted into the center of 1 or 2 cookies comes out clean, 15 to 20 minutes. Let the cookies cool for 5 minutes before eating.

STORAGE: Keep the cookies in a resealable glass or plastic container at room temperature for up to 5 days.

CONTINUED

Breakfast

TART CHERRY–ALMOND BREAKFAST COOKIES CONTINUED

FREEZE: Individually package each cookie in resealable plastic bags or wrap each cookie in plastic wrap and store for up to 2 months. Thaw at room temperature. The cookies can be eaten at room temperature, warmed in a toaster oven, or heated in the microwave for 20 to 30 seconds. Allow 2 minutes for the cookies to rest after heating in the microwave.

> **TOBY'S TIP:** Tart cherries aren't sold fresh because they're too tart. Instead you'll find them dried or turned into juice. These bad boys are packed with anthocyanin, a natural compound that gives the cherries their ruby-red color and distinctive sweet-sour flavor. Eating tart cherries helps decrease inflammation, reduces the risk of heart disease, and eases post-workout soreness.

Per Serving (1 cookie): Calories: 214; Fat: 6g; Saturated Fat: 1g; Protein: 6g; Total Carbs: 36g; Fiber: 4g; Sodium: 103mg

VEGETARIAN

APPLE WALNUT LOAF

MAKES 8 SERVINGS

PREP TIME: 15 minutes   COOK TIME: 50 to 55 minutes

When I was a little girl, my grandmother used to bake this loaf for me and my siblings. Her version, however, was made with lots of butter and only refined flour, resulting in a boatload of calories. My lighter version uses good-for-you ingredients.

Cooking spray

1 cup 100% whole-wheat flour

1 cup unrefined all-purpose flour

1 teaspoon baking soda

½ teaspoon salt

½ teaspoon cinnamon

½ cup unsweetened applesauce

½ cup honey

1 egg

½ cup unsweetened almond milk

1 Rome apple, chopped (about 1¼ cups)

½ cup raw walnuts, finely chopped

1. Preheat the oven to 325°F. Coat a 9-by-5-inch loaf pan with the cooking spray.

2. In a medium bowl, sift together the whole-wheat flour, all-purpose flour, baking soda, salt, and cinnamon.

3. In a large bowl, combine the applesauce and honey, and stir until well-combined. Add the egg and almond milk, and stir until thoroughly combined. Gently fold in the dry ingredients, being careful not to overmix the batter. Gently fold in the apples and walnuts, making sure to evenly distribute them throughout the batter. Pour the batter into the loaf pan and spread it into an even layer with a spatula.

4. Bake until a toothpick inserted in the center comes out clean, 50 to 55 minutes.

5. Let the loaf cool in the pan for 5 minutes. Transfer it from the pan onto a wire rack to finish cooling for 10 to 15 minutes. Slice the loaf into 1-inch slices.

STORAGE: Keep in a resealable glass or plastic container at room temperature for up to 5 days.

FREEZE: Individually package each slice in resealable plastic bags or wrapped in plastic wrap, and store for up to 2 months. Thaw at room temperature. The loaf can be eaten at room temperature, warmed in a toaster oven, or heated in the microwave for 20 to 30 seconds. Allow 2 minutes for the slices to rest after heating in the microwave.

Per Serving (one 1-inch slice): Calories: 206; Fat: 2g; Saturated Fat: 0g; Protein: 5g; Total Carbs: 45g; Fiber: 3g; Sodium: 272mg

VEGETARIAN

WILD BLUEBERRY WHOLE-GRAIN SCONES

MAKES 12 SCONES

PREP TIME: 15 minutes   **COOK TIME:** 15 minutes

I have a soft spot for pastries, so if left hungry and rushing to work, I'll fall victim to oversized muffins, donuts, and other baked goodies. Instead of falling into their sugary trap, I prepare my own healthier version at home using whole-wheat pastry flour, Greek yogurt, and fruit. They're perfect for making ahead and having on hand when I have to dash out the door.

Cooking spray

1¼ cups unbleached all-purpose flour

¾ cup whole-wheat pastry flour

4 teaspoons baking powder

½ teaspoon salt

¼ teaspoon baking soda

½ cup granulated sugar

1 large egg

3 tablespoons canola or safflower oil

1 cup nonfat plain Greek yogurt

½ cup low-fat milk

1 teaspoon vanilla extract

1 cup frozen dried wild blueberries, thawed

1. Preheat the oven to 400°F. Coat two baking sheets with the cooking spray.

2. In a medium bowl, sift together the all-purpose flour, whole-wheat pastry flour, baking powder, salt, and baking soda.

3. In a large bowl, whisk together the sugar, egg, oil, yogurt, milk, and vanilla extract.

4. Gently fold the dry ingredients into the wet ingredients until just combined. Be careful not to overmix the batter. Gently fold in the blueberries, making sure to evenly distribute them throughout the batter.

5. Drop generous ⅓ cups of batter onto the baking sheets, leaving about 2 inches of room all around each scone.

6. Bake until a toothpick inserted in the center of 1 or 2 scones comes out clean, about 15 minutes. Let the scones cool on the baking sheet for 5 minutes, then transfer them to a wire rack to finish cooling for 10 minutes more.

STORAGE: Keep the scones in a resealable glass or plastic container at room temperature for up to 3 days.

FREEZE: Individually package each scone in resealable plastic bags or wrap in plastic wrap, and store for up to 2 months. Thaw at room temperature. The scones can be eaten at room temperature, warmed in a toaster oven, or heated in the microwave for 20 to 30 seconds. Allow 2 minutes for the scone to rest after heating in the microwave.

> **TOBY'S TIP:** When fresh blueberries aren't in season, choose frozen ones. Wild blueberries are only found frozen, have a more intense blueberry flavor, and are packaged at their peak ripeness, which helps preserve important nutrients like antioxidants, fiber, and manganese.

Per Serving (1 scone): Calories: 160; Fat: 4g; Saturated Fat: 0g; Protein: 5g; Total Carbs: 26g; Fiber: 2g; Sodium: 293mg

DAIRY-FREE **GLUTEN-FREE** **VEGAN**

HOMEMADE GRANOLA

MAKES 12 SERVINGS

PREP TIME: 15 minutes   COOK TIME: 40 minutes

Many packaged granolas are made of healthy ingredients (nuts and fruit) but are combined with too much added sugar. A bowl at breakfast can weigh in at over 600 calories! This is why I like to make my own. My granola recipe uses a combo of oats, almonds, dried fruit, and a touch of 100% maple syrup. I enjoy my granola in controlled portions over oatmeal, Greek yogurt, fruit salad, or as a grab-and-go snack on its own.

Cooking spray

2 cups rolled oats

½ cup raw almonds, sliced

½ cup unsweetened dried apples, chopped

1 teaspoon ground cinnamon

¼ teaspoon salt

½ cup 100% maple syrup

½ cup water

1. Preheat the oven to 350°F. Line a baking sheet with parchment paper or aluminum foil and coat it with the cooking spray.

2. In a medium bowl, mix together the oats, almonds, and apples. Stir in the cinnamon and salt.

3. In a small bowl, whisk together the maple syrup and water. Pour this over the oat mixture, and then fold together to evenly coat the oats, almonds, and apples. Let stand for 5 minutes so the oats can absorb the liquid.

4. Stir the oat mixture to recombine the ingredients, then spread it in a thin, even layer onto the baking sheet. Bake for about 40 minutes, stirring the granola with a wooden spoon every 10 minutes. The finished granola should be golden brown. Let the granola cool for 15 minutes before eating.

STORAGE: Keep the cooled granola in a resealable plastic or glass container at room temperature for up to 1 month.

> **TOBY'S TIP:** When buying maple syrup, look for "100%" on the label to make sure you're getting the real deal. Those labeled 100% contain small amounts of nutrients like manganese, calcium, iron, and potassium. Imposters maple syrups are made from any number of ingredients, including liquid sucrose (aka sugar), and contain a laundry list of additives and preservatives.

Per Serving (¼ cup): Calories: 102; Fat: 3g; Saturated Fat: 0g; Protein: 2g; Total Carbs: 18g; Fiber: 2g; Sodium: 74mg

VEGETARIAN

PEAR-CINNAMON OAT MUFFINS

MAKES 12 MUFFINS

PREP TIME: 15 minutes **COOK TIME:** 20 minutes

Head to your corner bagel shop, and you'll find oversized muffins staring you in the face, tempting you into an impulse buy. These bad boys carry a hefty amount of calories, at least 400 each, and little nutritional value. With a little planning, meal prep, and a delicious recipe, muffins can also bring together highly nutritious ingredients like whole grains, fruits, vegetables, nuts, and seeds. Not to mention flavor!

Cooking spray
¼ cup oat bran
1 cup whole-wheat pastry flour
1 cup unbleached all-purpose flour
2 teaspoons baking powder
1 teaspoon baking soda
1 teaspoon cinnamon
¼ teaspoon salt
½ packed cup brown sugar
½ cup olive oil
1 cup nonfat plain Greek yogurt
1 egg
1 egg yolk
1 medium pear, chopped (about 1½ cups)
2 tablespoons rolled oats

1. Preheat the oven to 375°F. Coat a muffin tin with the cooking spray.

2. In a medium bowl, sift together the oat bran, pastry flour, all-purpose flour, baking powder, baking soda, cinnamon, and salt.

3. In a large bowl, whisk together the brown sugar and olive oil. Add the Greek yogurt, egg, and egg yolk, and whisk until smooth.

4. Gently fold the dry ingredients into the wet ingredients, being careful not to overmix the batter. Gently fold in the pear, making sure to evenly distribute it throughout the batter.

5. Scoop ¼ of batter into each muffin cup. Evenly sprinkle each muffin with the oats.

6. Bake until the muffins are golden brown on top and a toothpick inserted in the center comes out clean, about 20 minutes. Let the muffins cool for 5 minutes, then transfer them to a wire rack to finish cooling for another 10 minutes.

STORAGE: Keep the muffins in a resealable plastic container at room temperature for up to 7 days.

CONTINUED

PEAR-CINNAMON OAT MUFFINS CONTINUED

FREEZE: Individually wrap the muffins in plastic wrap or in individual freezer-safe containers for up to 3 months. Thaw at room temperature, then warm in the toaster oven or in a preheated 300°F oven for 5 minutes.

> **TOBY'S TIP:** For this muffin recipe, I use one of my favorite underappreciated fruit, pears, but you can substitute apples or peaches, too.

Per Serving (1 muffin): Calories: 223; Fat: 10g; Saturated Fat: 2g; Protein: 5g; Total Carbs: 29g; Fiber: 2g; Sodium: 214mg

VEGETARIAN

MEYER LEMON CRANBERRY-RICOTTA MUFFINS

MAKES 12 MUFFINS

PREP TIME: 15 minutes   COOK TIME: 25 minutes

I love experimenting with citrus fruit. There are so many fun varieties, and Meyer lemons, Cara Cara oranges, and Minneola tangelos pop up in supermarkets throughout the country. Once you're comfortable with being in the kitchen, start experimenting with these different delicious varieties of citrus. These muffins use Meyer lemons, which balance the flavor of cranberries and ricotta quite nicely.

Cooking spray

1¼ cups unbleached all-purpose flour

1 cup white whole-wheat flour, or 100% whole-wheat flour

2 teaspoons baking powder

½ teaspoon baking soda

½ teaspoon salt

1 cup whole-milk ricotta cheese

½ cup unsweetened applesauce

½ packed cup light brown sugar

Juice of 1 Meyer lemon

2 large eggs

1 cup dried cranberries

Zest of 1 Meyer lemon

1. Preheat the oven to 375°F. Coat a muffin tin with the cooking spray.

2. In a medium bowl, sift together the all-purpose flour, whole-wheat flour, baking powder, baking soda, and salt.

3. In a large bowl, mix together the ricotta and applesauce until well combined. Add the brown sugar, lemon juice, and eggs, and mix until smooth.

4. Gently fold the dry ingredients into the wet ingredients, being careful not to overmix the batter. Fold in the cranberries, making sure to evenly distribute them throughout the batter.

5. Scoop ¼ cup of batter into each muffin cup. Evenly sprinkle each muffin with the lemon zest.

6. Bake until the muffins are golden brown on top and a toothpick inserted in the center comes out clean, 18 to 22 minutes. Let the muffins cool for 5 minutes, then transfer the muffins to a wire rack to finish cooling for another 10 minutes.

CONTINUED

MEYER LEMON CRANBERRY-RICOTTA MUFFINS CONTINUED

FREEZE: Individually wrap the muffins in plastic wrap or in individual freezer-safe containers for up to 3 months. Thaw at room temperature, then warm in the toaster oven or in a preheated 300°F oven for 5 minutes.

> **TOBY'S TIP:** Meyer lemons are a cross between a regular lemon and a mandarin orange. They are sweeter than regular lemons, less acidic, and have a refreshing herbal scent. You can find Meyer lemons at your grocery store year-round. If unavailable, you can substitute regular lemons instead.

Per Serving (1 muffin): Calories: 198; Fat: 4g; Saturated Fat: 2g; Protein: 6g; Total Carbs: 36g; Fiber: 2g; Sodium: 213mg

GLUTEN-FREE   VEGETARIAN

TROPICAL GREEN SMOOTHIE

MAKES 12 SERVINGS

PREP TIME: 5 minutes   COOK TIME: 0 minutes

With 9 in 10 people not eating the daily recommended amounts of vegetables, smoothies are a perfect way to get in a serving first thing in the morning. Plus, with the combo of green veggies and different fruits, you'll be taking in a wide variety of good-for-you nutrients first thing in the morning. What better way to start your day!

- 2 cups chopped spinach or kale
- ½ banana
- ½ cup fresh or frozen unsweetened mango chunks
- ½ cup fresh or frozen unsweetened pineapple chunks
- 1 cup unsweetened almond milk
- ½ cup nonfat plain Greek yogurt
- 1 date, pitted

Add the spinach, banana, mango, pineapple, milk, yogurt, and date in a blender, and blend until smooth. Pour in a large glass or to-go cup and enjoy.

REFRIGERATE: To prep ahead of time, add the ingredients in the blender, cover it, and place in the refrigerator until ready to blend in the morning.

TOBY'S TIP: Keep a bag of pitted dates in your pantry. Toss 1 or 2 into smoothies for sweetness, in place of adding sugar.

Per Serving: Calories: 320; Fat: 4g; Saturated Fat: 0g; Protein: 16g; Total Carbs: 62g; Fiber: 8g; Sodium: 271mg

GLUTEN-FREE   VEGETARIAN

STRAWBERRY-CHOCOLATE-ALMOND SMOOTHIE JAR

MAKES 1 SERVING

PREP TIME: 5 minutes   **COOK TIME:** 0 minutes

When I was a beginner home chef, I put a ½ cup of almonds into the blender and burned the motor. I was so distraught that I went without smoothies for six months, refusing to invest in another blender! Over time, I learned that almond butter is much easier for the typical home blender to handle. I now leave the chopped almonds as a crunchy topping for smoothies.

- 1¼ cups fresh or frozen strawberries
- ½ cup plain nonfat Greek yogurt
- ½ cup 100% cranberry or pomegranate juice
- 1 tablespoon almond butter
- 1½ teaspoons unsweetened cocoa powder
- 4 teaspoons sweetened cacao nibs or mini dark chocolate chips, divided
- 1 tablespoon chopped raw almonds

Add the strawberries, yogurt, cranberry juice, almond butter, cocoa powder, and 2 teaspoons of cacao nibs in a blender, and blend until smooth. Pour into a 12-ounce glass jar and top the smoothie with the remaining 2 teaspoons of cacao nibs and the almonds.

REFRIGERATE: To prep ahead of time, add the same ingredients to the blender, cover it, and place in the refrigerator until ready to blend in the morning. Top with the remaining nibs and the almonds after blending.

> **TOBY'S TIP:** When purchasing juice, make sure it says 100% on the label. A small amount is a healthy way to add sweetness to dishes, plus it comes with a nice dose of vitamin C.

Per Serving: Calories: 418; Fat: 19g; Saturated Fat: 4g; Protein: 20g; Total Carbs: 47g; Fiber: 9g; Sodium: 96mg

DAIRY-FREE   GLUTEN-FREE   VEGETARIAN

QUINOA POWER BREAKFAST JAR

MAKES 1 SERVING

PREP TIME: 10 minutes, plus 8 hours to chill   COOK TIME: 0 minutes

You may be used to quinoa as a savory dish, but you can sweeten it, too! It's a fabulous way to take in a healthy dose of fiber and protein, as each ½ cup of cooked quinoa contains 2½ grams of fiber and 4 grams of protein. On days when I eat my Quinoa Power Breakfast Jar, I don't end up hungry and can focus on my morning routine.

- ½ banana, mashed (about ¼ cup)
- 1 tablespoon almond butter
- 1 teaspoon honey
- ½ cup unsweetened plain almond milk
- ½ cup cooked quinoa
- 4 tablespoons wild blueberries, frozen, divided

1. In a small bowl, mix the banana, almond butter, and honey until smooth and creamy. Add the almond milk, and whisk to thoroughly combine. Gently fold in the quinoa and 2 tablespoons of blueberries.

2. Pour the mixture into a 10-ounce glass jar and top with the remaining 2 tablespoons of blueberries. Seal the jar and refrigerate for at least 8 hours or overnight, allowing the flavors to combine.

3. When ready to eat, stir the mixture and enjoy.

REFRIGERATE: Store for up to 3 days. Give the mixture a stir before eating.

> **TOBY'S TIP:** Give dry quinoa a quick rinse before cooking to remove any bitter residue, called saponin, from the grain surface. You can also look for quinoa that has been prerinsed (it will say "prerinsed" on the label).

Per Serving: Calories: 337; Fat: 12g; Saturated Fat: 1g; Protein: 9g; Total Carbs: 52g; Fiber: 9g; Sodium: 99mg

VEGETARIAN

FRUIT SALSA AND YOGURT CRÊPES

MAKES 8 SERVINGS

PREP TIME: 15 minutes, plus 30 minutes to chill   COOK TIME: 20 minutes

Walking the streets of Paris, I love stopping at a local crêpe shop where they make fresh crêpes and fill them with sweet ingredients like chocolate-hazelnut spread or savory ingredients like chicken. Oftentimes, I cannot decide what I want! This combination of mouthwatering fruit, herbs, onions, and Greek yogurt is the perfect mix of both sweet and savory.

FOR THE SALSA
- 16 fresh strawberries, hulled and finely diced (about 1¾ cups)
- 3 kiwis, finely diced (about 1 cup)
- ½ red onion, diced (about ½ cup)
- 8 basil leaves, chopped
- Juice of 1 lemon
- ½ teaspoon salt
- ¼ teaspoon freshly ground black pepper

FOR THE CRÊPES
- 1¼ cups reduced-fat milk
- 4 large egg whites
- 1 tablespoon canola or safflower oil
- ¾ cup water
- 1 cup unbleached all-purpose flour
- Cooking spray
- 4 cups nonfat vanilla Greek yogurt

TO MAKE THE SALSA

Combine the strawberries, kiwi, onion, basil, lemon juice, salt, and black pepper in a medium bowl. Refrigerate for at least 30 minutes to allow the flavors to combine.

TO MAKE THE CRÊPES

1. In a medium bowl, whisk together the milk, egg whites, oil, and water. Gradually whisk in the flour until the mixture is well combined.

2. Coat a large skillet with the cooking spray, and place it over medium heat. When the skillet is hot, ladle in ⅓ cup of batter and cook, undisturbed, until the edges begin to slightly brown, 1 to 2 minutes. Using a spatula, flip the crêpe over and cook for 30 seconds more. Transfer the crêpe to a large plate and place a piece of parchment paper over the crêpe. Repeat with the remaining batter, placing parchment paper between each crêpe to prevent them from sticking together. You will have 8 crêpes.

3. Place 1 crêpe on a large plate and spoon ½ cup of Greek yogurt onto it and top with ⅓ cup of the fruit salsa. Fold in both sides and fold the crêpe in half to seal. Turn the crêpe over so the seam is on the bottom of the plate. Repeat with the remaining of the crêpes, salsa, and yogurt.

REFRIGERATE: Store the fruit salsa in a resealable container for up to 1 week. Place the crêpes, with parchment paper between each layer to prevent sticking, in a large container, and store at room temperature for up to 1 week.

> **TOBY'S TIP:** Use the fruit salsa to jazz-up grilled or baked chicken and fish.

Per Serving (1 crêpe): Calories: 235; Fat: 3g; Saturated Fat: 0g; Protein: 15g; Total Carbs: 41g; Fiber: 2g; Sodium: 231mg

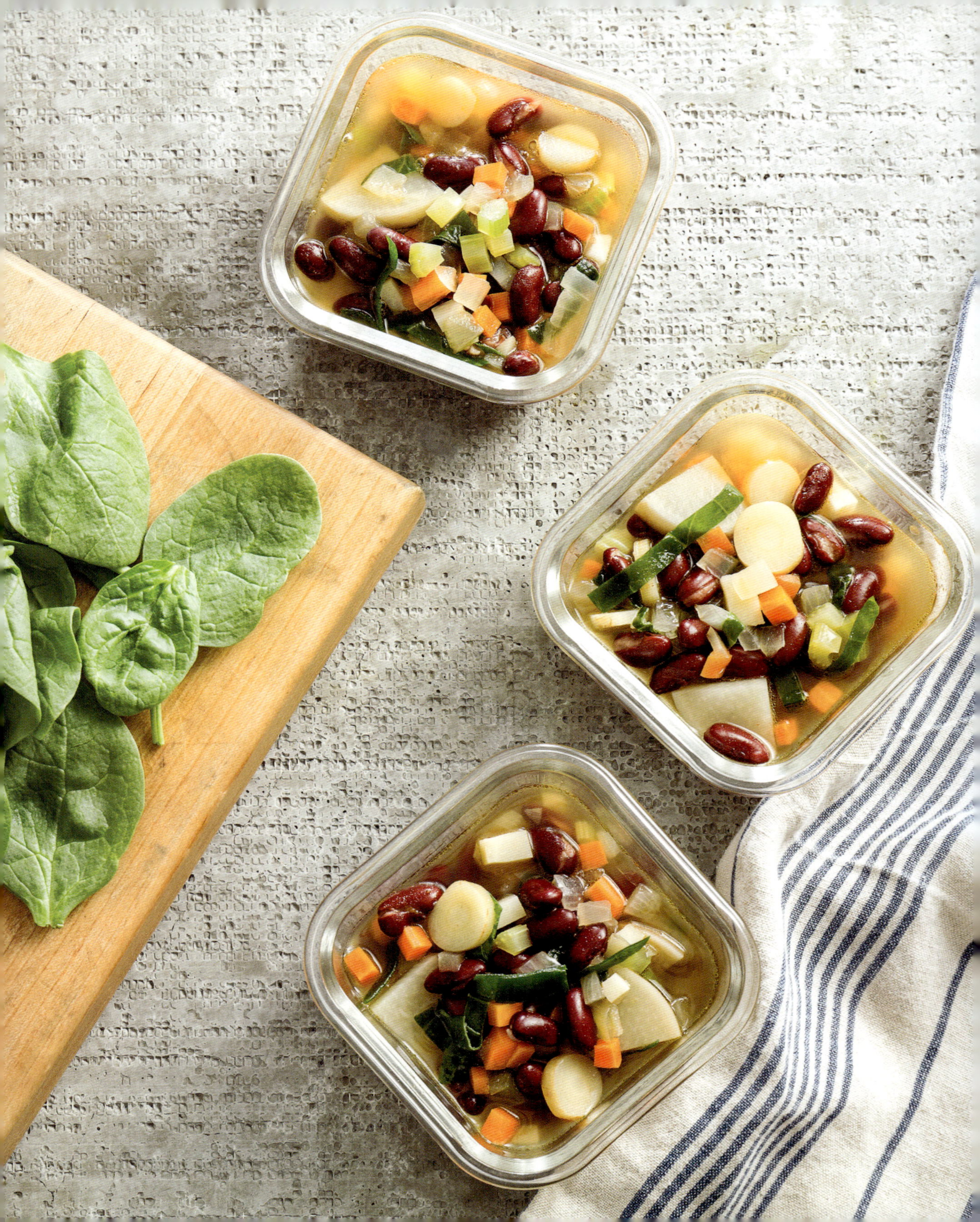

4 GRAINS & BEANS

- **96** Root Vegetable and Bean Soup
- **97** Turmeric Wild Rice and Black Beans
- **98** Oven-Roasted Tomato Quinoa
- **99** Balsamic Onion and Mango Quinoa
- **100** Farro Tabbouleh
- **101** Mushroom-Kale Brown Rice
- **102** Onion-Parsley Quinoa
- **103** Corn and Tomato Couscous
- **104** Indian-Style Sautéed Chickpeas
- **105** Asian "Fried" Brown Rice
- **106** Bulgur-Stuffed Tomatoes
- **107** Slow-Cooker Three-Bean Chili

« Root Vegetable and Bean Soup (page 96)

DAIRY-FREE **VEGAN**

ROOT VEGETABLE AND BEAN SOUP

MAKES 4 SERVINGS

PREP TIME: 15 minutes COOK TIME: 25 minutes

In the winter, when fewer fresh veggies are in season, my mom cooked us dishes using root vegetables. Oftentimes, she tossed whatever she could find into a pot and added beans, lentils, chicken, or turkey. This root-veggie soup makes me feel nostalgic and has become my go-to dish on those cold winter days.

- 1 packed cup baby spinach
- 1 tablespoon olive oil
- 1 medium onion, chopped
- 1 medium carrot, chopped
- 1 celery stalk, chopped
- 1 medium parsnip, chopped
- 1 medium turnip, chopped
- 1 (15-ounce) can low-sodium kidney beans, drained and rinsed
- 6 cups low-sodium vegetable broth
- 1 tablespoon mirin
- 2 bay leaves
- ¼ teaspoon freshly ground black pepper

1. Stack the spinach leaves, roll them up, and then slice into ribbons. Work in batches if needed.

2. In a large pot over medium heat, heat the olive oil until it shimmers. Add the onion, carrot, celery, parsnip, and turnip, and sauté until the onion is translucent, about 4 minutes. Add the beans, and stir to combine. Add the vegetable broth, mirin, and bay leaves, and stir to combine. Increase the heat to high and bring the liquid to a boil, then reduce the heat to low, cover the pot, and simmer until the beans are tender, about 20 minutes.

3. Remove and discard the bay leaves. Stir in the spinach ribbons and black pepper.

REFRIGERATE: Store the cold soup in a resealable container for up to 1 week. Reheat in a pot over medium-high heat. Bring the soup to a boil, then reduce the heat to low and simmer for 10 minutes. Single servings can be reheated in the microwave on high for 2 to 3 minutes.

FREEZE: Store the cooled soup in individual freezer-safe containers or in one large container for up to 2 months. Thaw in the refrigerator overnight. Reheat in a pot over medium-high heat. Bring soup to a boil, then reduce the heat to low and simmer for 10 minutes. Single servings can be reheated in the microwave on high for 2 to 3 minutes.

Per Serving (2 cups): Calories: 220; Fat: 4g; Saturated Fat: 1g; Protein: 9g; Total Carbs: 38g; Fiber: 10g; Sodium: 477mg

DAIRY-FREE **GLUTEN-FREE** **VEGAN**

TURMERIC WILD RICE AND BLACK BEANS

MAKES 6 SERVINGS

PREP TIME: 15 minutes   COOK TIME: 1 hour, 10 minutes

Rice and beans is a staple in my kitchen because I can repurpose it for many meals. I use it as a side dish to accompany a slice of chicken or fish, or I add it to my lunch bowl with sautéed greens, leftover chicken or beef, and top it with sliced avocado. I have added rice and beans to a wrap with a scrambled egg. The possibilities are endless, and all are delicious.

4 cups water

1 cup wild rice

2 teaspoons olive oil

½ onion, chopped

1 (10-ounce) package button mushrooms, chopped

2 garlic cloves, minced

1 (8-ounce) can reduced-sodium black beans, drained and rinsed

½ teaspoon ground turmeric

¼ teaspoon ground cumin

¼ teaspoon salt

1. In a medium pot, bring the water to a boil. Stir in the wild rice and reduce the heat to medium-low. Cover the pot and let the rice cook until it gets fluffy, about 1 hour. Drain any excess water from the rice.

2. Just before the rice is done, heat the olive oil in a large skillet over medium-low heat. When it is hot, add the onion, mushrooms, and garlic, and cook until the onions are translucent and the mushrooms are tender, about 3 minutes. Add the rice and beans, and stir to combine. Stir in the turmeric, cumin, and salt, and cook until the flavors are combined, about 3 minutes.

REFRIGERATE: Store the cooled rice and beans in a resealable container for up to 5 days. To reheat in the microwave, add 1 to 2 tablespoons of water to the dish before heating.

FREEZE: Store the cooled rice and beans in a freezer-safe container for up to 2 months. To reheat from frozen, add about ¼ cup of water to the pot along with the rice and beans.

> **TOBY'S TIP:** If you purchased regular beans (rather than reduced-sodium), rinse the beans well. Rinsing canned beans can reduce the amount of sodium up to 40%.

Per Serving (1 cup): Calories: 190; Fat: 2g; Saturated Fat: 0g; Protein: 10g; Total Carbs: 35g; Fiber: 7g; Sodium: 206mg

GLUTEN-FREE   VEGETARIAN

OVEN-ROASTED TOMATO QUINOA

MAKES 6 SERVINGS

PREP TIME: 15 minutes   **COOK TIME:** 40 minutes

Quinoa is a wonderful ingredient to deliver any number of flavors, whether sweet or savory. It takes on and enhances the flavors of the other ingredients in a recipe. This simple salad uses one of my favorite combinations of tomatoes and parsley, traditional to Mediterranean cuisine, which I grew up eating. The light and flavorful combination pairs perfectly with fish, alongside chicken, or over a green salad.

Cooking spray

2 cups cherry tomatoes, halved

½ cup chopped parsley, divided

3 tablespoons olive oil, divided

¼ teaspoon salt

⅛ teaspoon freshly ground black pepper

1 cup quinoa

2 cups low-sodium vegetable broth

¼ cup grated Parmesan cheese

1. Preheat the oven to 350°F. Coat a baking sheet with the cooking spray.

2. In a medium bowl, toss together the tomatoes, ¼ cup of chopped parsley, 1 tablespoon of olive oil, salt, and black pepper. Spread the tomatoes in a single layer on the baking sheet.

3. Bake for 15 to 20 minutes, or until the tomatoes are slightly browned.

4. In a medium saucepan, bring the quinoa and vegetable broth to a boil over high heat. Reduce the heat to low, cover the pan, and simmer until all the liquid has been absorbed, 12 to 15 minutes. Remove the pan from the heat and fluff the quinoa with a fork. Set aside to cool for 10 minutes.

5. Put the quinoa in a medium bowl. Toss it with the roasted tomatoes, the remaining ¼ cup of parsley, the remaining 2 tablespoons of olive oil, and Parmesan cheese.

REFRIGERATE: Store the cooled quinoa in a resealable container for up to 5 days. Serve cold.

> **TOBY'S TIP:** Bought way too many herbs? Freeze them! After chopping them, fill each pocket of an ice-cube tray ¼ full with the finely chopped herbs and top it with water. Once the cubes are frozen, store them in a resealable plastic bag or container.

Per Serving (¾ cup): Calories: 165; Fat: 8g; Saturated Fat: 2g; Protein: 6g; Total Carbs: 19g; Fiber: 3g; Sodium: 194mg

DAIRY-FREE   GLUTEN-FREE   VEGAN

BALSAMIC ONION AND MANGO QUINOA

MAKES 6 SERVINGS

PREP TIME: 15 minutes   COOK TIME: 25 minutes

I love getting creative by adding fruit into savory dishes like this one. One cup of sliced mango provides 3 grams of fiber and over 20 vitamins and minerals, including the antioxidant vitamins A and C. Mango also provides natural plant compounds called flavanoids, which may help control high blood pressure and reduce the risk of stroke and heart disease.

Cooking spray

1 cup quinoa

2 cups low-sodium vegetable broth or water

1 medium red onion, halved and thinly sliced into half-moons

2 tablespoons balsamic vinegar

1 tablespoon olive oil

1 teaspoon chopped fresh rosemary

¼ teaspoon salt

⅛ teaspoon freshly ground black pepper

1 mango, diced

2 scallions, chopped

1. Preheat the oven to 375°F. Coat a baking sheet with the cooking spray.

2. Put the quinoa and vegetable broth in a medium saucepan, and bring it to a boil over high heat. Reduce the heat to low, cover the pan, and simmer until all the liquid has been absorbed, 12 to 15 minutes. Remove the pan from the heat and fluff the quinoa with a fork.

3. In a small bowl, add the onions. Toss them with the vinegar, olive oil, rosemary, salt, and black pepper. Place in a single layer on the baking sheet and roast until the onions soften and begin to brown along the edges, about 12 minutes.

4. In a large bowl, combine the quinoa, balsamic onions, mango, and scallions. Gently toss to combine.

REFRIGERATE: Store the cooled quinoa in a resealable container for up to 5 days. Serve cold.

TOBY'S TIP: Shake things up by swapping 1½ cups of diced pineapple for the mango.

Per Serving (¾ cup): Calories: 134; Fat: 3g; Saturated Fat: 0g; Protein: 4g; Total Carbs: 24g; Fiber: 3g; Sodium: 127mg

Grains & Beans

DAIRY-FREE   **VEGAN**

FARRO TABBOULEH

MAKES 6 SERVINGS

PREP TIME: 20 minutes, plus 30 minutes to chill   COOK TIME: 30 minutes

I grew up on this Middle Eastern dish, which is customarily made with bulgur. Over the years, I've played around with the grain, and like the addition of nontraditional chickpeas. This version, made with farro, adds more protein without compromising the traditional flavors..

- 1 cup farro
- 3 cups water
- 1 cup reduced-sodium canned chickpeas, drained and rinsed
- ½ hothouse cucumber, chopped
- 1 cup cherry tomatoes, quartered
- ½ small onion, diced
- 1 bunch parsley, chopped
- 3 tablespoons extra-virgin olive oil
- Juice of 1 lemon (about 2 tablespoons)
- ½ teaspoon salt
- ¼ teaspoon freshly ground black pepper

1. In a medium pot, bring the water to a boil over high heat. Stir in the farro, then reduce the heat to medium-low and simmer until the water is absorbed and the grain is tender, about 30 minutes. Drain off any excess liquid. Let the farro cool for about 10 minutes, then transfer to a container, cover, and refrigerate for at least 30 minutes.

2. In a large bowl, combine the chickpeas, cucumber, tomatoes, and onions. Add the chopped parsley and toss to combine. Add the chilled farro and toss to evenly combine.

3. Add the olive oil, lemon juice, salt, and black pepper to the farro and toss to evenly coat.

REFRIGERATE: Store the tabbouleh in a resealable container for up to 5 days.

TOBY'S TIP: For another spin on this dish, swap the farro for traditional bulgur and swap half the parsley for mint.

Per Serving (1 cup): Calories: 236; Fat: 9g; Saturated Fat: 1g; Protein: 8g; Total Carbs: 34g; Fiber: 7g; Sodium: 277mg

DAIRY-FREE   **GLUTEN-FREE**   **VEGAN**

MUSHROOM-KALE BROWN RICE

MAKES 8 SERVINGS

PREP TIME: 20 minutes   COOK TIME: 50 minutes

My mom used to put mushrooms in everything, which I wasn't fond of as a kid. Now, however, I love the umami flavor they add to dishes and the fact that they go with pretty much everything—vegetables, chicken, fish, beef, and pork. Lucky for me, my kids love them, too.

- 3 cups water
- 1 cup brown rice
- 1 tablespoon olive oil
- 1 (10-ounce) container white mushrooms, chopped
- ½ medium onion, chopped
- 1 garlic clove, minced
- 3 cups chopped kale
- ½ teaspoon salt
- ¼ teaspoon freshly ground black pepper
- ¼ cup raw walnuts, chopped

1. In a medium pot, bring the water to a boil over high heat. Stir in the brown rice and reduce the heat to medium-low. Cover the pot and let the rice simmer, stirring it occasionally, until tender, about 40 minutes. Drain off any excess water. Transfer the rice to a large bowl and allow to cool slightly.

2. In a medium saucepan over medium heat, heat the olive oil until it shimmers. Add the mushrooms, onions, and garlic, and cook until the onion is translucent, about 5 minutes. Add the kale, cover the pan, and cook, stirring occasionally, until the kale is wilted, about 5 minutes.

3. Add the mushroom-kale mixture to the bowl with the rice and season with the salt and black pepper. Toss to combine. Top with the chopped walnuts.

REFRIGERATE: Store the cooled rice in a resealable container for up to 5 days. Reheat in a small saucepan over medium heat, or reheat individual portions in the microwave for 1 minute.

TOBY'S TIP: Have extra spinach? Use it instead of kale.

Per Serving (¾ cup): Calories: 149; Fat: 5g; Saturated Fat: 1g; Protein: 5g; Total Carbs: 23g; Fiber: 2g; Sodium: 163mg

DAIRY-FREE   GLUTEN-FREE   VEGAN

ONION-PARSLEY QUINOA

MAKES 6 SERVINGS

PREP TIME: 10 minutes   COOK TIME: 20 minutes

There are so many ways to flavor this protein-packed grain (technically a seed, but delicious, healthy, and versatile nonetheless). Sautéing the onions in a nice olive oil adds new levels of flavor to this quinoa and takes only minutes to cook. Top a green salad with it or wrap it in a whole-grain tortilla for an easy lunch.

- 1½ cups quinoa
- 3 cups low-sodium vegetable broth
- 2 teaspoons olive oil
- ½ sweet yellow onion, chopped (about ½ cup)
- ½ cup chopped parsley
- ¼ teaspoon salt
- ¼ teaspoon freshly ground black pepper
- 2 scallions, white parts only, sliced

1. In a medium pot, bring the quinoa and vegetable broth to a boil over high heat. Reduce the heat to low, cover the pot, and simmer until the water has been absorbed and the quinoa is soft and fluffy, about 15 minutes. Remove the pot from the heat and use a fork to fluff the quinoa.

2. While quinoa is cooking, heat the olive oil in a sauté pan over medium heat. Add the onions and cook until they are translucent, about 2 minutes. Turn off the heat and stir in the parsley.

3. Add the quinoa to the onion and parsley mixture, season with the salt and black pepper, and gently toss to combine. Top with sliced scallions.

REFRIGERATE: Store the room-temperature quinoa in a resealable container for up to 5 days. The quinoa can be eaten cold or reheated in the microwave or on the stove over low heat.

TOBY'S TIP: Have a rice cooker? Use it to cook the quinoa, using 2 cups of liquid for every 1 cup of quinoa (a 2:1 ratio). Prepping just got even easier.

Per Serving (1 cup): Calories: 155; Fat: 3g; Saturated Fat: 0g; Protein: 5g; Total Carbs: 27g; Fiber: 3g; Sodium: 182mg

DAIRY-FREE   **VEGAN**

CORN AND TOMATO COUSCOUS

MAKES 8 SERVINGS

PREP TIME: 15 minutes, plus 30 minutes to chill   COOK TIME: 10 minutes

Summer barbecues are one of my favorite activities. I cannot, however, take those side salads packed with artery-clogging mayonnaise and loads of refined carbs. Instead, I make this whole-grain side packed with veggies that helps add bulk and a ton of flavor. It's a welcome and appreciated addition to any summer barbecue.

- 1½ cups whole-wheat couscous
- ½ cup fresh parsley, chopped (stems saved)
- Zest of 1 lemon
- 2 cups water, divided
- 1 cup frozen corn kernels
- 1 cup cherry tomatoes, halved
- 2 scallions, chopped
- 1 tablespoon extra-virgin olive oil
- Juice of 1 lemon (about 2 tablespoons)
- ½ teaspoon salt
- ¼ teaspoon freshly ground black pepper

1. Put the couscous, parsley stems, and lemon zest in a medium, heat-proof bowl. Bring 1¾ cups of water to a boil and pour it over the couscous. Stir to separate any clumps. Cover the bowl until the water is absorbed, about 5 minutes. Fluff the couscous with a fork and remove and discard the zest and parsley stems.

2. In a small saucepan, bring ¼ cup of water to a boil over high heat. Add the corn, reduce the heat to low, and simmer until the corn is heated through, about 5 minutes.

3. Add chopped parsley, corn, tomatoes, and scallions to the couscous. Toss gently to combine. Add the olive oil, lemon juice, salt, and black pepper. Toss to evenly coat.

REFRIGERATE: Store the room-temperature couscous in a resealable container for up to 5 days. Serve cold.

TOBY'S TIP: Add some cheesy goodness to this couscous with ¾ cup diced part-skim mozzarella cheese.

Per Serving (¾ cup): Calories: 152; Fat: 3g; Saturated Fat: 0g; Protein: 5g; Total Carbs: 30g; Fiber: 4g; Sodium: 153mg

DAIRY-FREE **GLUTEN-FREE** **PALEO** **VEGAN**

INDIAN-STYLE SAUTÉED CHICKPEAS

MAKES 4 SERVINGS

PREP TIME: 10 minutes COOK TIME: 10 minutes

Chickpeas, or garbanzo beans, are a versatile side that I use throughout my meals. I add them to a bowl with lentils and sautéed greens, spoon them over baked salmon, or top them cold over a bed of greens. Here, combined with some traditional Indian spices, the chickpeas absorb tremendous flavor, making this wonderful as its own dish, or as a side with simply prepared chicken or fish.

2 tablespoons olive oil

1 red bell pepper, chopped

1 jalapeño pepper, halved, seeded, and chopped

1½ teaspoons cumin

1 teaspoon turmeric

1 teaspoon cardamom

2 (19-ounce) cans of reduced-sodium chickpeas, drained and rinsed

1½ cups low-sodium vegetable broth

2 tablespoons chopped fresh cilantro

Juice of 1 lemon (about 2 tablespoons)

¼ teaspoon salt

¼ teaspoon freshly ground black pepper

1. In a sauté pan over medium heat, heat the olive oil until it shimmers. Add the red pepper and jalapeño, and cook until softened, about 2 minutes. Add the cumin, turmeric, and cardamom, and stir until fragrant, about 1 minute.

2. Add the chickpeas and broth to the pan and bring them to a boil over high heat. Reduce the heat to low, and simmer until half the liquid has evaporated, about 5 minutes. Stir in the cilantro, lemon juice, salt, and black pepper.

REFRIGERATE: Store the room-temperature chickpeas and sauce in a resealable container for up to 1 week. Enjoy at room temperature or reheat in the microwave for 2 minutes or in a small pot over medium-low heat for 5 minutes.

FREEZE: Store the chickpeas with the sauce in individual freezer-safe containers for up to 2 months. Thaw overnight in the refrigerator. For a single portion, reheat for 2 minutes in the microwave or in a small pot over medium-low heat for 5 minutes.

TOBY'S TIP: This dish is fantastic with other traditional Indian legumes. Swap out the chickpeas for black-eyed peas, adzuki beans, or kidney beans.

Per Serving (½ cup): Calories: 230; Fat: 9g; Saturated Fat: 1g; Protein: 13g; Total Carbs: 39g; Fiber: 10g; Sodium: 577mg

DAIRY-FREE   GLUTEN-FREE   VEGETARIAN

ASIAN "FRIED" BROWN RICE

MAKES 4 SERVINGS

PREP TIME: 10 minutes   COOK TIME: 45 minutes

Instead of getting caught mid-week without food to prepare and ordering Chinese takeout, I make one of my favorite Chinese dishes at home. This "fried" rice is made with brown rice, adding lots of filling fiber. It pairs perfectly with a stir-fry or grilled fish, and costs a heck of a lot less than any takeout!

3 cups water

1 cup brown rice

1 cup frozen shelled edamame

Cooking spray

1 scallion, sliced

1 teaspoon freshly grated ginger

½ teaspoon salt

4 large eggs

1 teaspoon toasted sesame oil

1. In a medium pot, bring the water to a boil over high heat. Add the brown rice and reduce the heat to medium-low. Cover the pot and simmer the rice, stirring it occasionally, until tender, about 40 minutes. Drain off any excess water.

2. While the rice is cooking, fill a small pot half full with water and bring it to a boil over high heat. Add the edamame, and then reduce the heat to low and simmer, uncovered, until cooked through, about 5 minutes. Drain well.

3. Coat a large skillet with the cooking spray and place it over medium heat. Once the pan is hot, add the scallion and cook until softened, about 1 minute. Add the cooked rice, edamame, ginger, and salt, and cook, stirring occasionally, until heated through.

4. In a small bowl, whisk the eggs. Pour them over the rice. Stir continuously until the eggs are cooked through, about 5 minutes. Break up any large pieces of egg and stir to incorporate. Top with sesame oil.

REFRIGERATE: Store the rice in a resealable container for up to 5 days. Reheat in the microwave for about 2 minutes or in a small pot over medium-low heat. Add 1 to 2 tablespoons of water if the rice is dry.

> **TOBY'S TIP:** Edamame are baby soybeans. Each ½ cup provides 11 grams of protein, 9 grams of fiber, 10% of your daily vitamin C, and 8% of the recommended daily amount of vitamin A. Shelled edamame can be added to rice, pasta, and stir-fry dishes.

Per Serving (1 cup): Calories: 299; Fat: 9g; Saturated Fat: 2g; Protein: 14g; Total Carbs: 40g; Fiber: 3g; Sodium: 379mg

DAIRY-FREE   **VEGAN**

BULGUR-STUFFED TOMATOES

MAKES 8 SERVINGS

PREP TIME: 20 minutes   COOK TIME: 45 minutes

Bulgur is an ancient grain that originated in the Mediterranean region. The process of turning wheat into bulgur has been around for thousands of years. It has a nutty flavor, chewy texture, and it is a nutrition powerhouse. This whole grain is brimming with energy-boosting B vitamins like niacin, folate, and thiamine, and provides 10 percent of the recommended daily amount of iron. One cooked cup also provides 8 grams of fiber and 6 grams of protein.

Cooking spray

1 cup low-sodium vegetable broth

½ cup bulgur

8 medium tomatoes

1 cup chopped fresh parsley

½ cup chopped fresh mint

1 scallion, chopped

1½ tablespoons extra-virgin olive oil

Juice of 1 lemon (about 2 tablespoons)

½ teaspoon salt

1. Preheat the oven to 350°F. Coat a baking sheet with the cooking spray.

2. In a medium pot over high heat, bring the vegetable broth to a boil. Add the bulgur, cover the pot, reduce the heat to medium-low, and simmer until the grain is tender and the liquid is absorbed, 15 to 25 minutes. Drain off any excess liquid.

3. While the bulgur cooks, cut the top third off the tomatoes and set them aside. Using a spoon, remove the seeds and pulp from the center of the tomatoes. Set the tomato "bowls" aside.

4. Dice the tomato tops and place them in a large bowl. Add the bulgur and stir to combine. Add the parsley, mint, scallion, olive oil, lemon juice, and salt. Stir to combine thoroughly.

5. Spoon 2 heaping tablespoons of the bulgur mixture into the hollow of each tomato. Place the tomatoes 2 inches apart on the baking sheet. Bake until the tomatoes are slightly browned, about 20 minutes.

REFRIGERATE: Store the tomatoes in a single layer in resealable containers for up to 5 days. The stuffed tomatoes can be eaten cold, at room temperature, or reheated in the microwave for about 1 minute.

TOBY'S TIP: Have extra quinoa? Use it instead of bulgur. Many of the grains in these dishes are interchangeable.

Per Serving (1 tomato): Calories: 87; Fat: 3g; Saturated Fat: 0g; Protein: 3g; Total Carbs: 14g; Fiber: 3g; Sodium: 175mg

DAIRY-FREE   GLUTEN-FREE   VEGAN

SLOW-COOKER THREE-BEAN CHILI

MAKES 6 SERVINGS

PREP TIME: 15 minutes   COOK TIME: 5 minutes, plus 8 hours

Sunday night is family dinner night in my house, and this bean chili is a favorite of all. I toss in whichever beans I have on hand, cover, and press the "cook" button. Now that the slow cooker is doing all the work, I'm free to spend quality time with my kids—usually playing a little 2-on-2 basketball.

- 1 tablespoon olive oil
- 1 medium onion, diced
- 2 garlic cloves, minced
- 2 (14.5-ounce) cans crushed tomatoes
- 2 (15-ounce) cans reduced-sodium black beans, drained and rinsed
- 1 (15-ounce) can reduced-sodium kidney beans, drained and rinsed
- 1 (15-ounce) can reduced-sodium cannellini beans, drained and rinsed
- 1¾ cups low-sodium vegetable broth
- 1 tablespoon chili powder
- 1 tablespoon ground cumin
- 2 teaspoons Worcestershire sauce
- ½ teaspoon salt
- ¼ teaspoon freshly ground black pepper

1. In a medium skillet over medium heat, heat the olive oil until it shimmers. Add the onion and garlic and sauté until the onions are translucent, about 2 minutes. Add the onion mixture to the slow cooker.

2. Add the crushed tomatoes, black beans, kidney beans, cannellini beans, vegetable broth, chili powder, cumin, Worcestershire sauce, salt, and black pepper to the slow cooker. Stir to combine.

3. Cover and cook on low for 8 hours.

REFRIGERATE: Let the chili cool for 1 to 2 hours before storing in a resealable container for up to 1 week.

FREEZE: Store the cooled chili in individual containers or one large freezer-safe container for up to 2 months. Thaw in the refrigerator overnight. Reheat in the microwave for several minutes (depending on the portion size), or reheat in a pot over medium-low heat for 10 to 15 minutes.

> **TOBY'S TIP:** Switch things up by adding 1 diced sweet potato to the slow cooker when you're cooking this chili.

Per Serving (1 cup): Calories: 271; Fat: 4g; Saturated Fat: 1g; Protein: 14g; Total Carbs: 47g; Fiber: 15g; Sodium: 757mg

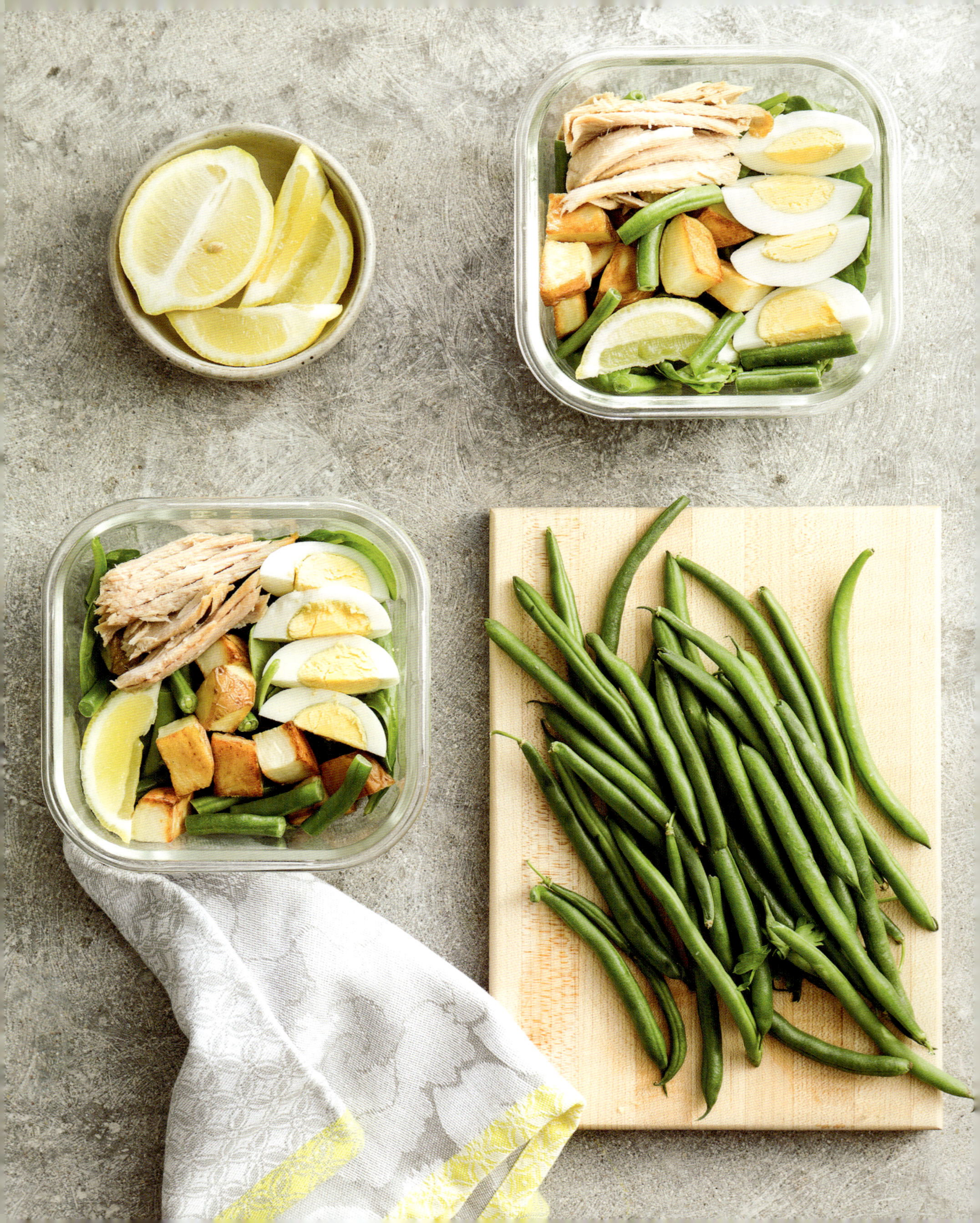

5 SALADS & VEGETABLES

- **110** Roasted Root Vegetable Salad with Kale
- **111** Arugula Salad with Salmon
- **112** Mason Jar Cobb Salad
- **114** Grilled Asian Steak Salad
- **115** Tuna Niçoise Salad
- **116** Quinoa-Kale Salad Bowl
- **117** Lighter Panzanella Salad
- **118** Citrus Broccoli Slaw
- **119** Chopped Salad with Feta and Lentils
- **120** Artichoke and White Bean Salad
- **121** Carrot-Cabbage Slaw
- **122** Eggplant Zucchini Provençal
- **123** Cauliflower-Rice Mushroom Risotto
- **124** Lemony Green Beans with Almonds
- **125** Maple Orange Glazed Baby Carrots
- **126** Steamed Asparagus with Bacon
- **128** Balsamic Brussels Sprouts
- **129** Lighter Creamed Spinach

« Tuna Niçoise Salad (page 115)

GLUTEN-FREE   VEGETARIAN

ROASTED ROOT VEGETABLE SALAD WITH KALE

MAKES 4 SERVINGS

PREP TIME: 15 minutes   COOK TIME: 30 minutes

During the winter, the hearty comfort of root vegetables like parsnips, yams, sweet potatoes, beets, and turnips warms me on the coldest of days. My favorite way to cook root vegetables is by roasting them in the oven. This gives the natural sugars and starches in the vegetables a chance to brown, resulting in a nice, deep flavor.

Cooking spray
¾ pound sweet potatoes, peeled and diced
¾ pound parsnips, peeled and diced
1 tablespoon olive oil
¼ teaspoon salt
⅛ teaspoon freshly ground black pepper
⅓ cup raw almonds, sliced
6 cups chopped kale
¼ cup grated Parmesan cheese
Herbed Vinaigrette (page 208)

1. Preheat the oven to 400°F. Coat a baking sheet with the cooking spray.

2. Put the sweet potatoes and parsnips in a large bowl and drizzle them with the olive oil, and season with the salt and black pepper. Spread the vegetables in a single layer on the baking sheet. Roast until softened and slightly browned, 25 to 30 minutes.

3. In a small sauté pan over low heat, toast the almond slices for about 2 minutes. Stir or shake the pan frequently to prevent the nuts from burning. Remove the pan from the heat and let the almonds cool for 5 minutes.

4. Put 1½ cups of kale in each of four individual resealable containers and top each with ½ cup of roasted vegetables, 1 heaping tablespoon of almonds, and 1 teaspoon of Parmesan cheese. When ready to eat, top each with 1½ tablespoons of dressing.

REFRIGERATE: Store the undressed salad in a resealable container for up to 5 days. Store the dressing in a resealable container for up to 1 week.

> **TOBY'S TIP:** Roast double the amount of root vegetables, or add ¾ pound each of beets and turnips to the mix. Use the extra servings as an easy side dish for the week.

Per Serving: Calories: 413; Fat: 24g; Saturated Fat: 3g; Protein: 9g; Total Carbs: 45g; Fiber: 12g; Sodium: 391mg

DAIRY-FREE **GLUTEN-FREE** **PALEO**

ARUGULA SALAD WITH SALMON

MAKES 4 SERVINGS

PREP TIME: 15 minutes   COOK TIME: 20 minutes

I love going to a local restaurant for lunch where I order a green salad topped with salmon. But for a fraction of the price, I make this arugula salad with salmon and an herb vinaigrette.

Cooking spray
1 pound salmon fillet
¼ teaspoon salt, divided
¼ teaspoon freshly ground black pepper, divided
2 tablespoons unseasoned rice vinegar
1 garlic clove, minced
Juice of ½ lemon (about 1 tablespoon)
1 teaspoon Dijon mustard
¼ teaspoon dried tarragon
¼ cup extra-virgin olive oil
7 ounces of arugula, washed (about 6 cups)
2 cups cherry tomatoes, halved
¼ cup raw walnuts, chopped

1. Preheat the oven to 425°F. Coat a baking sheet with the cooking spray.

2. Place the salmon skin-side down on the baking sheet. Sprinkle the fish with ⅛ teaspoon each of the salt and black pepper. Bake until the salmon is flaky and cooked through, reaching an internal temperature of 145°F, 20 to 22 minutes. Let the salmon cool for 10 minutes, then cut it into 4 even pieces.

3. In a small bowl, whisk together the rice vinegar, garlic, lemon juice, mustard, tarragon, and the remaining ⅛ teaspoon each of salt and black pepper. While whisking, slowly drizzle in the olive oil to combine.

4. Into each of four resealable containers, put 1½ cups of arugula, ½ cup of cherry tomato halves, 1 tablespoon of chopped walnuts, and a piece of salmon. Before serving, top each salad with 1 tablespoon of dressing.

REFRIGERATE: Store the undressed salad in the refrigerator for up to 5 days. Refrigerate the dressing in a resealable plastic or glass container for up to 2 weeks. When ready to eat, top each salad with 1 tablespoon of dressing. Alternatively, the dressing can be placed at the bottom of a Mason jar and then topped with the salad ingredients and salmon. Shake before eating.

> **TOBY'S TIP:** Don't want four salads this week? Make two instead, and keep the two additional pieces of salmon for other meals throughout the week with sides like Citrus Broccoli Slaw (page 118) or Turmeric Wild Rice and Black Beans (page 97).

Per Serving: Calories: 361; Fat: 27g; Saturated Fat: 4g; Protein: 26g; Total Carbs: 6g; Fiber: 2g; Sodium: 246mg

GLUTEN-FREE

MASON JAR COBB SALAD

MAKES 4 SERVINGS

PREP TIME: 30 minutes COOK TIME: 20 minutes

The colorful array of vegetables makes eating this salad not only a tasty experience but also a visually appealing one. After all, we eat with our eyes first. Bring this salad to work and your co-workers will be jealous they didn't spend time over the weekend prepping meals. It's a great way to share your tips with them.

Cooking spray

4 (1-ounce) slices lean turkey bacon

4 large eggs

1 cup frozen corn kernels

1 avocado

Juice of ½ lemon (about 1 tablespoon)

Lighter Blue Cheese Dressing (page 209)

2 cups shredded romaine lettuce

1 cup grape tomatoes, halved

1 cucumber, diced (about 1 cup)

1. Coat a medium skillet with the cooking spray and place it over medium heat until hot. Add the turkey bacon and cook until crispy, 3 to 5 minutes, flipping the slices over halfway through. Transfer the bacon to a paper towel–lined plate. Set aside to cool for 10 minutes.

2. Place the eggs in a medium pot and cover them with water. Place the pot over high heat and bring the water to a boil. Cook the eggs for 3 minutes, then remove the pot from the heat, cover it, and let the eggs stand for 15 minutes. Drain the water from the pot, and run cold water over the eggs until they are completely cool, about 10 minutes. Peel the eggs.

3. In a small pot over medium heat, add ¼ cup of water and the corn and cook until the corn is heated through, about 5 minutes. Drain any excess water and set aside to cool for 10 minutes.

4. When you're ready to assemble the salads, cube the avocado and drizzle it with the lemon juice to prevent browning. Coarsely chop each egg and crumble the turkey bacon.

5. In the bottom of each of four Mason jars, add 2 tablespoons of the dressing. Next, add ½ cup of lettuce and ¼ cup each of the tomatoes, corn, and cucumber. If the salad begins to get close to the top of the jar, gently push down on the vegetables with your fingertips. Top each salad with 1 coarsely chopped egg, ¼ of the cubed avocado, and 1 slice of crumbled turkey bacon. Seal the jar and store in the refrigerator until ready to eat.

REFRIGERATE: Store the jars for up to 5 days. Shake the Mason jar to evenly distribute the dressing before eating.

> **TOBY'S TIP:** Look for uncured turkey bacon, which may appear to have a duller color compared to regular cured turkey bacon. The nitrites found in cured meats have been linked to various types of cancer. Sodium nitrite is a preservative added to cured and processed meats to help prevent bacterial growth and lengthen shelf life.

Per Serving: Calories: 337; Fat: 21g; Saturated Fat: 6g; Protein: 18g; Total Carbs: 21g; Fiber: 6g; Sodium: 679mg

DAIRY-FREE **PALEO**

GRILLED ASIAN STEAK SALAD

MAKES 4 SERVINGS

PREP TIME: 15 minutes, plus 30 minutes to marinate   **COOK TIME:** 10 minutes

I love the taste of beef, and a few ounces over a green salad makes my day without an ounce of guilt. Because of the increased trimming practices of beef over the past few decades, many cuts of lean beef are available at the market.

- 1 pound flank steak or skirt steak
- Soy-Sesame Dressing (page 210)
- Nonstick cooking spray or canola oil
- 1 (9-ounce) package spring mix greens or other mixed greens (about 6 cups)
- 1 cup cherry tomatoes, halved
- 1 medium cucumber, halved lengthwise and cut into half-moons
- 1 carrot, grated

1. In a large bowl, add the steak and drizzle it with ¼ cup of the dressing. Use your fingers to makes sure the entire surface of the steak is covered by the dressing. Cover the bowl and marinate the steak in the refrigerator for at least 30 minutes and up to 24 hours.

2. Place a grill pan over high heat or preheat the grill. Coat the grill pan with the cooking spray or brush the grill grates with the canola oil. Place the steak on the grill and discard the leftover marinade. Grill until the steak's internal temperature reaches 145°F, 3 to 5 minutes on each side. Transfer the steak to a plate and let it rest for 10 minutes. Slice the steak into 1-inch-thick strips.

3. Place 1½ cups of the greens into each of four individual containers. Top each with equal amounts of the tomatoes, cucumbers, and carrots. Layer the sliced steak across each salad (about 4 ounces per salad). Drizzle each salad with 2 tablespoons of the dressing just before eating.

REFRIGERATE: Store the undressed salad for up to 5 days. Store the dressing in a resealable container or glass jar for up to 2 weeks. When ready to eat, top each salad with 2 tablespoons of dressing. Alternatively, put the dressing serving in the bottom of a Mason jar and then add the salad ingredients and steak slices. Refrigerate for up to 5 days and shake the jar before eating to evenly coat the salad.

TOBY'S TIP: You can make your own mixed greens with any combination of spinach, radicchio, red leaf lettuce, butter lettuce, and arugula.

Per Serving: Calories: 433; Fat: 35g; Saturated Fat: 8g; Protein: 24g; Total Carbs: 10g; Fiber: 2g; Sodium: 306mg

DAIRY-FREE   **GLUTEN-FREE**   **PALEO**

TUNA NIÇOISE SALAD

MAKES 4 SERVINGS

PREP TIME: 30 minutes   COOK TIME: 30 minutes

Making a lighter niçoise salad is all about portion control. My version uses traditional niçoise ingredients like potatoes, green beans, eggs, and tuna, but in smaller portions so you get the nutrition and flavor you want for a reasonable amount of calories.

Cooking spray

2 small red potatoes, sliced into 1-inch cubes (about 1 cup)

1 teaspoon olive oil

¼ teaspoon salt

4 large eggs

5 ounces fresh spinach, chopped (about 4 cups)

1 cup fresh green beans, trimmed and cut into thirds

1 cup grape tomatoes, halved

2 (4-ounce) cans tuna packed in olive oil, undrained

⅛ teaspoon freshly ground black pepper

1 lemon, quartered

1. Preheat the oven to 350°F. Coat a baking sheet with the cooking spray.

2. In a small bowl, add the potatoes, olive oil, and salt. Toss to evenly coat. Spread the potatoes in a single layer on the baking sheet. Roast until golden brown and tender, 20 to 25 minutes. Set aside to cool for 10 minutes.

3. While the potatoes are roasting, place the eggs in a medium pot and cover them with water. Place the pot over high heat and bring the water to a boil. Cook the eggs for 3 minutes, then remove the pot from the heat, cover it, and let stand for 15 minutes. Drain and run cold water over the eggs until they are completely cool, about 10 minutes. Peel and slice into quarters lengthwise.

4. Into each of four glass containers, place 1 cup of the spinach. Top each with ¼ cup of the potatoes, 4 egg quarters, ¼ cup each of green beans and tomatoes, and ½ can of tuna with the oil. Sprinkle each with the black pepper and add a lemon wedge. When ready to eat, squeeze the lemon juice on the tuna.

REFRIGERATE: Store each sealed jar for up to 5 days.

> **TOBY'S TIP:** Instead of making a separate dressing, this salad uses the oil from the tuna and adds a squeeze of lemon juice and black pepper. It's a quick, easy, and healthy way to flavor the salad.

Per Serving: Calories: 278; Fat: 12g; Saturated Fat: 3g; Protein: 23g; Total Carbs: 19g; Fiber: 3g; Sodium: 508mg

Salads & Vegetables

DAIRY-FREE **GLUTEN-FREE** **VEGETARIAN**

QUINOA-KALE SALAD BOWL

MAKES 6 SERVINGS

PREP TIME: 20 minutes **COOK TIME:** 15 minutes

Sometimes I crave a salad with protein, but I'm not in the mood for chicken or meat. That's when I whip up this vegetarian salad made with quinoa, which contains all the essential amino acids (building blocks of protein) that the body needs. It's one of the only plant-based sources of complete protein.

- 1 cup quinoa
- 2 cups low-sodium vegetable broth
- 6 cups chopped kale
- 3 plum tomatoes, chopped
- 1 hothouse cucumber, chopped
- ¼ pineapple, cut into small cubes
- ½ cup raw walnuts, chopped
- ½ cup extra-virgin olive oil
- 2 tablespoons apple cider vinegar
- 2 teaspoons honey
- ½ teaspoon salt
- ¼ teaspoon freshly ground black pepper

1. In a medium pot over high heat, bring the quinoa and vegetable broth to a boil. Reduce the heat to low, cover the pot, and simmer until the broth has evaporated and the quinoa is soft and fluffy, about 15 minutes. Remove the pot from the heat, and using a fork fluff the quinoa. Let the quinoa cool for about 5 minutes.

2. While quinoa is cooking, put the kale, tomatoes, cucumber, pineapple, and walnuts in a large bowl and toss to combine.

3. In a small bowl, whisk together the olive oil, apple cider vinegar, honey, salt, and black pepper.

4. In each of six resealable containers, add 2 cups of the salad and ⅓ cup of the quinoa. When ready to eat, add 2 tablespoons of dressing to each salad and toss to combine.

REFRIGERATE: Store the undressed salad in a resealable container for up to 5 days. Store the dressing in a resealable container or glass jar. Alternatively, the dressing can also be placed at the bottom of a glass Mason jar and topped with the salad and quinoa to take on the go. Shake the Mason jar to evenly distribute the dressing before eating.

> **TOBY'S TIP:** Buying fresh kale and chopping it yourself is cheaper. However, in a pinch or if it is on sale, save a little time by purchasing pre-chopped, bagged kale.

Per Serving: Calories: 418; Fat: 27g; Saturated Fat: 3g; Protein: 10g; Total Carbs: 39g; Fiber: 7g; Sodium: 274mg

VEGETARIAN

LIGHTER PANZANELLA SALAD

MAKES 4 SERVINGS

PREP TIME: 30 minutes   COOK TIME: 10 minutes

I was recently at a business meeting where I tried a panzanella salad. I was in love with the flavor but wanted to make my own croutons and make it using my favorite vegetables. This lighter version is the result, and now it's a go-to salad in my lunch repertoire.

FOR THE CROUTONS

- Cooking spray
- 4 slices 100% whole-wheat bread, cut into 1-inch squares
- 2 tablespoons olive oil
- 2 teaspoons dried rosemary
- ¼ teaspoon sea salt

FOR THE SALAD

- 4 cups shredded romaine lettuce
- 2 cups cherry tomatoes, halved
- 1 yellow or orange bell pepper, cut into 1-inch-wide strips
- 1 medium cucumber, sliced into ½-inch-thick rounds
- ½ small red onion, thinly sliced
- ¼ cup fresh basil leaves, sliced into ¼-inch-thick ribbons
- 4 ounces part-skim mozzarella cheese, cut into 1-inch cubes
- White Balsamic Vinaigrette (page 207)

TO MAKE THE CROUTONS

1. Preheat the oven to 325°F. Coat a baking sheet with the cooking spray. Put the bread in a medium bowl.
2. In a small bowl whisk together the olive oil, rosemary, and sea salt. Drizzle the mix over the bread and toss to combine.
3. Put the bread on the baking sheet in a single layer. Bake until dry and golden brown, 8 to 10 minutes. Let cool for 10 minutes.

TO PREPARE THE SALAD

1. In a large bowl, add the romaine lettuce, tomatoes, bell peppers, cucumber, and onion and toss to combine. Sprinkle with the basil and mozzarella and stir to evenly distribute.
2. Place 2¾ cups of salad in each of four large bowls or individual resealable containers. Top each bowl with ⅔ cup of croutons and 2 tablespoons of dressing.

REFRIGERATE: Store the undressed salad in a resealable container for up to 5 days. Store the dressing in a separate resealable container or glass jar for up to 1 month. Before eating, drizzle 2 tablespoons of the dressing on an individual serving and toss to combine. Alternatively, the dressing can be placed at the bottom of a glass Mason jar and topped with the salad. Shake the Mason jar before eating to evenly distribute.

> **TOBY'S TIP:** Want to up your protein? Add leftover chicken or turkey and enjoy this salad for lunch or dinner.

Per Serving: Calories: 443; Fat: 30g; Saturated Fat: 6g; Protein: 14g; Total Carbs: 31g; Fiber: 6g; Sodium: 706mg

`GLUTEN-FREE` `VEGETARIAN`

CITRUS BROCCOLI SLAW

MAKES 6 SERVINGS

PREP TIME: 20 minutes, plus 2 hours to chill   **COOK TIME:** 0 minutes

I can't enjoy any kind of slaw where the vegetables are hidden under a heavy dressing. Instead, I make my slaws with a light, citrus dressing so I can taste the flavor of the delicious, seasonal veggies. This recipe uses a little light mayo complimented with Greek yogurt, so you still get some of the creaminess without drowning the gorgeous vegetables.

- 1 pound fresh broccoli
- 2 tablespoons nonfat plain Greek yogurt
- 2 tablespoons reduced-fat mayonnaise
- 1 tablespoon freshly squeezed orange juice
- 1 tablespoon unseasoned rice vinegar
- Juice of ½ lemon (about 1 tablespoon)
- ¼ teaspoon salt
- ⅛ teaspoon freshly ground black pepper
- 1 medium carrot, grated
- ½ red onion, chopped (about ½ cup)
- ¼ cup sunflower seeds
- 2 tablespoons pomegranate arils

1. Cut the broccoli into florets. Thinly slice the broccoli stems and florets using a chef's knife or mandolin.

2. In a small bowl, whisk together the Greek yogurt, mayonnaise, orange juice, rice vinegar, lemon juice, salt, and black pepper.

3. In a large bowl, toss together the broccoli, carrots, onion, sunflower seeds, and pomegranate arils. Add the Greek yogurt dressing and toss to evenly coat. Cover the bowl and refrigerate for at least 2 hours before eating.

REFRIGERATE: Store the slaw in a resealable container for up to 5 days.

TOBY'S TIP: When substituting Greek yogurt for mayo-based dressings, I like to use a 1:1 ratio. This means equal amounts of Greek yogurt and reduced-fat mayo. This way I can still get the mayo flavor without all the calories.

Per Serving (1 cup): Calories: 83; Fat: 4g; Saturated Fat: 0g; Protein: 4g; Total Carbs: 10g; Fiber: 3g; Sodium: 174mg

GLUTEN-FREE   **VEGETARIAN**

CHOPPED SALAD WITH FETA AND LENTILS

MAKES 4 SERVINGS

PREP TIME: 15 minutes   COOK TIME: 0 minutes

As a young girl, I spent most of my summers in Israel where we ate chopped salad at most meals. As an adult, I have created different versions of this salad including this Mediterranean-style version with fiber-filled lentils deliciously balanced with feta cheese. It's the perfect salad to make use of any extra vegetables taking up room in your refrigerator.

- ½ hothouse cucumber, chopped
- 1 plum tomato, chopped
- ½ red bell pepper, chopped
- ¼ red onion, chopped
- 1 cup canned lentils, drained and rinsed
- 2 tablespoons chopped parsley
- 1 tablespoon extra-virgin olive oil
- Juice of 1 lemon
- ¼ teaspoon salt
- ⅛ teaspoon freshly ground black pepper
- ⅓ cup crumbled feta cheese

1. In a medium bowl, add the cucumber, tomato, bell pepper, onion, lentils, and parsley. Toss to combine.
2. Add the olive oil, lemon juice, salt, and black pepper and toss evenly to coat the vegetables. Sprinkle the feta cheese over the salad.

REFRIGERATE: Store the salad in a resealable container for up to 5 days.

> **TOBY'S TIP:** Swap the lentils for chickpeas or white beans for variety or if those are what you have in your pantry.

Per Serving (1 cup): Calories: 134; Fat: 6g; Saturated Fat: 2g; Protein: 7g; Total Carbs: 14g; Fiber: 5g; Sodium: 266mg

GLUTEN-FREE   VEGETARIAN

ARTICHOKE AND WHITE BEAN SALAD

MAKES 4 SERVINGS

PREP TIME: 20 minutes   **COOK TIME:** 0 minutes

During warmer weather I enjoy a cold salad for lunch. This combo provides protein from the beans and gets me a few steps closer to the recommended daily amount of vegetables. I love pairing this salad with an antioxidant-packed berry-fruit salad sprinkled with chopped almonds.

- 1 (15-ounce) can low-sodium cannellini beans, drained and rinsed
- 1 (15-ounce) can artichoke hearts, drained
- 1 cup cherry tomatoes, halved
- ½ cup shredded Parmesan cheese
- ½ red onion, finely diced (about ⅓ cup)
- 3 tablespoons finely chopped parsley
- ¼ cup red wine vinegar
- ¼ garlic clove, minced
- 1 teaspoon Dijon mustard
- ¼ teaspoon salt
- ⅛ teaspoon freshly ground black pepper
- 2 tablespoons extra-virgin olive oil

1. In a large bowl, add the beans, artichokes, tomatoes, Parmesan cheese, onion, and parsley. Toss to combine.

2. In a small bowl, whisk together the vinegar, garlic, mustard, salt, and black pepper. Continue whisking and slowly drizzle in the olive oil until the dressing is emulsified.

3. Pour the dressing over the salad and toss to combine. Cover and refrigerate for at least 30 minutes before eating. When ready to serve, stir the salad to recombine the ingredients.

REFRIGERATE: Store the salad in a resealable container for up to 5 days.

TOBY'S TIP: Fresh artichokes are pricey and not always in season. Frozen artichokes are best when used in cooked dishes. Compare canned artichoke labels and choose the one with the least amount of sodium. You can also rinse them before adding them to the salad to reduce the sodium levels even further.

Per Serving (1¼ cups): Calories: 211; Fat: 9g; Saturated Fat: 2g; Protein: 9g; Total Carbs: 22g; Fiber: 8g; Sodium: 656mg

DAIRY-FREE   **GLUTEN-FREE**   **VEGAN**

CARROT-CABBAGE SLAW

MAKES 6 SERVINGS

PREP TIME: 20 minutes   COOK TIME: 0 minutes

My 12-year-old daughter has loved cabbage since she was 5 years old. In elementary school she took shredded cabbage with her for lunch but always insisted eating it plain. After a while, I convinced her to add a little flavor. This light, lemony oil dressing is the result. It's great just with the cabbage or used to dress a more complex slaw like this one.

- ¼ head napa cabbage, shredded
- 2 carrots, shredded
- 1 large zucchini, shredded
- 3 tablespoons extra-virgin olive oil
- Juice of 1½ lemons (about 3 tablespoons)
- 1 teaspoon brown sugar
- ¼ teaspoon salt
- ⅛ teaspoon freshly ground black pepper

1. In a large bowl, add the cabbage, carrots, and zucchini. Toss to combine.

2. In a small bowl, whisk together the olive oil, lemon juice, brown sugar, salt, and black pepper. Whisk until the sugar and salt are dissolved and the dressing has emulsified. Drizzle the dressing over the vegetables and toss to combine.

REFRIGERATE: Store the slaw in a resealable container for up to 1 week.

TOBY'S TIP: Use a food processor to shred vegetables. Alternatively, use a vegetable peeler, rotating the vegetable each time you peel. Slice larger slivers in half lengthwise.

Per Serving (1¼ cups): Calories: 91; Fat: 7g; Saturated Fat: 1g; Protein: 1g; Total Carbs: 7g; Fiber: 2g; Sodium: 124mg

DAIRY-FREE   GLUTEN-FREE   PALEO   VEGAN

EGGPLANT ZUCCHINI PROVENÇAL

MAKES 6 SERVINGS

PREP TIME: 20 minutes   COOK TIME: 50 minutes

You can't go wrong with roasted vegetables. They are a perfect side to chicken, fish, and beef, or they can be tossed over a green salad or over whole-grain pasta or quinoa. If you have other veggies hanging out in the refrigerator, don't waste them—roast them instead! It's all about versatility.

Cooking spray

2 small onions, cut lengthwise into ¼-inch rounds

2 red bell peppers, cut into 2-inch-wide strips

1 medium eggplant, cut into ½-inch-thick rounds, then quartered

2 medium zucchini, cut into ¼-inch rounds

10 garlic cloves

¼ cup olive oil

2 tablespoons Herbes de Provence

½ teaspoon salt

4 medium tomatoes, cut into 8 wedges each

1. Preheat the oven to 400°F. Coat two baking sheets with the cooking spray.

2. In a large bowl, add the onions, bell peppers, eggplant, zucchini, garlic cloves, olive oil, Herbes de Provence, and salt. Toss to combine. Spread the vegetables in a single layer on the baking sheets. Roast for 30 minutes, giving the vegetables a stir halfway through. After 30 minutes, stir the vegetables again and add the tomatoes to the baking sheets. Continue roasting until the vegetables are soft and slightly browned, 15 to 20 minutes more.

REFRIGERATE: Store the cooled vegetables in a resealable container for up to 5 days. Reheat single-serving portions in the microwave for 1½ minutes, and let sit for 2 minutes before eating.

FREEZE: Store the cooled vegetables in individual freezer-safe containers for up to 2 months. Thaw overnight in the refrigerator. Reheat in the microwave for about 1½ minutes, and let cool for 2 minutes before eating.

TOBY'S TIP: Be sure to cut the vegetables into the thickness indicated in the recipe. You do not want them too thin because they shrink in the oven as the water in them evaporates. Also make sure they're evenly cut so they cook evenly. If you're unsure of the measurements, use a ruler or measuring tape until you get the hang of the sizes.

Per Serving (1 cup): Calories: 157; Fat: 10g; Saturated Fat: 1g; Protein: 3g; Total Carbs: 17g; Fiber: 6g; Sodium: 211mg

GLUTEN-FREE **VEGETARIAN**

CAULIFLOWER-RICE MUSHROOM RISOTTO

MAKES 4 SERVINGS

PREP TIME: 15 minutes   COOK TIME: 13 minutes

A good bowl of risotto always hits the spot. What doesn't hit the spot, though, is all those carbs and calories. Plus, risotto takes forever to cook. I've discovered riced cauliflower, which provides tons of vitamins, minerals, and antioxidants without all the calories. It also takes fewer than 30 minutes to whip up. It's everything that's good about risotto but with more nutrition and less work.

- 1 tablespoon unsalted butter
- ½ white onion, diced
- 1 (8-ounce) package brown mushrooms
- 1 garlic clove, minced
- 1 (12-ounce) package frozen riced cauliflower, thawed
- 1 cup cherry tomatoes, halved
- ¾ cup low-sodium vegetable or chicken broth
- ¼ cup grated Parmesan cheese

1. In a medium skillet over medium heat, heat the butter. Add the onion, mushrooms, and garlic, and sauté until the onions are translucent and the mushrooms are fragrant, about 5 minutes.

2. Add the cauliflower rice and tomatoes and stir to combine. Add the broth and bring it to a boil over high heat. Reduce the heat to low and simmer, stirring occasionally, until the liquid has reduced by half, about 7 minutes.

3. Remove the skillet from the heat and stir in the Parmesan cheese.

REFRIGERATE: Store the cooled risotto in a resealable container for up to 5 days. Reheat it in a medium saucepan over medium heat with 2 tablespoons of water. Heat single risotto portions in the microwave for 1½ minutes and let each cool for 2 minutes before eating.

FREEZE: Store in individual freezer-safe containers for up to 2 months. Reheat from frozen with 2 tablespoons of water in a medium saucepan over medium heat until warmed through, about 5 minutes.

> **TOBY'S TIP:** Make your own cauliflower rice by cutting 1 head of cauliflower into large chunks. Place it into a food processor and pulse until the cauliflower looks like rice grains.

Per Serving (1¼ cups): Calories: 102; Fat: 5g; Saturated Fat: 3g; Protein: 7g; Total Carbs: 10g; Fiber: 3g; Sodium: 198mg

DAIRY-FREE **GLUTEN-FREE** **PALEO** **VEGAN**

LEMONY GREEN BEANS WITH ALMONDS

MAKES 4 SERVINGS

PREP TIME: 15 minutes   **COOK TIME:** 10 minutes

Green beans are brimming with nutrients as 1 cup of fresh green beans has 34 calories and 15 percent of the recommended daily amount of fiber. They're also an excellent source of vitamins C and K, and a good source of vitamin A, folate, and manganese.

2 tablespoons olive oil

2 garlic cloves, thinly sliced

1 shallot, chopped

1½ pounds green beans, trimmed

¼ cup raw almonds, chopped

¼ teaspoon salt

⅛ teaspoon freshly ground black pepper

Zest of ½ lemon (about 2 teaspoons)

1. In a medium skillet over medium heat, heat the olive oil until it shimmers. Add the garlic and shallot and cook until fragrant, about 2 minutes. Add the green beans, cover, and cook, stirring occasionally, until softened, 6 to 8 minutes. Turn off the heat.

2. Add the almonds, salt, black pepper, and lemon zest and toss to combine.

REFRIGERATE: Store the cooled beans in a large resealable container for up to 1 week. To reheat, coat a medium skillet with cooking spray and place over medium heat. Add the green beans and cook, stirring occasionally, until heated through, about 5 minutes. Reheat a single serving in the microwave for 45 seconds to 1 minute.

FREEZE: Store the cooled beans in freezer-safe containers for up to 2 months. Thaw in the refrigerator overnight. To reheat, coat a medium skillet with cooking spray and place over medium heat. Add the green beans and cook, stirring occasionally, until heated through, about 5 minutes. Reheat a single serving in the microwave for 45 seconds to 1 minute.

TOBY'S TIP: The zest (peel) of citrus fruit adds a ton of flavor for few calories. Use a microplane to easily zest a lemon. Switch things up by substituting orange zest for lemon zest in this green-bean recipe.

Per Serving: Calories: 174; Fat: 12g; Saturated Fat: 1g; Protein: 5g; Total Carbs: 16g; Fiber: 6g; Sodium: 159mg

DAIRY-FREE **GLUTEN-FREE** **VEGAN**

MAPLE ORANGE GLAZED BABY CARROTS

MAKES 6 SERVINGS

PREP TIME: 10 minutes   COOK TIME: 15 minutes

In the 1980s, a California farmer was unable to sell many of his carrots because they weren't the size or shape typically sold at grocery stores. They were categorized as "ugly" even though they were fresh and delicious. So he used an industrial bean cutter to shape the carrots into what we now call baby carrots. As a result, carrot consumption increased by 30 percent by 1987.

1 tablespoon olive oil
1 (1-pound) bag baby carrots
¼ teaspoon salt
¼ cup 100% maple syrup
2 tablespoons freshly squeezed orange juice
⅛ teaspoon nutmeg

1. In a large skillet over medium heat, heat the olive oil until it shimmers. Add the carrots and salt and toss to combine. Cook, stirring occasionally, until the carrots are heated through, about 5 minutes.

2. Add the maple syrup and orange juice and toss to combine. Bring the mixture to a boil over high heat, then reduce the heat to medium-low, cover the skillet, and simmer until the carrots begin to soften, about 5 minutes. Uncover the skillet and continue cooking until the liquid is reduced by half, about 5 minutes more. Add nutmeg and toss to incorporate.

REFRIGERATE: Store the cooled carrots in a resealable container for up to 1 week. Reheat in a medium skillet coated with cooking spray over medium heat until heated through, about 5 minutes. Reheat a single serving in the microwave for 45 seconds.

FREEZE: Store the cooled carrots in freezer-safe containers for up to 2 months.. Thaw in the refrigerator overnight. Reheat in a medium skillet coated with cooking spray over medium heat until heated through, about 5 minutes. Reheat a single serving in the microwave for 45 seconds.

TOBY'S TIP: Baby carrots are packaged in 1-pound bags. Alternatively, purchase a bunch of carrots and slice them into quarters.

Per Serving (¾ cup): Calories: 84; Fat: 2g; Saturated Fat: 0g; Protein: 1g; Total Carbs: 16g; Fiber: 2g; Sodium: 159mg

Salads & Vegetables

DAIRY-FREE   **PALEO**

STEAMED ASPARAGUS WITH BACON

MAKES 4 SERVINGS

PREP TIME: 15 minutes   COOK TIME: 15 minutes

Just because you're on a healthy eating plan, doesn't mean you can't enjoy bacon on occasion. Bacon has a strong flavor, so you need just one slice to get the flavor you need. In this recipe I used turkey bacon, but you can choose Canadian or even the real deal. Just remember, a little goes a long way.

- 1 bunch asparagus (1 pound), trimmed and cut into thirds
- Cooking spray
- 2 slices turkey bacon or Canadian bacon
- Juice of ½ lemon (about 1 tablespoon)
- ¼ teaspoon salt
- ⅛ teaspoon freshly ground black pepper

1. Fill a medium pot with 1 cup of water, fit it with a steamer basket, and bring the water to a boil over high heat. Add the asparagus, cover, and steam until tender, about 6 minutes. Remove the pot from the heat, remove the steamer basket, and set the asparagus aside.

2. Coat a medium skillet with the cooking spray and place it over medium heat until hot. Add the bacon and cook until it is brown and crisp, about 4 minutes per side. Transfer the bacon to a paper towel–lined plate and let it cool. Chop the bacon into small pieces.

3. Add the asparagus to the same skillet with the bacon drippings and place it over medium heat. Add the lemon juice, salt, and black pepper and toss to evenly coat. Add the bacon pieces and toss to combine. Reduce the heat to medium-low and let the flavors combine, about 1 minute.

REFRIGERATE: Store the cooled asparagus in a resealable container for up to 1 week. Reheat in a medium skillet coated with cooking spray over medium-low heat until heated through, about 5 minutes. Reheat a single serving in the microwave for 45 seconds to 1 minute.

FREEZE: Store the cooled asparagus in freezer-safe containers for up to 2 months. Thaw the refrigerator overnight. Reheat in a medium skillet coated with cooking spray over medium-low heat until heated through, about 5 minutes. Reheat a single serving in the microwave for 45 seconds to 1 minute.

> **TOBY'S TIP:** Large spears of asparagus can have tough skins. Use a veggie peeler to remove them.

Per Serving (¾ cup): Calories: 59; Fat: 3g; Saturated Fat: 1g; Protein: 5g; Total Carbs: 5g; Fiber: 2g; Sodium: 322mg

DAIRY-FREE **GLUTEN-FREE** **PALEO** **VEGAN**

BALSAMIC BRUSSELS SPROUTS

MAKES 4 SERVINGS

PREP TIME: 15 minutes   **COOK TIME:** 10 minutes

I used to find Brussels sprouts intimidating to cook. I always used to order them at my favorite tapas restaurant, but I rarely made them at home. Then one day I roasted them in the oven and overcame my fear of cooking this delicious veggie. I don't even remember why I found them so intimidating. They're super easy to prepare and oh-so delicious.

Cooking spray
2 tablespoons olive oil
2 tablespoons balsamic vinegar
½ teaspoon salt
¼ teaspoon freshly ground black pepper
1½ pounds Brussels sprouts, trimmed

1. Preheat the oven to 400°F. Coat a baking sheet with the cooking spray.

2. In a small bowl, whisk together the olive oil, vinegar, salt, and black pepper.

3. Place the Brussels sprouts in a large bowl. Drizzle them with the balsamic dressing and toss to combine.

4. Put the Brussels sprouts in a single layer on the baking sheet. Roast until slightly browned, 10 to 15 minutes.

REFRIGERATE: Store the cooled Brussels sprouts in a resealable container for up to 1 week. Reheat in a medium skillet coated with cooking spray over medium heat until heated through, about 5 minutes. Reheat a single serving in the microwave for 45 seconds to 1 minute.

FREEZE: Store the cooled Brussels sprouts in freezer-safe containers for up to 2 months. Thaw in the refrigerator overnight. Reheat in a medium skillet coated with cooking spray over medium heat until heated through, about 5 minutes. Reheat a single serving in the microwave for 45 seconds to 1 minute.

> **TOBY'S TIP:** Clean Brussels sprouts thoroughly to remove the soil that can cling to them. To do so, remove a few outer leaves of the sprouts and wash under cold running water.

Per Serving (1 cup): Calories: 77; Fat: 7g; Saturated Fat: 1g; Protein: 1g; Total Carbs: 4g; Fiber: 1g; Sodium: 306mg

GLUTEN-FREE   VEGETARIAN

LIGHTER CREAMED SPINACH

MAKES 4 SERVINGS

PREP TIME: 10 minutes   COOK TIME: 5 minutes

Creamed spinach is usually laden with calories and artery-clogging saturated fats thanks to butter and heavy cream. Just 1 cup of heavy cream contains a whopping 800 calories, so you can imagine the hundreds of calories that are in a traditional version of the recipe. My lighter version uses Greek yogurt and a touch of Parmesan cheese to add creaminess and mouthwatering flavor.

- 1 (10-ounce) package frozen chopped spinach, thawed and well-drained
- 3 tablespoons low-fat plain Greek yogurt
- ½ teaspoon garlic powder
- ¼ teaspoon salt
- ⅛ teaspoon freshly ground black pepper
- 1 teaspoon grated Parmesan cheese

1. Place the spinach in a medium saucepan with ¼ cup of water. Bring it to a boil over high heat, then reduce the heat to medium-low. Cook until the spinach is heated through, about 5 minutes. Allow to cool for 5 minutes.

2. Place the spinach on a clean dish towel or cheesecloth and squeeze it over the sink to remove any excess liquid.

3. Put the spinach in a medium bowl. Add the Greek yogurt, garlic powder, salt, and black pepper and stir to combine. Add the Parmesan cheese and stir to incorporate.

REFRIGERATE: Store the cooled spinach in a resealable container for up to 5 days. Reheat in a medium saucepan over medium-low heat for 5 to 8 minutes. Reheat individual portions in the microwave for 45 seconds to 1 minute.

> **TOBY'S TIP:** Buy frozen chopped spinach where the spinach is the only ingredient. The nutrients are equivalent to fresh spinach as it's frozen at the peak of freshness, but is quicker to prep and cook.

Per Serving (¾ cup): Calories: 29; Fat: 0g; Saturated Fat: 0g; Protein: 3g; Total Carbs: 3g; Fiber: 1g; Sodium: 301mg

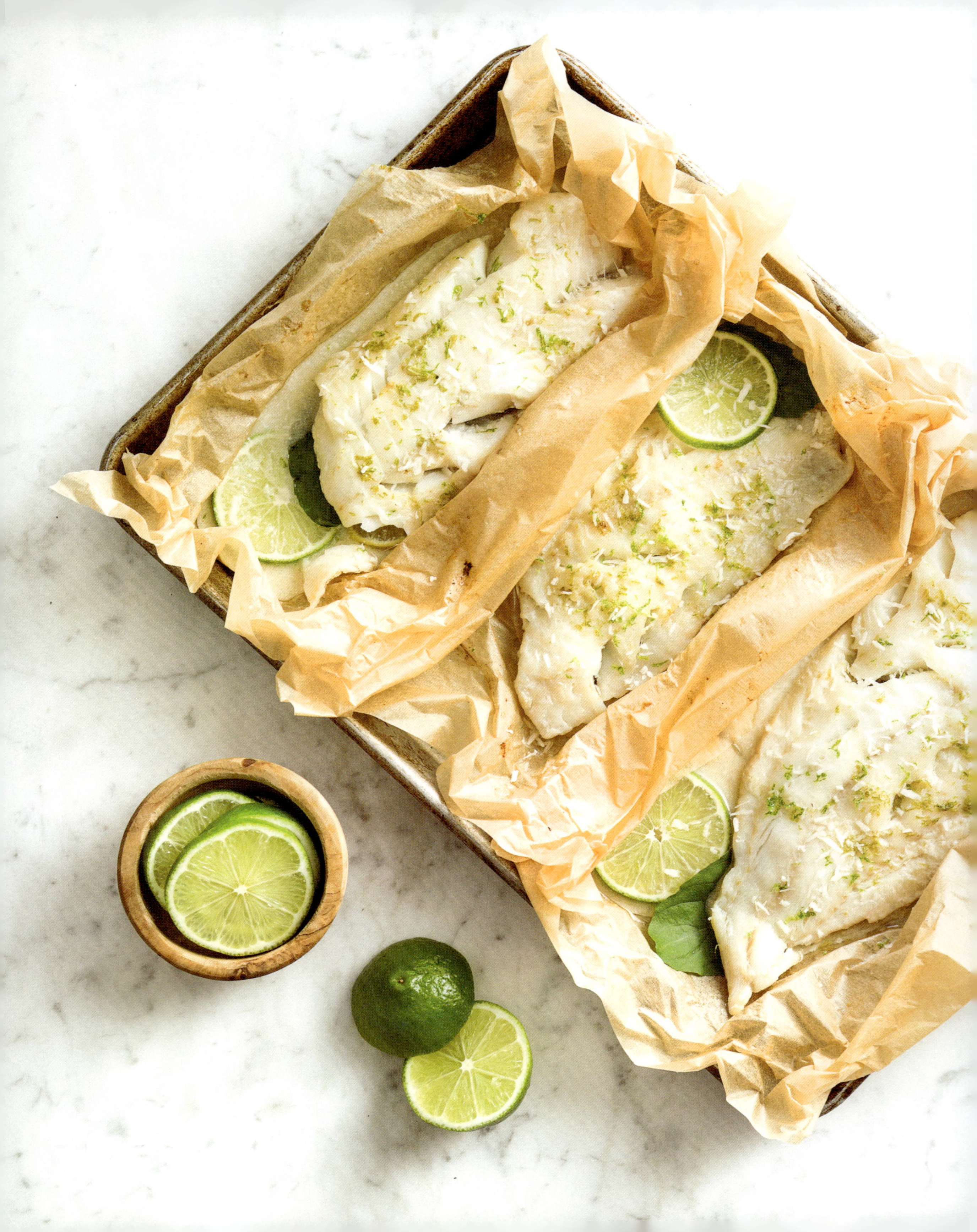

6 FISH & SEAFOOD

132 Spicy Tuna with Edamame

133 Poached Salmon with Chimichurri Sauce

134 Roasted Trout with Green Olive Tapenade

135 Ginger Soy Tuna Packets with Snap Peas and Bok Choy

137 Coconut Lime Flounder in Parchment Paper

138 Farro, Sardines, and Greens

139 Lime Shrimp with Tomato Salsa

140 Lighter Fish Cakes

142 Crab-Stuffed Flounder

143 Grilled Halibut with Anchovy-Caper Dressing

« Coconut Lime Flounder in Parchment Paper (page 137)

GLUTEN-FREE

SPICY TUNA WITH EDAMAME

MAKES 4 SERVINGS

PREP TIME: 15 minutes **COOK TIME:** 5 minutes

I grew up eating tuna every week. With five kids in the house, it was a simple dish to prepare and make sandwiches with. As an adult and registered dietitian, I like to add creative, healthy foods to my tuna salad. In this version, I add baby soybeans (aka edamame) for a boost of protein and fiber. Plus, there's jalapeño and sriracha for a spicy kick. If spice isn't your thing, just leave them out.

- ½ cup frozen shelled edamame
- 2 (6-ounce) cans chunky light tuna in water, drained
- ½ medium onion, chopped
- ½ jalapeño, sliced lengthwise, seeded, and finely diced (optional)
- 1 celery stalk, chopped
- 1 scallion, chopped
- 2 tablespoons light mayonnaise
- 2 tablespoons nonfat plain Greek yogurt
- 1 tablespoon Dijon mustard
- 1 teaspoon freshly squeezed lemon juice
- ½ teaspoon sriracha (optional)
- ⅛ teaspoon salt
- ⅛ teaspoon freshly ground black pepper

1. Bring a small pot of water to a boil over high heat. Add the edamame and cook until heated through, about 5 minutes. Drain, then set aside to cool for at least 10 minutes.

2. In a medium bowl, add the tuna, onion, jalapeño (if using), celery, and scallion. Mix to evenly combine.

3. In a small bowl, mix together the mayonnaise, Greek yogurt, mustard, lemon juice, sriracha (if using), salt, and black pepper. Spoon the mayonnaise dressing over the tuna, and mix to evenly coat.

REFRIGERATE: Store the tuna in a resealable container for up to 5 days.

TOBY'S TIP: After handling any chile pepper like jalapeños, wash your hands thoroughly. If you touch your eyes or skin after handling them, they can become irritated (it's really unpleasant!).

Per Serving (¾ cup): Calories: 152; Fat: 5g; Saturated Fat: 0g; Protein: 22g; Total Carbs: 5g; Fiber: 1g; Sodium: 631mg

DAIRY-FREE   **GLUTEN-FREE**   **PALEO**

POACHED SALMON WITH CHIMICHURRI SAUCE

MAKES 4 SERVINGS

PREP TIME: 5 minutes   COOK TIME: 5 minutes

My 12-year-old, who loves to cook, had me show her how I poached this salmon, and she was pleasantly shocked at how easy it is. I explained to her how you can poach eggs and chicken, too. She now plans on making poaching part of her healthy-cooking repertoire, just like mom. I love nothing more than passing these skills down to my kids.

2 bay leaves
3 black peppercorns
1¼ pounds salmon fillet
Chimichurri Sauce (page 212)

1. In a medium saucepan or high-sided skillet over high heat, bring 8 cups of water to a boil. Add the bay leaves and peppercorns. Add the salmon, making sure it's completely covered by the water, and bring the water back to a boil. Cook the salmon for 1 minute, then turn off the heat and cover the pan. Let the salmon poach for 20 minutes. Carefully remove the fish from the pan and let it cool. Discard the liquid.

2. Slice the salmon into 4 (5-ounce) pieces. When ready to eat, top each with 2 tablespoons of chimichurri sauce.

REFRIGERATE: Store the cooled salmon and chimichurri sauce in separate resealable containers for up to 5 days. Reheat 1 to 2 pieces at a time in the microwave for 1 to 2 minutes.

FREEZE: Store the cooled salmon, without the sauce, in a freezer-safe container for up to 2 months. Thaw overnight in the refrigerator. Reheat 1 to 2 pieces at a time in the microwave for 1 to 2 minutes.

> **TOBY'S TIP:** Once you are done prepping raw fish, meat, or poultry, thoroughly clean the cutting board, knife, and working surface with soap and warm water. Always use clean hands, cutting boards, utensils, and surfaces once the food is cooked.

Per Serving (5 ounces salmon, plus 2 tablespoons chimichurri sauce): Calories: 373; Fat: 27g; Saturated Fat: 4g; Protein: 29g; Total Carbs: 2g; Fiber: 1g; Sodium: 169mg

DAIRY-FREE **GLUTEN-FREE** **PALEO**

ROASTED TROUT WITH GREEN OLIVE TAPENADE

MAKES 4 SERVINGS

PREP TIME: 5 minutes   **COOK TIME:** 10 minutes

One day, my youngest daughter told me she was sneaking leftover fish out of the refrigerator. She was trying to admit something "bad" that she did, though I was smiling on the inside. If my kid is going to "sneak" food outside mealtime, fish would be ideal, don't you agree? I then realized how much this girl loves fish, and since then the mild-flavored rainbow trout has been on my menu rotation.

Cooking spray

1 bunch rosemary

4 (5-ounce) rainbow trout fillets

Green Olive Tapenade (page 216)

1. Preheat the oven to 400°F. Coat a baking sheet with the cooking spray.

2. Place the rosemary in a single layer on the baking sheet. Place the fish, skin-side down, on the rosemary. Coat the top of the fish with the cooking spray. Bake until the fish is opaque and reaches an internal temperature of 145°F, about 10 minutes.

3. Top the fish with 2 tablespoons of olive tapenade.

REFRIGERATE: Store the cooled fish and tapenade in separate resealable containers for up to 5 days. Reheat one piece at a time in the microwave for 1 to 1½ minutes.

FREEZE: Store the cooled fish, without the tapenade, in a freezer-safe container for up to 2 months. Thaw in the refrigerator overnight. Reheat the fish one piece at a time in the microwave for 1 to 1½ minutes.

> **TOBY'S TIP:** For about $10 a bimetallic stemmed kitchen thermometer is extremely handy to check the temperature of fish, poultry, and meat. It's hard to tell if fish, chicken, and beef are cooked through just by looking at the meat. Using a thermometer is your best bet to prevent foodborne illness in your home.

Per Serving: Calories 306; Fat: 20g; Saturated Fat: 3g; Protein: 28g; Total Carbs: 2g; Fiber: 0g; Sodium: 269mg

DAIRY-FREE

GINGER SOY TUNA PACKETS WITH SNAP PEAS AND BOK CHOY

MAKES 4 SERVINGS

PREP TIME: 20 minutes, plus 30 minutes to marinate   COOK TIME: 10 minutes

Cooking in parchment paper, or en papillote, means wrapping and cooking food like fish and vegetables in parchment paper. The paper is folded like an envelope, allowing the liquid inside to essentially steam the food, making it a moist, tender meal cooked to perfection. Cooking fish, like tuna, en papillote takes 10 minutes. You can even eat it right out of the paper, making it a no-dish meal!

2 tablespoons olive oil

¼ cup reduced-sodium soy sauce

¼ cup toasted sesame oil

2 tablespoons agave

2 garlic cloves, minced

2 tablespoons freshly grated ginger

1¼ pounds (½-inch-thick) tuna steak, cut into 4 equal portions

2 bunches baby bok choy

1 pound sugar snap peas, trimmed

4 scallions, chopped

1. If cooking the fish right away, preheat the oven to 400°F.

2. In a large bowl, whisk together the olive oil, soy sauce, sesame oil, agave, garlic, and ginger. Add the tuna steaks and toss to coat. Cover the container and let the tuna marinate for 30 minutes in the refrigerator, flipping the steaks after 15 minutes.

3. Lay 1 piece of parchment paper flat on the counter. In the lower half of the sheet, place a layer of the bok choy and a layer of the snap peas. Place 1 piece of tuna on top of the vegetables. Top the tuna with 1 teaspoon of the marinade, and sprinkle it with 1 of the chopped scallions. Fold the parchment paper in half over the fish. Working your way around, gently roll the edges of the open sides of the paper, tucking the ends under the packet. Repeat for the remaining 3 packets.

4. At this time, you can store the raw-fish packets in the refrigerator and cook as needed.

5. To cook, place up to two packets on a baking sheet and bake until the fish is opaque and reaches an internal temperature of 145°F, about 10 minutes. Using a sharp knife, carefully cut several 3-inch slits in the top of the packets. Be careful of the hot steam that is released from the open packet.

CONTINUED

GINGER SOY TUNA PACKETS WITH SNAP PEAS AND BOK CHOY CONTINUED

REFRIGERATE: Store the uncooked packets for up to 3 days. Once cooked, transfer the fish and vegetables to a resealable container and refrigerate for up to 5 days.

> **TOBY'S TIP:** If you're new to cooking en papillote, you can opt to purchase parchment-paper bags. Place the food inside the parchment bag, and just tuck the top underneath before cooking.

Per Serving: Calories: 381; Fat: 16g; Saturated Fat: 2g; Protein: 42g; Total Carbs: 20g; Fiber: 5g; Sodium: 525mg

DAIRY-FREE **GLUTEN-FREE**

COCONUT LIME FLOUNDER IN PARCHMENT PAPER

MAKES 4 SERVINGS

PREP TIME: 15 minutes   COOK TIME: 15 minutes

Coconut imparts a lovely flavor on many different foods, especially fish. In this simple parchment paper–cooked dish, coconut cream is combined with lime, soy sauce, and basil to give you a melt-in-your mouth fish.

- ¼ cup coconut cream (not coconut milk)
- Zest of 2 limes
- 2 teaspoons low-sodium soy sauce
- 2 limes, cut into 6 rounds each
- 12 fresh basil leaves
- 4 (5-ounce) flounder or cod fillets
- 4 tablespoons unsweetened shredded coconut, divided

1. If cooking the fish right away, preheat the oven to 400°F.

2. In a small bowl, whisk together the coconut cream, lime zest, and soy sauce.

3. Place 1 piece of parchment paper flat on the counter. On the lower half lay down 3 rings of lime and then a layer of 3 basil leaves. Place the fish on top of the basil and lime. Spoon 2 teaspoons of the coconut mixture over the fish and sprinkle it with 1 tablespoon of shredded coconut. Fold the parchment paper in half over the fish. Working your way around, gently roll the edge of the open sides of the paper, tucking the ends under the packet. Repeat this step for the remaining three packets.

4. At this time, you can store the raw-fish packets in the refrigerator and cook as needed.

5. To cook, place up to two packets on a baking sheet and roast until the fish is opaque and reaches an internal temperature of 145°F, about 10 minutes. Using a sharp knife, carefully cut several 3-inch slits in the packets.

REFRIGERATE: Store the uncooked packets for up to 3 days. Once cooked, transfer the fish and seasonings to a resealable container and refrigerate for up to 5 days.

> **TOBY'S TIP:** Coconut cream is the liquid expressed from the grated meat of the coconut fruit. Look for it in stores like Trader Joe's, Whole Foods, or in the Asian section of your grocery store.

Per Serving: Calories: 212; Fat: 9g; Saturated Fat: 6g; Protein: 19g; Total Carbs: 15g; Fiber: 2g; Sodium: 545mg

Fish & Seafood

DAIRY-FREE   GLUTEN-FREE

FARRO, SARDINES, AND GREENS

MAKES 4 SERVINGS

PREP TIME: 15 minutes   **COOK TIME:** 40 minutes

My dad is one of the biggest sardine lovers I know. He'll pop open a can and chomp on these little guys like they're going out of style. My dad aside, however, these tiny, soft-boned, saltwater fish are underappreciated by most. Sardines are a powerhouse of nutrition, providing omega-3 fatty acids, vitamin B_{12}, selenium, and 350 percent of the recommended daily amount of vitamin D. Delicious and nutritious.

- 3 cups low-sodium vegetable broth
- 1 cup farro
- 2 (4.5-ounce) cans sardines packed in extra-virgin olive oil (at least 12 sardines)
- 1 garlic clove, minced
- 1 pound fresh spinach

1. In a medium pot over high heat, bring the vegetable broth to a boil. Stir in the farro, reduce the heat to medium-low, and simmer until the water is absorbed and the grain is tender, about 30 minutes. Drain off any excess liquid. Let the farro cool for about 10 minutes.

2. While the farro cooks, open the sardine cans halfway. Keeping the fish in the can, pour the oil from the cans into a medium pot. Place the pot over medium heat and once hot, add the garlic and sauté until fragrant, about 1 minute. Add the spinach and cook, stirring occasionally, until the spinach is wilted and tender, about 10 minutes. Cover the pot when not stirring the spinach.

3. In each of four resealable containers, place ½ cup of farro, 3 sardines, and ¾ cup of spinach.

REFRIGERATE: Once cooled, cover the containers and store for up to 3 days. To reheat, microwave for 1 to 2 minutes.

TOBY'S TIP: Change up this dish by switching around the grains and greens. Swap the farro for wild rice, quinoa, or brown rice, and the spinach for kale, bok choy, or collards.

Per Serving: Calories: 390; Fat: 12g; Saturated Fat: 4g; Protein: 27g; Total Carbs: 45g; Fiber: 11g; Sodium: 388mg

DAIRY-FREE **GLUTEN-FREE**

LIME SHRIMP WITH TOMATO SALSA

MAKES 6 SERVINGS

PREP TIME: 10 minutes   COOK TIME: 10 minutes

If you shy away from shrimp because you've heard it's bad for your cholesterol, it's time to dig in. The 2015 Dietary Guidelines for Americans removed the long-standing recommendation for eating a maximum of 300 milligrams of cholesterol per day.

- 2 tablespoons olive oil
- 2 garlic cloves, minced
- 2 pounds large shrimp (40 or 60 count), peeled and deveined
- Juice of 3 limes (about ⅓ cup)
- 1 (15-ounce) can white beans, drained and rinsed
- ¾ cup pitted black olives, chopped
- ¼ teaspoon salt
- ⅛ teaspoon freshly ground black pepper
- Simple Tomato Salsa (page 217)

1. In a large skillet over medium heat, heat the olive oil until it shimmers. Add the garlic and cook until fragrant, about 1 minute. Add the shrimp and cook, stirring occasionally, until they turn opaque, about 5 minutes.

2. Add the lime juice and toss to coat the shrimp. Raise the heat to high and bring the liquid to a boil. Add the beans and stir to combine. Reduce the heat to low, cover the skillet, and simmer until flavors combine, 3 to 5 minutes. Stir in the olives, salt, and black pepper.

3. Serve the shrimp with ½ cup of tomato salsa on the side.

REFRIGERATE: Store the cooled shrimp in resealable containers for up to 5 days. Reheat single servings in the microwave for 1 to 2 minutes, or reheat in a skillet over medium-low heat until the shrimp and sauce are heated through, about 10 minutes.

FREEZE: Store the cooled shrimp in freezer-safe containers for up to 2 months. Thaw in the refrigerator overnight. Reheat single servings in the microwave for 1 to 2 minutes. Or reheat in a skillet over medium-low heat until the shrimp and sauce are heated through, about 10 minutes.

TOBY'S TIP: Frozen shrimp is a good alternative to fresh and can last several months in your freezer. Look for frozen shrimp that has been peeled and deveined.

Per Serving (1 cup shrimp mixture, plus ½ cup tomato salsa): Calories: 323; Fat: 11g; Saturated Fat: 1g; Protein: 37g; Total Carbs: 22g; Fiber: 5g; Sodium: 512mg

DAIRY-FREE

LIGHTER FISH CAKES

MAKES 6 SERVINGS

PREP TIME: 20 minutes   COOK TIME: 20 minutes

I am one of five children, and my mom was always finding new favorites to serve for dinner. Fish sticks happened to be a favorite back in the 80's, so she served them to us several times a month. Although I am still a fan of fish sticks (the homemade kind), I am not a fan of the breading. Fish cakes are a perfect answer, as they use just a touch of bread crumbs, plus I can grate or chop veggies to use in them, too.

Cooking spray
1 pound cod fillet
¼ teaspoon salt
¼ teaspoon freshly ground black pepper
1 medium yellow squash, shredded
2 large eggs, beaten
½ cup finely chopped parsley
2 scallions, chopped
Juice of 1 lemon (about 2 tablespoons)
1 cup plain bread crumbs
¼ teaspoon smoked paprika
Avocado Lime Mayonnaise (page 215)

1. Preheat the oven to 375°F. Coat a baking sheet with the cooking spray.

2. Season both sides of the fish with the salt and black pepper and put it on the baking sheet. Bake until the fish is opaque and reaches an internal temperature of 145°F, about 10 minutes. Let the fish cool for 10 minutes.

3. Using a fork, flake the fish into bite-size pieces and place them in a large bowl. Add the squash, eggs, parsley, scallions, lemon juice, bread crumbs, and paprika to the bowl and toss to combine. Let the mixture sit for 10 minutes so the flavors can combine.

4. Using clean hands, form 1 heaping tablespoon into a round patty and place it on a large plate. Repeat this step to create 12 patties.

5. Coat a large frying pan with the cooking spray and place it over medium heat. When the oil is shimmering, add each patty to the pan, gently pressing down on it with your fingers to slightly flatten it. Leave 1 inch of space between each patty in the pan. Cook the patties until they are slightly browned and cooked through, about 5 minutes per side.

6. Serve 2 patties with 2 tablespoons of Avocado Lime Mayonnaise.

REFRIGERATE: Store the cooled fish cakes in a resealable container for up to 5 days. Store the Avocado Lime Mayonnaise in a separate container or glass jar for up to 1 week. Reheat 2 patties in the microwave for 45 seconds to 1 minute.

FREEZE: Store the patties in a freezer-safe container for up to 1 month. Thaw in the refrigerator overnight. Reheat 2 patties in the microwave for 45 seconds to 1 minute.

> **TOBY'S TIP:** To make your own bread crumbs, tear 4 slices of 100% whole-wheat bread into small pieces. Place them in a food processor and pulse until fine crumbs form, about 30 seconds. Sprinkle the crumbs across an ungreased baking sheet and toast them in a 350°F preheated oven until slightly browned, about 10 minutes. Remove from the oven and set aside to cool.

Per Serving: Calories: 264; Fat: 13g; Saturated Fat: 2g; Protein: 20g; Total Carbs: 19g; Fiber: 4g; Sodium: 417mg

DAIRY-FREE

CRAB-STUFFED FLOUNDER

MAKES 4 SERVINGS

PREP TIME: 20 minutes   COOK TIME: 30 minutes

If you take this recipe to work, the double dose of seafood will have your co-workers salivating. Be warned, however, and keep a close eye on who's taking what out of that communal work refrigerator.

Cooking spray

¼ onion, diced (about ¼ cup)

1 celery stalk, diced (about ¼ cup)

1 large egg, beaten

1½ teaspoons Dijon mustard

1 teaspoon Worcestershire sauce

½ teaspoon Old Bay Seasoning

1 pound crab meat (drained and gently rinsed, if canned)

½ cup plain bread crumbs

2 tablespoons low-fat milk

4 (4-ounce) flounder fillets

1 teaspoon dried basil

1. Preheat the oven to 400°F. Coat a baking dish with the cooking spray.

2. Coat a small sauté pan with the cooking spray and place it over medium heat. When the oil is shimmering, add the onion and celery, and cook until the onion is translucent, 3 to 4 minutes. Let the mixture cool for 5 minutes.

3. In a medium bowl, add the cooled onion mixture, egg, mustard, Worcestershire sauce, Old Bay Seasoning, and crab meat. Stir to combine. Add the bread crumbs and milk and stir to combine.

4. Using clean hands, divide the filling into four 1-cup portions and gently form each into a ball. Wrap one flounder fillet around each ball and place each in the baking dish seam-side down. Spray the top of the flounder with the cooking spray and sprinkle with the dried basil.

5. Bake until the fish is opaque and reaches an internal temperature of 155°F, 20 to 25 minutes.

REFRIGERATE: Store the cooled stuffed fish in resealable plastic containers for up to 5 days. Reheat individual portions in the microwave for about 2 minutes.

FREEZE: Store the cooled stuffed fish in freezer-safe containers for up to 1 month. Reheat from frozen in a preheated 350°F oven. Cover the fish with aluminum foil and bake for about 30 minutes. Remove the foil and continue to bake for about 10 minutes more. Alternatively, thaw overnight in the refrigerator, and reheat individual portions in the microwave for about 2 minutes.

Per Serving: Calories: 245; Fat: 6g; Saturated Fat: 1g; Protein: 36g; Total Carbs: 11g; Fiber: 1g; Sodium: 1,072mg

DAIRY-FREE **GLUTEN-FREE** **PALEO**

GRILLED HALIBUT WITH ANCHOVY-CAPER DRESSING

MAKES 4 SERVINGS

PREP TIME: 15 minutes   COOK TIME: 10 minutes

When cooking fish, it's all about the flavors you impart. Herbs, spices, citrus, and various flavored vinegars are usually what I love to toss in an easy-to-make dressing or sauce. The dressing in this recipe uses anchovies and capers, which are the Mediterranean flavors I grew up with. The flavors compliment the halibut beautifully.

Juice of 2 lemons

Zest of 2 lemons

¼ cup white wine vinegar

2 tablespoons anchovy paste

1 tablespoon chopped parsley

¼ cup plus 2 tablespoons olive oil, divided

2 tablespoons capers, divided

⅛ teaspoon freshly ground black pepper

Cooking spray

4 (5-ounce) halibut fillets

1. In a large bowl, whisk together the lemon juice and zest, vinegar, anchovy paste, and parsley. While continuing to whisk, slowly add ¼ cup of olive oil. Add 1 tablespoon of capers and crush them into the sauce, then stir in the remaining 1 tablespoon of capers and the black pepper.

2. Preheat a grill or coat a grill pan with the cooking spray and place it over high heat. Brush both sides of the fillets with the remaining 2 tablespoons of olive oil. Grill the fish until they are opaque and the internal temperature reaches 145°F, about 5 minutes per side.

3. Serve each fillet with ¼ cup of the caper sauce.

REFRIGERATE: Store the cooled fish in individual resealable containers and top each with ¼ cup of sauce. Refrigerate for up to 5 days. Reheat in the microwave for about 1 minute.

FREEZE: Store the cooled fish in individual freezer-safe containers and top each with ¼ cup of sauce. Freeze for up to 1 month. Thaw in the refrigerator overnight. Reheat in the microwave for about 1 minute.

> **TOBY'S TIP:** Substitute the Anchovy Caper Dressing with Kale Pesto (page 206), Chimichurri Sauce (page 212), or Avocado Lime Mayonnaise (page 215). If using the mayonnaise, refrigerate it separately from the fish.

Per Serving (1 fillet plus ¼ cup caper sauce): Calories: 328; Fat: 23g; Saturated Fat: 4g; Protein: 27g; Total Carbs: 1g; Fiber: 0g; Sodium: 800mg

Fish & Seafood

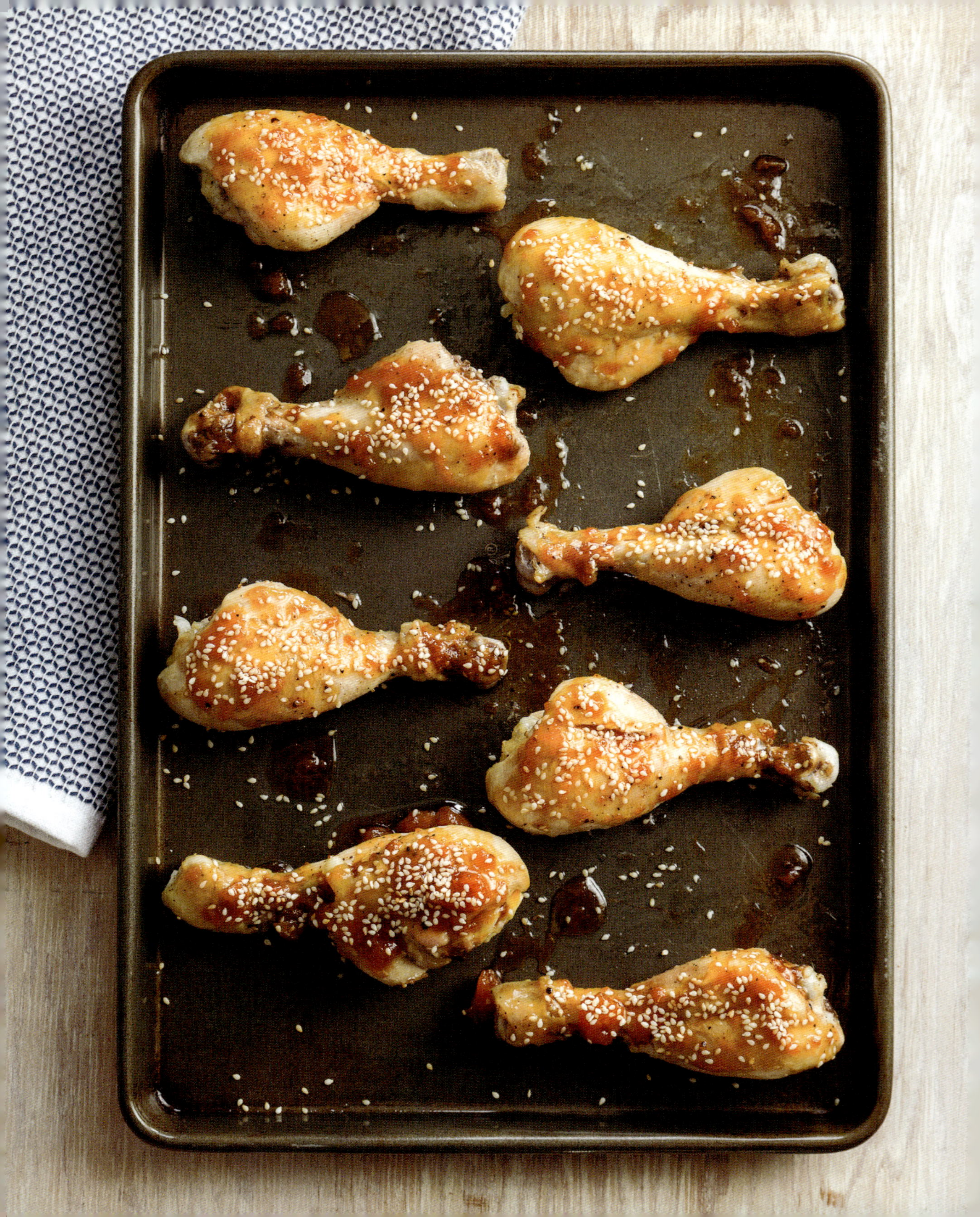

7 POULTRY

146 Turkey-Walnut Salad with Cranberries
147 Mediterranean Turkey Burgers
148 Baked Turkey Meatballs
150 Pesto Chicken
151 Thai Chicken Thighs
152 One-Pot Mediterranean Chicken and Quinoa
154 Thai Chicken Stir-Fry
155 Hawaiian Chicken Skewers
157 Apricot Chicken Drumsticks
159 Lemony Chicken Breasts
160 Rosemary Chicken Breasts
161 Slow-Cooker Tuscan Chicken
162 Slow-Cooker White Chicken Chili
163 White Chicken Chili and Spinach Quesadillas
164 Slow-Cooker Barbecue Chicken
165 Barbecue Chicken Pizza

« Apricot Chicken Drumsticks (page 157)

GLUTEN-FREE

TURKEY-WALNUT SALAD WITH CRANBERRIES

MAKES 4 SERVINGS

PREP TIME: 15 minutes

How often do you have leftover Thanksgiving turkey that you don't know what to do with? Or maybe some leftover rotisserie or an extra cooked chicken breast? This is the easiest (and tastiest) way to put it to good use. If you want to make this salad and don't have leftovers, many groceries' ready-to-eat counters sell homemade roasted turkey breast, oftentimes already seasoned with herbs.

- 8 ounces cooked skinless turkey or rotisserie chicken, minced
- ½ medium yellow onion, finely chopped
- 1 celery stalk, finely chopped
- ¼ cup walnuts, chopped
- 3 tablespoons dried cranberries
- 2 tablespoons light mayonnaise
- 2 tablespoons nonfat plain Greek yogurt
- 1 tablespoon Dijon mustard
- 1 teaspoon freshly squeezed lemon juice
- 2 teaspoons chopped fresh parsley
- ¼ teaspoon salt
- ⅛ teaspoon freshly ground black pepper

1. In a medium bowl, combine the turkey, onion, celery, walnuts, and cranberries. Set aside.

2. In a small bowl, whisk together the mayonnaise, Greek yogurt, mustard, lemon juice, parsley, salt, and black pepper until well combined. Add this to the turkey mixture and stir until well combined.

REFRIGERATE: Store the salad in a resealable container for up to 5 days.

> **TOBY'S TIP:** To reduce the amount of mayo in salads, I substitute half for nonfat plain Greek yogurt. Although you can replace all of the mayo for Greek yogurt, I still like the mayo flavor that you get with a 1:1 mayo-to-Greek yogurt ratio.

Per Serving (⅔ cup): Calories: 175; Fat: 8g; Saturated Fat: 1g; Protein: 17g; Total Carbs: 8g; Fiber: 1g; Sodium: 450mg

GLUTEN-FREE

MEDITERRANEAN TURKEY BURGERS

MAKES 4 SERVINGS

PREP TIME: 20 minutes   COOK TIME: 10 minutes

In these babies, spinach and feta bind the burgers while boosting the flavor. Enjoy with the yogurt sauce, babaganoush, or tzatziki.

FOR THE BURGERS

- 1 pound ground turkey
- 6 ounces frozen spinach, thawed and gently squeezed (about 1½ cups)
- ¼ red onion, finely chopped
- ¼ cup crumbled feta
- 1 garlic clove, minced
- 1 teaspoon dried oregano
- ¼ teaspoon freshly ground black pepper
- Cooking spray

FOR THE YOGURT SAUCE

- 1 cup nonfat plain Greek yogurt
- Juice of 1 lemon (about 2 tablespoons)
- 1 tablespoon chopped fresh dill
- ¼ teaspoon salt
- ½ garlic clove, minced

TO MAKE THE BURGERS

1. In a large bowl, combine the turkey, spinach, onion, feta, garlic, oregano, and black pepper. Gently mix to combine.
2. Using clean hands, form the mixture into 4 patties.
3. Coat a grill pan or sauté pan with the cooking spray and place it over medium heat. When hot, place the burgers in the pan. Cook until the turkey has reached an internal temperature of 165°F, about 5 minutes per side.

TO MAKE THE YOGURT SAUCE

1. In a small bowl, add the Greek yogurt, lemon juice, dill, salt, and garlic. Stir to combine.
2. Serve each burger with ¼ cup of yogurt sauce.

REFRIGERATE: Store the cooled burgers and yogurt sauce in separate resealable containers for up to 1 week. To reheat, microwave each burger for 1 to 2 minutes. The burgers can also be reheated on a grill or grill pan for 4 minutes on each side.

FREEZE: Store the cooled burgers in a freezer-safe container for up to 2 months. Thaw in the refrigerator overnight. To reheat, microwave each burger for 1 to 2 minutes. Burgers can also be reheated on a grill or grill pan for 4 minutes on each side. The yogurt sauce will not freeze well.

> **TOBY'S TIP:** Enjoy your burger in a whole-grain bun with lettuce and tomato or sliced over a salad.

Per Serving: Calories: 248; Fat: 12g; Saturated Fat: 4g; Protein: 30g; Total Carbs: 6g; Fiber: 2g; Sodium: 364mg

GLUTEN-FREE

BAKED TURKEY MEATBALLS

MAKES 24 MEATBALLS

PREP TIME: 20 minutes   COOK TIME: 25 minutes

I'm probably one of the messiest meal preppers you'll ever meet. During an afternoon in the kitchen it looks like a hurricane passed through. I'm also not the neatest cook, so though delicious, the food itself isn't always the prettiest. But I have learned small tricks to help up my creative abilities. One skill that isn't my strongest is rolling meatballs evenly. Using a mini muffin tray helps guide me so the meatballs all come out the same size.

Cooking spray

1½ cups low-sodium canned chickpeas, drained and rinsed

1 pound ground turkey

¼ cup part-skim ricotta

¼ cup grated Parmesan cheese

½ serrano chile, seeded and finely chopped

1 teaspoon dried oregano

1 tablespoon chopped fresh parsley

½ teaspoon salt

¼ teaspoon freshly ground black pepper

1. Preheat the oven to 375°F. Coat a 24-cup mini muffin tin with the cooking spray.

2. In a food processor, pulse the chickpeas until they become paste-like.

3. In a large bowl, add the chickpea paste, turkey, ricotta, Parmesan, serrano chile, oregano, parsley, salt, and black pepper. Mix until well combined and the mixture almost appears to be one large ball.

4. Using clean hands, form 1 heaping teaspoon of the turkey mixture into a 2-inch ball and place it in one of the muffin cups. Repeat this with the rest of the turkey mixture. You should have 24 meatballs.

5. Bake until the meatballs are golden brown, about 25 minutes. Let cool for 5 minutes, then use a teaspoon to transfer each meatball to a container.

REFRIGERATE: Store the cooled meatballs in a resealable container for up to 1 week. To reheat, microwave one serving (4 meatballs) for about 1 minute. The meatballs can also be reheated in a saucepan along with the Speedy Tomato Sauce (page 213).

FREEZE: Store the cooled meatballs in a freezer-safe container for up to 2 months. Thaw in the refrigerator overnight and reheat one serving (4 meatballs) in the microwave for about 1 minute.

> **TOBY'S TIP:** Ground turkey breast is the leanest, but I like to mix it with a little higher-fat ground turkey. Look for ground turkey that's at least 90% lean. If the ground turkey is too lean, then the meatballs will come out dry.

Per Serving (4 meatballs): Calories: 201; Fat: 9g; Saturated Fat: 3g; Protein: 20g; Total Carbs: 10g; Fiber: 3g; Sodium: 404mg

DAIRY-FREE **GLUTEN-FREE** **PALEO**

PESTO CHICKEN

MAKES 4 SERVINGS

PREP TIME: 5 minutes   COOK TIME: 1 hour to 1 hour, 15 minutes

I dread the same old chicken dish night after night. That's why I love using versatile sauces to liven up my taste buds. This pesto sauce is delicious, healthy, and busting with flavor. Even better, it takes only a few minutes to flavor my chicken, and there's only one baking dish to clean. I love those one-and-done meals!

1 (3.75-pound) whole chicken, cut in 8 pieces, skin removed

Kale Pesto (page 206)

1. Preheat the oven to 350°F.

2. Add ¼ cup of pesto to a small bowl. Brush the pesto all over the chicken pieces and place them in a single layer in a 9-by-13-inch baking dish. Discard any unused pesto.

3. Bake until the chicken is cooked through and a thermometer inserted into the center of a piece of chicken reads 165°F, about 60 to 75 minutes.

4. Serve 2 pieces of chicken (1 large and 1 small) with 2 tablespoons of pesto.

REFRIGERATE: Store the cooled chicken and pesto in separate resealable containers for up to 1 week. Reheat single-serve portions of chicken in the microwave for 1½ to 2 minutes.

FREEZE: Store the cooled chicken in a freezer-safe container for up to 2 months. To reheat, thaw in the refrigerator overnight. Reheat single portions of chicken in the microwave for 1½ to 2 minutes. The pesto does not freeze well.

> **TOBY'S TIP:** To significantly cut back on artery-clogging saturated fat, trim any fat and take the skin off the chicken before cooking it, as I suggest in this recipe. This saves 51 calories and 7 grams of saturated fat per each 3-ounce portion.

Per Serving (1 large and 1 small piece): Calories: 370; Fat: 21g; Saturated Fat: 4g; Protein: 42g; Total Carbs: 4g; Fiber: 1g; Sodium: 551mg

DAIRY-FREE

THAI CHICKEN THIGHS

MAKES 4 SERVINGS

PREP TIME: 5 minutes, plus 2 hours to chill   COOK TIME: 25 minutes

Dark-meat chicken has a bad reputation for having a lot of artery-clogging saturated fat. In reality, once you take off the skin, most of the saturated fat is gone. What's left is heart-healthy monounsaturated fat. Plus, chicken thighs are less expensive than chicken breasts and can be a tasty part of your chicken repertoire.

1½ pounds boneless, skinless chicken thighs

⅓ cup Thai Marinade (page 214)

1. Put the chicken thighs in a large bowl. Pour the marinade over the thighs and toss to coat the chicken. Cover the bowl and refrigerate for at least 2 hours or up to overnight.

2. Preheat the oven to 350°F.

3. Place the marinated chicken thighs in a roasting pan, and bake until the thighs are cooked through and a thermometer inserted into one or two thighs reads 165°F, about 25 minutes.

REFRIGERATE: Store the cooled chicken in a resealable container for up to 1 week. To reheat, microwave each thigh for 1 minute.

FREEZE: Store the cooled chicken in a freezer-safe container for up to 2 months. Thaw in the refrigerator overnight and reheat each thigh in the microwave for 1 minute.

> **TOBY'S TIP:** I purchase my chicken thighs from my butcher on Tuesdays when they have a manager's special. All that means is that the chicken needs to be cooked that night or the next day, but it's still safe to eat and is a high-quality protein.

Per Serving (6 ounces chicken): Calories: 298; Fat: 14g; Saturated Fat: 5g; Protein: 42g; Total Carbs: 3g; Fiber: 0g; Sodium: 397mg

DAIRY-FREE   GLUTEN-FREE

ONE-POT MEDITERRANEAN CHICKEN AND QUINOA

MAKES 6 SERVINGS

PREP TIME: 20 minutes   COOK TIME: 30 minutes

Since my parents emigrated from Israel to the United States, I was raised on the Mediterranean-style foods typical to my home country. Olives, tomatoes, olive oil, and oregano are flavors I grew up with and have incorporated into this lovely dish. I added the versatile quinoa for more protein and fiber. Because of the tomato-based sauce, it also freezes and reheats beautifully.

2 tablespoons olive oil

1¼ pounds boneless, skinless chicken breasts, cut into bite-size pieces

1 garlic clove, minced

1 medium yellow onion, chopped

1½ cups low-sodium chicken broth

¾ cup pitted Kalamata olives, sliced

2 (14.5-ounce) cans low-sodium diced tomatoes

2 teaspoons dried oregano

¼ teaspoon freshly ground black pepper

⅛ teaspoon smoked paprika

1½ cups quinoa

1. In a large skillet over medium heat, heat the olive oil until it shimmers. Add the chicken and cook until the pieces are browned on all sides, about 8 minutes. Transfer the chicken to a plate and set aside.

2. In the same skillet over medium heat, add the garlic and onion and cook until the onions are soft and translucent, about 3 minutes. Add the broth, olives, tomatoes, oregano, black pepper, and paprika and stir to incorporate. Raise the heat to high and bring the mixture to a boil, then reduce the heat to low and simmer until the olives begin to soften, about 5 minutes.

3. Return the chicken to the skillet and stir to combine. Add the quinoa, increase the heat to medium-high, and bring the mixture to a boil. Then reduce the heat to low and simmer, covered but stirring occasionally, until the chicken is cooked through and the quinoa is tender, about 15 minutes.

REFRIGERATE: Store the cooled chicken and quinoa in a resealable container for up to 1 week. To reheat individual portions, microwave for 2 minutes. The entire dish can be reheated in a saucepan over medium heat. Add ¼ cup of water to the pan to prevent the bottom from burning.

FREEZE: Store the cooled chicken and quinoa in individual freezer-safe containers for up to 2 months. Thaw in the refrigerator overnight. To reheat, microwave for 2 minutes. The entire dish can be reheated in a saucepan over medium heat. Add ¼ cup of water to the pan to prevent the bottom from burning.

> **TOBY'S TIP:** Buy bulk portions of skinless chicken breast from warehouse clubs, then repackage into recipe portions when you get home. This can help save money on many proteins like beef, chicken, and fish.

Per Serving (1 cup): Calories: 380; Fat: 12g; Saturated Fat: 1g; Protein: 29g; Total Carbs: 27g; Fiber: 4g; Sodium: 457mg

DAIRY-FREE

THAI CHICKEN STIR-FRY

MAKES 4 SERVINGS

PREP TIME: 20 minutes, plus 30 minutes to marinate   COOK TIME: 55 minutes

Once I started having kids, I lived on stir-fries. With a little planning to marinate the chicken, beef, or tofu for at least 30 minutes, they are super quick to cook. They are also a perfect way to get rid of any leftover fresh, frozen, or canned veggies. Stir-fries are also a great way to introduce different flavors into your meals, making regular ingredients sing.

- 1¼ pounds skinless, boneless chicken breast, cut into 1½-inch strips
- ⅓ cup Thai Marinade (page 214), divided
- 3 cups water
- 1 cup long-grain brown rice
- 1 tablespoon canola or safflower oil
- ½ head broccoli, cut into bite-size florets
- 1 (8-ounce) package white mushrooms, sliced
- 1 red bell pepper, sliced into 1-inch strips

1. In a large bowl, add the chicken strips and ⅓ cup of marinade and toss to coat the chicken. Cover the bowl and refrigerate for at least 30 minutes or up to overnight.

2. In a medium pot over high heat, bring the water to a boil. Add the brown rice and lower the heat to medium-low. Cover and simmer the rice, stirring occasionally, until it is tender, about 40 minutes. Drain any excess water. Transfer the rice to a large bowl and let it cool slightly.

3. In a large wok or skillet over medium heat, heat the oil until it shimmers. Add the chicken (discarding the marinade) and cook until it is browned on all sides, about 6 minutes. Add the broccoli, mushrooms, and bell pepper and stir-fry until the vegetables start to soften, about 8 minutes. Add the remaining ⅓ cup of marinade to the stir-fry and cook until heated through, about 1 minute.

REFRIGERATE: Store the cooled stir-fry and rice together or separately in a resealable container for up to 1 week. To reheat, microwave for 1½ to 2 minutes.

> **TOBY'S TIP:** I live by my rice cooker, which I use to cook up more than rice. Besides white and brown rice, I use it to prepare farro, quinoa, and other grains, too. My rice cooker even has the capability to keep the grain warm after cooking.

Per Serving (1½ cups stir-fry plus ⅔ cup rice): Calories: 357; Fat: 9g; Saturated Fat: 3g; Protein: 24g; Total Carbs: 46g; Fiber: 3g; Sodium: 226mg

DAIRY-FREE   **GLUTEN-FREE**   **PALEO**

HAWAIIAN CHICKEN SKEWERS

MAKES 6 SERVINGS

PREP TIME: 30 minutes, plus 30 minutes to chill   COOK TIME: 25 minutes

These Hawaiian-inspired skewers are made with a coconut marinade and chunks of pineapple. They remind me of my two trips to these gorgeous islands, where the weather was incredible and everyone was frolicking in the water. Now every time I pack them in my lunchbox, I remember scuba diving and surfing in Hawaii and the amazing food.

12 skewers, wooden or metal

Cooking spray

1 (13.5-ounce) can light coconut milk

¼ cup honey

Juice of 2 limes (about ¼ cup)

2 teaspoons freshly grated ginger

2 tablespoons freshly chopped chives

½ teaspoon salt

¼ teaspoon freshly ground black pepper

1½ pounds skinless, boneless chicken breast, cut into 2-inch cubes

24 cherry tomatoes

⅞ pineapple, cut into large cubes (about 24 chunks)

1. Preheat the oven to 375°F. If using wooden skewers, soak them in water while preparing the chicken. Coat a baking sheet with the cooking spray or line it with parchment paper.

2. In a medium bowl, whisk together the coconut milk, honey, lime juice, ginger, chives, salt, and black pepper.

3. Put the chicken in a large bowl. Pour 1 cup of the coconut mixture over the chicken and toss to coat. Cover and refrigerate for at least 30 minutes or up to overnight. Put the remaining coconut mixture in a separate resealable container and refrigerate it.

4. To assemble the skewers, thread a piece of chicken, followed by a cherry tomato and then a pineapple chunk. Repeat once more on the same skewer. Prepare the remaining 11 skewers the same way. Discard the used marinade.

5. Place the skewers on the baking sheet in a single layer. Bake until the chicken is cooked through, about 20 minutes.

6. While the chicken is baking, heat the remaining coconut mixture in a small saucepan over medium-low heat until bubbling, about 5 minutes.

CONTINUED

HAWAIIAN CHICKEN SKEWERS CONTINUED

REFRIGERATE: Cool the skewers to room temperature. Use a fork to slide the food off two skewers into a resealable container. Top this with 4 teaspoons of the coconut mixture. Repeat this for the remaining skewers and coconut mixture. Store in the refrigerator for up to 1 week. Reheat individual portions in the microwave for about 1 minute. Do not heat wooden or metal skewers in the microwave.

> **TOBY'S TIP:** When it comes to coconut milk, choose those that are light. Regular coconut milk has almost 2½ times more calories and saturated fat than its light counterpart.

Per Serving (4 skewers): Calories: 433; Fat: 11g; Saturated Fat: 5g; Protein: 40g; Total Carbs: 44g; Fiber: 4g; Sodium: 360mg

DAIRY-FREE

APRICOT CHICKEN DRUMSTICKS

MAKES 4 SERVINGS

PREP TIME: 15 minutes   COOK TIME: 40 minutes

When I was right out of my master's program in nutrition, I taught at a culinary school in New York City. It so happened that my mother, a fellow registered dietitian, asked me to work there so I could substitute for her when she wanted to go on vacation. I ended up teaching there for 10 years. During my tenure, they asked me to do many media interviews. This recipe was the first one that ever got published in the New York Daily News, back in 2006.

Cooking spray

8 skinless chicken drumsticks

2 tablespoons canola or safflower oil

¼ teaspoon salt

⅛ teaspoon freshly ground black pepper

2 tablespoons sesame seeds

¼ cup apricot jam

2 tablespoons low-sodium soy sauce

1. Preheat the oven to 400°F. Coat a shallow 9-by-9-inch baking dish with the cooking spray.

2. Brush the chicken with the oil and sprinkle it with the salt and black pepper. Put the chicken in the baking dish and bake until a thermometer inserted in the center of a drumstick reads 165°F, about 35 to 40 minutes.

3. Just before the chicken is ready, in a small skillet over medium-low heat, toast the sesame seeds until slightly browned, stirring them frequently so they don't burn, about 5 minutes.

4. In a small saucepan over medium heat, whisk together the apricot jam and soy sauce. Cook, stirring frequently, until it boils, about 5 minutes. Remove the pan from the stove.

5. Let the chicken cool for 5 minutes, then drizzle the apricot sauce over it and sprinkle with the toasted sesame seeds.

CONTINUED

APRICOT CHICKEN DRUMSTICKS CONTINUED

REFRIGERATE: Store the cooled chicken with the sauce and seeds in a resealable container for up to 1 week. To reheat, microwave for 1½ minutes. It can also be reheated in a saucepan over medium heat.

FREEZE: Store the cooled chicken with the sauce and seeds in a freezer-safe container for up to 2 months. Thaw in the refrigerator overnight and reheat in the microwave for 1 minute. It can also be reheated in a saucepan over medium heat.

> **TOBY'S TIP:** Pair the drumsticks with my Oven-Roasted Tomato Quinoa (page 98) and Lemony Green Beans with Almonds (page 124). First roast the tomatoes for the quinoa. When they're done, remove them from the oven and add the drumsticks. While the chicken bakes, cook the quinoa in a saucepan and prepare the green beans in a skillet. When the quinoa is done cooking, fluff it and let it cool before mixing it with the roasted tomatoes and other finishing ingredients.

Per Serving (2 drumsticks with 1 tablespoon sauce and 1½ teaspoons sesame seeds): Calories: 541; Fat: 32g; Saturated Fat: 7g; Protein: 46g; Total Carbs: 14g; Fiber: 1g; Sodium: 766mg

DAIRY-FREE   GLUTEN-FREE   PALEO

LEMONY CHICKEN BREASTS

MAKES 4 SERVINGS

PREP TIME: 15 minutes   COOK TIME: 40 minutes

I always make sure to have a few fresh lemons in the house. Their juice and zest are some of the easiest ways to enhance the flavor of foods from chicken to salads to cooked asparagus to a refreshing glass of water. I always keep a few on hand in a bowl on my countertop. If it's in sight, then it will be top of my mind to use.

Cooking spray

4 (5-ounce) skinless, boneless chicken breasts

¼ teaspoon salt

⅛ teaspoon freshly ground black pepper

3 tablespoons olive oil, divided

1 garlic clove, minced

½ cup dry white wine

⅓ cup low-sodium chicken broth

Zest of ½ lemon

Juice of ½ lemon (about 1 tablespoon)

1 teaspoon dried rosemary

1 lemon, sliced

1. Preheat the oven to 400°F. Coat an 8-by-11-inch baking dish with the cooking spray.

2. Coat the chicken breasts with the cooking spray and season them with the salt and black pepper. Place them in the baking dish.

3. In a small saucepan over medium heat, heat 1 tablespoon of olive oil until it shimmers. Add the garlic and cook until fragrant, about 30 seconds. Add the wine, chicken broth, lemon juice and zest, and rosemary, and bring it to a boil. Reduce the heat to low and continue cooking until the flavors combine, about 3 to 4 minutes.

4. Pour the lemon sauce over the chicken and tuck the lemon slices around the chicken. Bake for 25 minutes, then cover the dish with aluminum foil and continue baking for 10 minutes more, until the chicken is browned and a thermometer inserted into the center of a breast reads 165°F.

REFRIGERATE: Store the cooled chicken and sauce in a resealable container for up to 1 week. Reheat in the microwave for 1 minute.

FREEZE: Store the cooled chicken and sauce in a freezer-safe container for up to 2 months. Thaw in the refrigerator overnight. Reheat in the microwave for 1 minute. It can also be reheated in a baking dish in a preheated 375°F oven for 15 to 20 minutes, or until heated through.

Per Serving: Calories: 276; Fat: 14g; Saturated Fat: 2g; Protein: 32g; Total Carbs: 1g; Fiber: 0g; Sodium: 262mg

DAIRY-FREE   GLUTEN-FREE   PALEO

ROSEMARY CHICKEN BREASTS

MAKES 4 SERVINGS

PREP TIME: 15 minutes   COOK TIME: 20 minutes

When my children were younger, I took them to Martha's Vineyard for a few summers. Nobody likes to cook on vacation, but it's expensive to eat out with three kids for an entire week. I needed quick, easy, and tasty food that both my kids and I would enjoy. In the cabinet of the beach house, I came across a jar of dried rosemary. That's how these quick chicken breasts came to be.

4 (5-ounce) skinless, boneless chicken breasts

¼ teaspoon salt

⅛ teaspoon freshly ground black pepper

1 tablespoon chopped fresh rosemary

2 tablespoons olive oil

Juice of 1 lemon (about 2 tablespoons)

1. Loosely wrap each chicken breast in plastic wrap and place on a cutting board. Using a mallet or heavy-bottomed pan, pound the chicken until each breast is 1 inch thick. Unwrap the chicken and throw the plastic wrap away.

2. Season the chicken breast on both sides with the salt, black pepper, and rosemary.

3. In a large skillet over medium heat, heat the olive oil until it shimmers. Add the chicken breasts and cook until they're browned, about 10 minutes. Flip the chicken over and drizzle with the lemon juice. Continue cooking until the chicken is cooked through and a thermometer inserted in the center of a breast reads 165°F, about 10 minutes.

REFRIGERATE: Store the cooled chicken in a resealable container for up to 1 week. To reheat, microwave one breast for 1 minute.

FREEZE: Store the cooled chicken in a freezer-safe container for up to 2 months. Thaw in the refrigerator overnight and reheat one breast in the microwave for 1 minute.

> **TOBY'S TIP:** Toss the chicken breasts on the grill for a quick and easy barbecue or cookout dish.

Per Serving: Calories: 217; Fat: 11g; Saturated Fat: 2g; Protein: 29g; Total Carbs: 1g; Fiber: 0g; Sodium: 393mg

DAIRY-FREE   GLUTEN-FREE   PALEO

SLOW-COOKER TUSCAN CHICKEN

MAKES 4 SERVINGS

PREP TIME: 15 minutes   COOK TIME: 4 to 6 hours

One of my favorite kitchen toys is my slow cooker. In the morning, it takes me 15 minutes to prep and toss my ingredients into it. I cover the pot, press the "cook" button, and the cooker does the rest. Nothing beats coming home to a warm, delicious meal that I know is good for me.

- 4 (5-ounce) skinless chicken breasts
- 1 (28-ounce) can crushed tomatoes
- 1 (8-ounce) container button mushrooms, sliced
- 1 garlic clove, minced
- ½ yellow onion, sliced
- 1 teaspoon Italian seasoning
- ¼ teaspoon salt
- ⅛ teaspoon freshly ground black pepper
- 1 cup fresh basil leaves, roughly chopped
- ¼ cup pitted black olives, sliced

1. In the slow cooker, add the chicken, tomatoes, mushrooms, garlic, onion, Italian seasoning, salt, and black pepper. Stir to combine. Cover and cook on low for 4 to 6 hours.

2. Turn off the slow cooker and stir in the basil and olives.

REFRIGERATE: Store the cooled chicken and vegetables in a resealable container for up to 1 week. Reheat in a saucepan. Bring to a boil, then reduce the heat and simmer until the chicken is warmed through, about 5 minutes. Individual portions can be reheated in the microwave for 1½ to 2 minutes.

FREEZE: Store the cooled chicken and vegetables in a freezer-safe container for up to 2 months. Thaw in the refrigerator overnight. Reheat in a saucepan. Bring to a boil, then reduce the heat and simmer until the chicken is warmed through, about 5 minutes. Individual portions can be reheated in the microwave for 1½ to 2 minutes.

> **TOBY'S TIP:** When shopping for basil, look for bright green leaves without brown or yellow spots. To store, place the cut stems in a container of water for up to 1 week, changing the water every other day. Basil can also be stored in the refrigerator wrapped in a damp paper towel for up to 4 days.

Per Serving (1 chicken breast with 1¼ cups sauce): Calories: 266; Fat: 6g; Saturated Fat: 1g; Protein: 37g; Total Carbs: 19g; Fiber: 5g; Sodium: 638mg

GLUTEN-FREE

SLOW-COOKER WHITE CHICKEN CHILI

MAKES 4 SERVINGS

PREP TIME: 15 minutes   COOK TIME: 4 hours

Saturday is a busy day in my home, and the slow cooker is the answer to my prayers. After lunch, I toss all the ingredients in my slow cooker, and I don't have to worry about getting dinner on the table when I'm driving all my kids to their activities. By the time they come home from gymnastics, tennis, and basketball, I have a warm meal on the table.

- 1 pound skinless, boneless chicken tenders, cut into 1-inch pieces
- 2 (15-ounce) cans low-sodium Northern beans, drained and rinsed
- 2 (8-ounce) cans chile peppers (mild, hot, or one of each), drained
- 1 (14-ounce) bag frozen corn kernels
- 1 large yellow onion, diced
- 2 garlic cloves, minced
- 2 teaspoons ground cumin
- 1 teaspoon chili powder
- 2 cups low-sodium chicken broth
- 1 cup low-fat milk
- 2 tablespoons cornstarch

1. In the slow cooker, add the chicken, beans, chiles, corn, onion, garlic, cumin, chili powder, and broth. Cover and cook on low for 4 hours.

2. Right before serving or when still warm, whisk together the milk and cornstarch in a small bowl. Pour this into the chili and stir until thoroughly combined. Let the chili sit until it has thickened, about 2 to 3 minutes.

REFRIGERATE: Store the cooled chili in a resealable container for up to 1 week. Reheat in a saucepan. Bring the chili to a boil, then reduce the heat and simmer until the chicken is warmed through, about 5 minutes. Individual portions can be reheated in the microwave for 1½ to 2 minutes.

FREEZE: Store the cooled chili in a freezer-safe container for up to 2 months. Thaw in the refrigerator overnight. Reheat in a saucepan. Bring the chili to a boil, then reduce the heat and simmer until the chicken is warmed through, about 5 minutes. Individual portions can be reheated in the microwave for 1½ to 2 minutes.

> **TOBY'S TIP:** If you don't like your chili too thick or want to make it dairy-free, skip the milk and cornstarch. Those are added to help thicken the chili.

Per Serving (about 2 cups): Calories: 397; Fat: 6g; Saturated Fat: 1g; Protein: 36g; Total Carbs: 47g; Fiber: 12g; Sodium: 875mg

WHITE CHICKEN CHILI AND SPINACH QUESADILLAS

MAKES 4 SERVINGS

PREP TIME: 15 minutes   COOK TIME: 8 minutes

Quesadillas are one of the easiest meals to make to get rid of leftovers. You can stick almost anything between two tortillas with some cheese. How many times do you have a little leftover chili in the refrigerator? I found the perfect solution—I just made it into a quesadilla. My son begged me for seconds.

- 3 cups Slow-Cooker White Chicken Chili (page 162)
- 2 cups baby spinach leaves, cut into ribbons
- 1 cup shredded low-salt Cheddar cheese
- 4 (10-inch) whole-wheat tortillas
- Cooking spray
- ¼ cup reduced-fat sour cream

1. In a medium skillet over medium heat, add the chili. Cook until the chili is bubbling. Reduce the heat to medium-low and stir in the spinach. Cook, stirring occasionally, until the spinach is wilted, about 2 minutes.

2. Lay 1 tortilla on a flat surface and top it with ¼ cup of cheese. Top the cheese with half the chili and then sprinkle it with another ¼ cup of cheese. Top with a second tortilla. Repeat this step with the remaining tortillas, cheese, and chili.

3. Coat a large skillet with the cooking spray and place it over medium heat. Carefully add 1 quesadilla to the pan and cook until the bottom tortilla is golden brown, about 3 minutes. Carefully flip the quesadilla over and cook until the cheese is melted and the tortilla is slightly browned, about 3 minutes. Transfer the quesadilla to a plate or cutting board and cook the second one.

4. Slice each quesadilla into four quarters. Serve two quarters with 1 tablespoon of the sour cream.

REFRIGERATE: Store the cooled quesadilla quarters in a resealable container or individually wrapped in plastic or aluminum foil for up to 1 week. Reheat in the microwave for 30 seconds or in a preheated 350°F oven for about 10 minutes.

Per Serving (2 quesadilla quarters and 1 tablespoon sour cream): Calories: 482; Fat: 21g; Saturated Fat: 9g; Protein: 29g; Total Carbs: 49g; Fiber: 11g; Sodium: 865mg

DAIRY-FREE   GLUTEN-FREE

SLOW-COOKER BARBECUE CHICKEN

MAKES 4 SERVINGS

PREP TIME: 15 minutes   COOK TIME: 2 hours, 15 minutes

Every summer my mom would roll out her grill and toss on barbecue chicken. I sometimes crave those barbecue flavors, and now I can enjoy it all year round due to my beloved slow cooker and my indoor grill pan.

- 1 teaspoon salt
- ½ teaspoon freshly ground black pepper
- 1 tablespoon smoked paprika
- 1 teaspoon garlic powder
- 1 teaspoon onion powder
- 8 skinless chicken drumsticks
- ¼ cup 100% apple juice
- ¼ cup Speedy Tomato Sauce (page 213)
- 1 tablespoon honey
- 1 teaspoon apple cider vinegar

1. In a small bowl, combine the salt, black pepper, paprika, garlic powder, and onion powder. Rub the mix all over the chicken drumsticks and put them into the slow cooker. Cover and cook on high for 2 hours, or on low for 4 hours.

2. About 10 minutes before the chicken is done, preheat the grill or heat a grill pan coated with cooking spray over medium-high heat.

3. To make the sauce, in a small saucepan over high heat, combine the apple juice, tomato sauce, honey, and apple cider vinegar. Bring to a boil, then reduce the heat to medium-low and simmer until the sauce is slightly reduced, about 10 minutes.

4. When the chicken is done, dip each drumstick into the barbecue sauce and place it on the grill. Grill them until they are slightly browned, then flip them over, about 2 minutes per side.

REFRIGERATE: Store the cooled chicken in a resealable container for up to 1 week. Reheat in the microwave for 1 minute.

FREEZE: Store the cooled chicken in a freezer-safe container for up to 2 months. Thaw in the refrigerator overnight and reheat in the microwave for 1 minute.

> **TOBY'S TIP:** Don't have time to prepare my Speedy Tomato Sauce? You can find a variety of jarred sauces with fewer additives and preservatives. It just takes a little patience and diligent label reading at the market. Keep 1 or 2 jars in your pantry in case you're in a pinch.

Per Serving (2 drumsticks): Calories: 318; Fat: 9g; Saturated Fat: 2g; Protein: 48g; Total Carbs: 9g; Fiber: 1g; Sodium: 724mg

DAIRY-FREE

BARBECUE CHICKEN PIZZA

MAKES 4 SERVINGS

PREP TIME: 15 minutes   COOK TIME: 15 minutes

Every time I offer to pick up pizza for my kids, they always request barbecue chicken pizza. It was such a frequent request, I started to make it on my own. Now my kids don't stop asking for it, and they'll warm up leftovers on their own.

Cooking spray

1 (10-ounce) ready-made whole-wheat thin-crust pizza crust

1 tablespoon canola or safflower oil

1 cup Speedy Tomato Sauce (page 213)

1½ cups shredded part-skim mozzarella cheese

2 Slow-Cooker Barbecue Chicken drumsticks (page 164)

1. Preheat the oven to 375°F. Coat a pizza pan or baking sheet with the cooking spray.

2. Place the pizza crust on the pan and brush it with the oil. Evenly spread the tomato sauce over the crust. Sprinkle evenly with the cheese.

3. Using a fork and knife, shred the chicken off the drumsticks. Top the pizza with the shredded chicken.

4. Bake until the crust is crisp and browned around the edges, about 15 minutes. Let cool slightly before cutting into 8 slices.

REFRIGERATE: Wrap the cooled pizza slices in aluminum foil or place in a resealable container and refrigerate for up to 5 days. Reheat each slice in the microwave for 30 seconds.

TOBY'S TIP: Play around with ready-made pizza crusts until you find what you like best. You can find whole-wheat versions in the frozen or refrigerated section of your grocery store, or try naan bread or even whole-grain English muffins.

Per Serving (¼ of the pizza): Calories: 412; Fat: 15g; Saturated Fat: 5g; Protein: 30g; Total Carbs: 44g; Fiber: 7g; Sodium: 693mg

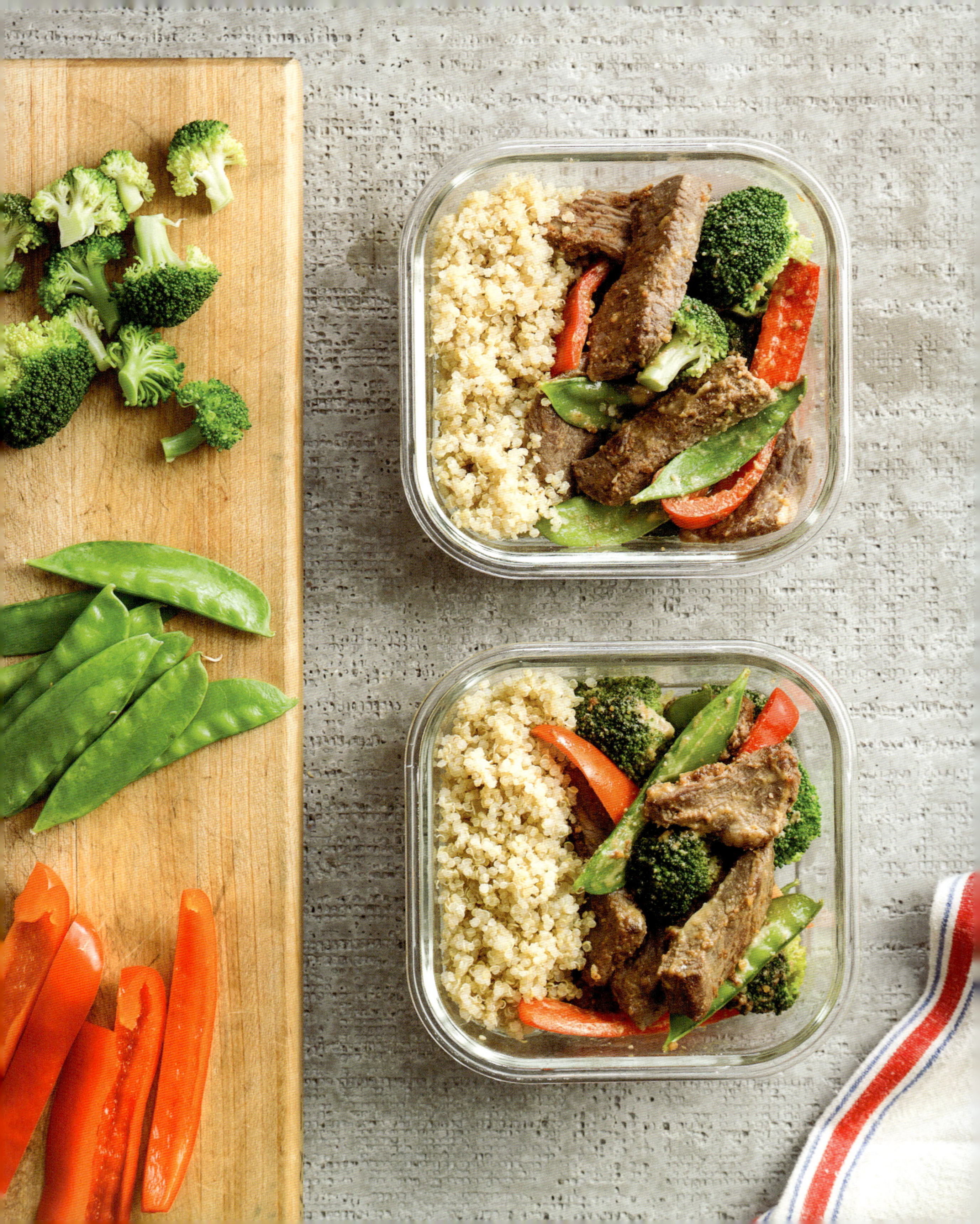

8 MEAT

168 Skirt Steak with Asian Peanut Sauce
169 Tex-Mex Burgers
170 Beef-Mushroom Meatballs
171 Lentil-Beef Meatloaf
172 Mediterranean Stuffed Peppers
174 Beef Stir-Fry with Asian Peanut Sauce
175 Beef Kebobs with Chimichurri Sauce
177 Slow-Cooker Beef Stew
178 Slow-Cooker Beer Brisket
179 Beer Brisket Tacos
180 Shawarma Steak
181 Easy Tricolored Pepper Steak
182 Lamb Chops with Mint-Yogurt Sauce
183 Herbed Pork Loin
184 Roasted Thai Pork Tenderloin
185 Slow-Cooker Barbecue Pulled Pork

« Beef Stir-Fry with Asian Peanut Sauce (page 174)

DAIRY-FREE

SKIRT STEAK WITH ASIAN PEANUT SAUCE

MAKES 4 SERVINGS

PREP TIME: 15 minutes, plus 30 minutes to chill   COOK TIME: 15 minutes

Beef is packed with lots of good-for-you nutrients for optimal health. It is an excellent source of protein, zinc, selenium, niacin, vitamins B_6 and B_{12}, phosphorus, iron, riboflavin, and choline. Beef has a bad reputation of being high in fat, but about half the fatty acids in beef are monounsaturated fatty acids, the same kind found in olive oil.

- ⅓ cup light coconut milk
- 1 teaspoon curry powder
- 1 teaspoon coriander powder
- 1 teaspoon reduced-sodium soy sauce
- 1¼ pound skirt steak
- Cooking spray
- ½ cup Asian Peanut Sauce (page 211)

1. In a large bowl, whisk together the coconut milk, curry powder, coriander powder, and soy sauce. Add the steak and turn to coat. Cover the bowl and refrigerate for at least 30 minutes and no longer than 24 hours.

2. Preheat the barbecue or coat a grill pan with cooking spray and place the steak over medium-high heat. Grill the meat until it reaches an internal temperature of 145°F, about 3 minutes per side. Remove the steak from the grill and let it rest for 5 minutes. Slice the steak into 5-ounce pieces and serve each with 2 tablespoons of the Asian Peanut Sauce.

REFRIGERATE: Store the cooled steak in a resealable container for up to 1 week. Reheat each piece in the microwave for 1 minute.

> **TOBY'S TIP:** I order my meat from the butcher's counter, where I can request an exact portion of meat. This helps me keep the portions and my food budget under control.

Per Serving (5 ounces steak and 2 tablespoons dressing): Calories: 361; Fat: 22g; Saturated Fat: 7g; Protein: 36g; Total Carbs: 8g; Fiber: 2g; Sodium: 349mg

DAIRY-FREE   GLUTEN-FREE

TEX-MEX BURGERS

MAKES 4 SERVINGS

PREP TIME: 15 minutes   COOK TIME: 10 minutes

Beef is an important part of my healthy eating plan. Besides being filled with good-for-you nutrients, evidence shows that nutrients in beef, such as protein, can help satisfy your hunger and maintain a healthy weight, build and maintain muscle, and fuel a healthy and active lifestyle.

- 1 pound lean ground beef (90% or leaner)
- ¼ red onion, finely chopped
- ¼ green bell pepper, finely chopped
- ¼ cup chopped cilantro
- 2 garlic cloves, minced
- 1 teaspoon ground cumin
- 1 teaspoon smoked paprika
- ¼ teaspoon salt
- ⅛ teaspoon freshly ground black pepper
- ⅛ teaspoon allspice
- Cooking spray
- ½ cup Avocado Lime Mayonnaise (page 215)

1. In a medium bowl, combine the ground beef, onion, bell pepper, cilantro, garlic, cumin, paprika, salt, black pepper, and allspice. Using clean hands, form the mixture into 4 patties.

2. Coat a grill pan or sauté pan with the cooking spray and place it over medium heat. When the oil is shimmering, add the burgers and cook until a thermometer inserted into the center of a burger reads 155°F, about 5 minutes per side.

3. Top each burger with 2 tablespoons of the Avocado Lime Mayonnaise before eating.

REFRIGERATE: Store the cooled burgers and mayonnaise in separate resealable containers for up to 1 week. Reheat the burgers in the microwave for 1 to 2 minutes. They also can be reheated on the barbecue or in a grill pan for about 4 minutes per side. Top with the mayonnaise before eating.

FREEZE: Place the cooled burgers in a freezer-safe container for up to 2 months. Thaw in the refrigerator overnight and reheat in the microwave for 1 to 2 minutes. They can also be reheated on the grill or in a grill pan for about 4 minutes per side. The mayonnaise will not freeze well.

> **TOBY'S TIP**: Purchasing lean ground beef will help keep the calories down. You do want a little fat in your meat, though, so no need for 97% lean. Choose 90% or 93% lean ground beef, as a small amount of fat will help keep the burgers moist.

Per Serving (1 hamburger and 2 tablespoons mayonnaise): Calories: 267; Fat: 17g; Saturated Fat: 5g; Protein: 24g; Total Carbs: 5g; Fiber: 3g; Sodium: 253mg

DAIRY-FREE

BEEF-MUSHROOM MEATBALLS

MAKES 24 MEATBALLS

PREP TIME: 15 minutes   **COOK TIME:** 30 minutes

First the mushrooms are sautéed to bring out their tantalizing umami flavor, then they are mixed in with lean beef. The refreshing flavor of the parsley helps balance the flavors and provides a kick of freshness.

- 1 tablespoon canola or safflower oil
- 1 (8-ounce) container Portobello mushrooms, finely chopped
- Cooking spray
- 1 pound lean ground beef (90% or higher)
- ¾ cup unseasoned bread crumbs
- ½ cup chopped fresh parsley
- 2 garlic cloves, minced
- 1 egg, beaten
- ¼ teaspoon salt
- ⅛ teaspoon freshly ground black pepper

1. In a medium skillet over medium heat, heat the oil until it shimmers. Add the mushrooms and sauté until they soften, about 5 minutes. Set aside to slightly cool for 5 minutes.

2. Preheat the oven to 350°F. Coat a mini muffin tin with the cooking spray.

3. In a large bowl, combine the mushrooms, beef, bread crumbs, parsley, garlic, egg, salt, and black pepper. Using clean hands, mix until well combined.

4. Form 1 heaping teaspoon of the beef mixture into a 2-inch ball. Place it into a muffin cup and continue forming meatballs.

5. Bake until the meatballs are golden brown, about 25 minutes. Let cool for 5 minutes, then use a teaspoon to transfer each meatball into a storage container.

REFRIGERATE: Store the cooled meatballs in a resealable container for up to 1 week. To reheat, microwave for 1 minute. The meatballs also can be reheated in a saucepan over medium heat along with the Speedy Tomato Sauce (page 213).

FREEZE: Store the cooled meatballs in a freezer-safe container for up to 2 months. Thaw in the refrigerator overnight and reheat in the microwave for 1 minute. The meatballs also can be reheated in a saucepan over medium heat along with the Speedy Tomato Sauce (page 213).

> **TOBY'S TIP:** When mixing mushrooms together with ground meat, you can go up to a 1:1 ratio of beef to mushrooms. In this recipe, that would mean ¾ pound lean beef and ¾ pound mushrooms.

Per Serving (4 meatballs): Calories: 232; Fat: 12g; Saturated Fat: 4g; Protein: 19g; Total Carbs: 12g; Fiber: 1g; Sodium: 276mg

DAIRY-FREE

LENTIL-BEEF MEATLOAF

MAKES 8 SERVINGS

PREP TIME: 15 minutes   COOK TIME: 1 hour

Ground beef blends very well with chopped vegetables and legumes—it's one of my go-to "Toby Tricks." The flavor of this meatloaf bursts in your mouth, and you'll never suspect the secret ingredients are mushrooms and lentils.

Cooking spray

1 pound lean ground beef (90% lean or higher)

1 (8-ounce) container mushrooms, finely chopped

½ onion, finely chopped

1 garlic clove, minced

1 (15-ounce) can low-sodium lentils, drained and rinsed

½ cup chopped fresh cilantro

1 large egg, beaten

1 cup whole-wheat panko bread crumbs

½ teaspoon salt

¼ teaspoon freshly ground black pepper

¾ cup Speedy Tomato Sauce (page 213)

1. Preheat the oven to 350°F. Coat a 9-by-5-inch loaf pan with the cooking spray.

2. In a large bowl, combine the beef, mushrooms, onions, garlic, lentils, cilantro, egg, panko, salt, and black pepper. Mix until thoroughly combined.

3. Place the meat mixture into the loaf pan, making sure the top is even. Pour the tomato sauce over the top of the meatloaf.

4. Bake until a thermometer reads 155°F when inserted into the center of the meatloaf, about 1 hour to 1 hour, 10 minutes.

5. Let cool and slice into 8 equal portions.

REFRIGERATE: Store the cooled meatloaf slices in a resealable container for up to 1 week. Reheat in the microwave for 1 to 1½ minutes.

FREEZE: Store the cooled meatloaf slices in a freezer-safe container for up to 2 months. Thaw in the refrigerator overnight. Reheat in the microwave for 1 to 1½ minutes.

> **TOBY'S TIP:** Panko is Japanese bread crumbs. If you have extra homemade bread crumbs ready to go, use those instead.

Per Serving: Calories: 210; Fat: 7g; Saturated Fat: 3g; Protein: 19g; Total Carbs: 18g; Fiber: 5g; Sodium: 224mg

GLUTEN-FREE

MEDITERRANEAN STUFFED PEPPERS

MAKES 8 STUFFED PEPPERS

PREP TIME: 30 minutes, plus 30 minutes to chill   COOK TIME: 1 hour, 40 minutes

My grandma Hannah made the best stuffed peppers with rice and ground beef. Thirty years later, I still love a good stuffed pepper, but with more whole grains, veggies, and legumes. Playing around with the stuffing is all part of the fun! Almost anything works and it keeps your taste buds delighted.

3 cups water

1 cup farro

Cooking spray

1 pound lean ground beef (90% lean or higher)

1 cup reduced-sodium canned chickpeas, drained and rinsed

1 cup cherry tomatoes, quartered

1 bunch parsley, chopped

½ small yellow onion, chopped

⅓ cup crumbled feta cheese

3 tablespoons olive oil

Juice of ½ lemon (about 1 tablespoon)

½ teaspoon salt

¼ teaspoon freshly ground black pepper

8 red, yellow, or green bell peppers

1. In a medium pot over high heat, bring the water to a boil. Stir in the farro, then reduce the heat to medium-low and simmer until the water is absorbed and the grain is tender, about 30 minutes. Drain off any excess liquid. Let cool for about 10 minutes, then transfer to a container, cover, and refrigerate for at least 30 minutes.

2. Preheat the oven to 350°F. Coat a 9-by-13-inch baking dish with the cooking spray.

3. In a large bowl, combine the beef, chickpeas, tomatoes, parsley, and onion and stir until well mixed. Add the chilled farro and feta cheese and stir to combine.

4. In a small bowl, whisk together the olive oil, lemon juice, salt, and black pepper. Pour this into the beef-farro mixture and stir to incorporate.

5. Slice the tops off the peppers. Using a paring knife, remove the membranes and seeds from inside each pepper. Spoon ¾ cup of the beef mixture into each pepper and arrange the peppers in the baking dish, leaving about 2 inches between them. Cover the dish with aluminum foil.

6. Bake for 50 minutes. Then remove the foil and continue baking for another 20 minutes.

REFRIGERATE: Store the cooled peppers in a resealable container for up to 1 week. Reheat one pepper in the microwave for 1 to 2 minutes. To reheat more evenly, slice the pepper in quarters.

FREEZE: Store the cooled peppers in a freezer-safe container for up to 2 months. Thaw in the refrigerator overnight. Reheat one pepper in the microwave for 1 to 2 minutes. To reheat more evenly, slice the pepper in quarters.

Per Serving (1 stuffed pepper): Calories: 320; Fat: 14g; Saturated Fat: 4g; Protein: 19g; Total Carbs: 30g; Fiber: 7g; Sodium: 291mg

DAIRY-FREE

BEEF STIR-FRY WITH ASIAN PEANUT SAUCE

MAKES 4 SERVINGS

PREP TIME: 20 minutes, plus 30 minutes to marinate   COOK TIME: 35 minutes

When I lived in New York City, it was easy to pick up the phone and order Chinese delivery. These days it's just as easy to order it right on your smartphone. But who wants all the calories and oil that go along with Chinese takeout? I would rather make my own, like in this simple stir-fry.

- 1 pound top sirloin, cut into 1½-inch strips
- 6 tablespoons Asian Peanut Sauce (page 211), divided
- 2 cups water
- 1 cup quinoa
- 1 tablespoon canola or safflower oil
- ½ head broccoli, cut into bite-size florets
- 1 red bell pepper, cut into 1-inch-wide strips
- 1 cup snow peas

1. In a large bowl, add the beef strips and 4 tablespoons of the Asian Peanut Sauce and toss to coat the meat. Cover the bowl and refrigerate for at least 30 minutes or up to overnight.

2. In a medium pot over high heat, bring the water to a boil. Stir in the quinoa and reduce the heat to medium-low. Cover and simmer the quinoa, stirring occasionally, until the liquid is absorbed and the grains are tender, about 15 minutes. Transfer the quinoa to a large bowl and let cool lightly.

3. In a large wok or skillet over medium heat, heat the oil until it shimmers. Add the beef and cook until it is browned on all sides, about 8 minutes. Discard the leftover beef marinade. Add the broccoli, bell pepper, and snow peas, stirring occasionally, until the vegetables have started to soften, about 8 minutes. Add the remaining 2 tablespoons of Asian Peanut Sauce to the stir-fry and cook, stirring frequently, until heated through, about 2 minutes. Enjoy with the quinoa right away, or store for later.

REFRIGERATE: Store the cooled stir-fry and quinoa together or separately in resealable containers for up to 1 week. Reheat in the microwave for 1½ to 2 minutes.

TOBY'S TIP: Out of olive oil? Canola oil is the perfect substitute. It's filled with healthy omega-3s and can be used in cooking, baking, and as is (like in dressings).

Per Serving (1½ cups stir-fry plus ½ cup quinoa): Calories: 522; Fat: 25g; Saturated Fat: 7g; Protein: 35g; Total Carbs: 39g; Fiber: 5g; Sodium: 223mg

DAIRY-FREE **GLUTEN-FREE** **PALEO**

BEEF KEBOBS WITH CHIMICHURRI SAUCE

MAKES 6 SERVINGS

PREP TIME: 20 minutes, plus 30 minutes to marinate   COOK TIME: 20 minutes

My summers have always been filled with kebobs (shee-poo-deem in Hebrew) for lunch or dinner. As summers are extremely hot in Israel, the easiest way to feed a large family is to toss skewers on the grill. Lamb, chicken, and beef skewers were my typical meal during the summer, and today I still enjoy kebobs regularly. Served with a chopped salad and couscous on the side, it's a healthy, satisfying meal.

- 1½ pounds top sirloin, cut into 1-inch cubes
- 1 cup Chimichurri Sauce (page 212), divided
- Cooking spray
- 12 medium mushrooms, halved
- 24 cherry tomatoes
- 1 yellow bell pepper, cut into 2-inch pieces

1. Place the sirloin strips in a medium bowl. Top with ¼ cup of chimichurri sauce and toss to coat the beef. Cover the bowl and refrigerate for at least 30 minutes or up to 24 hours.

2. Preheat the oven to 375°F. If using wooden skewers, soak them in water while preparing the beef. Coat a baking sheet with the cooking spray or line it with parchment paper.

3. Remove the sirloin from the marinade, allowing the excess to drip off. Thread each skewer with 2 to 3 pieces of the sirloin, 2 mushrooms, 2 tomatoes, and 2 pieces of bell pepper. Discard the used beef marinade. Place the skewers on the baking sheet in a single layer.

4. Bake until the beef is cooked through, about 20 minutes.

5. Serve 2 tablespoons of Chimichurri Sauce per 2 skewers.

CONTINUED

BEEF KEBOBS WITH CHIMICHURRI SAUCE CONTINUED

REFRIGERATE: Let the skewers cool to room temperature. Using a fork, slide the beef and vegetables off 2 skewers into a resealable container. Repeat this for all the skewers. Store for up to 1 week. Store the Chimichurri Sauce in a separate resealable container for up to 5 days. Reheat the beef and vegetables in the microwave for about 1 minute. Do not heat wooden or metal skewers in the microwave. Serve with 2 tablespoons of sauce.

> **TOBY'S TIP:** When shopping for mushrooms, choose fresh mushrooms that are firm and evenly colored. Avoid those that are damaged, broken, or have soft spots. If all the gills are showing, the mushroom is no longer fresh. Once you get home, store unwashed loose mushrooms in a paper bag in the refrigerator for up to 6 days.

Per Serving (2 skewers and 2 tablespoons sauce): Calories: 385; Fat: 27g; Saturated Fat: 5g; Protein: 28g; Total Carbs: 8g; Fiber: 2g; Sodium: 202mg

DAIRY-FREE

SLOW-COOKER BEEF STEW

MAKES 4 SERVINGS

PREP TIME: 15 minutes   COOK TIME: 4 to 6 hours

During the bone-chilling winter, I love to cozy up to a warming bowl of stew. I grew up with carrots and peas in my stew, but these days I add whatever extra veggies I have lying around, including sweet potatoes, parsnips, and turnips. I also add extra legumes like chickpeas, black beans, or cannellini beans. It's a great way to prevent food waste and help save my food dollar.

- 1½ pounds beef stew meat
- 1 (15-ounce) can low-sodium chickpeas, drained and rinsed
- 1¼ pounds sweet potatoes (about 3 medium), diced
- 1 cup baby carrots (about 20)
- 1 cup frozen peas
- 1 yellow onion, diced
- 1 celery stalk, diced
- 2 garlic cloves, minced
- 3 bay leaves
- 2½ cups low-sodium beef broth
- 2 tablespoons tomato paste
- 1 tablespoon Worcestershire sauce
- 1 teaspoon dried thyme
- 1 teaspoon paprika
- ¼ teaspoon salt
- ¼ teaspoon freshly ground black pepper

1. Place the meat, chickpeas, sweet potatoes, carrots, peas, onion, celery, garlic, and bay leaves in the slow cooker.

2. In a medium bowl, whisk together the beef broth, tomato paste, Worcestershire sauce, thyme, paprika, salt, and black pepper. Pour this into the slow cooker and stir to combine. Cover and cook on high for 4 to 6 hours.

REFRIGERATE: Store the cooled stew in a resealable container for up to 1 week. Reheat single or multiple portions in a saucepan over medium-high heat until the stew is warmed through, about 5 minutes. Individual portions can also be reheated in the microwave for 1½ to 2 minutes.

FREEZE: Store the cooled stew in a freezer-safe container for up to 2 months. Thaw in the refrigerator overnight. Reheat in a saucepan over medium-high heat until the stew is warmed through, about 5 minutes. Individual portions can also be reheated in the microwave for 1½ to 2 minutes.

> **TOBY'S TIP:** I prefer a thin stew, almost soupy, but traditional stews have a thicker sauce. To thicken, once the stew has cooked, put ½ cup of the liquid in a small bowl. Whisk in ¼ cup of unbleached all-purpose flour. Stir this back in to the stew, cover, and cook for an additional 30 minutes.

Per Serving (2 cups): Calories: 518; Fat: 10g; Saturated Fat: 4g; Protein: 49g; Total Carbs: 59g; Fiber: 13g; Sodium: 903mg

DAIRY-FREE

SLOW-COOKER BEER BRISKET

MAKES 4 SERVINGS

PREP TIME: 15 minutes   **COOK TIME:** 6 hours

My mom makes a killer brisket which marinates in beer for 24 hours. As I'm always in a time crunch, I developed this easy slow-cooker version, which only takes 15 minutes of my prep time and is just as tasty.

- 1 tablespoon brown sugar
- 1 teaspoon instant coffee crystals
- ½ teaspoon smoked paprika
- ½ teaspoon ground cumin
- ½ teaspoon salt
- ¼ teaspoon freshly ground black pepper
- 1 (3-pound) beef brisket, fat trimmed
- 1 (12-ounce) bottle lager beer

1. In a small bowl, combine the brown sugar, coffee crystals, paprika, cumin, salt, and black pepper. Using clean hands, rub the mixture all over the brisket. Place the brisket in the slow cooker. Pour the beer into the slow cooker around the brisket.

2. Cover and cook on high for 6 hours. Let the brisket cool for at least 10 minutes, then slice or shred the meat, discarding any visible fat.

REFRIGERATE: Store the cooled shredded or sliced brisket with about half the liquid from the slow cooker in a resealable container for up to 1 week. Reheat the beef and sauce in a saucepan over medium-high heat until heated through, about 5 minutes. Single portions can be reheated in the microwave for about 1½ to 2 minutes.

FREEZE: Store the cooled shredded or sliced brisket with about half the liquid from the slow cooker in a freezer-safe container for up to 2 months. Thaw in the refrigerator overnight. Reheat the beef and sauce in a saucepan over medium-high heat until heated through, about 5 minutes. Single portions can be reheated in the microwave for about 1½ to 2 minutes.

TOBY'S TIP: Use the brisket to top a salad, a baked potato, or for Beer Brisket Tacos (page 179).

Per serving (1¼ cups shredded beef): Calories 459; Fat 13g; Saturated Fat 5g; Protein 74g; Total Carbs 3g; Fiber 0g; Sodium 475mg

BEER BRISKET TACOS

MAKES 4 SERVINGS

PREP TIME: 15 minutes   COOK TIME: 10 minutes

The first time I had brisket tacos was at a delicious Mexican restaurant in Connecticut. They were so good, I actually waited an hour to be seated without complaining. Soon I realized I didn't have to wait at all if I made my own.

Cooking spray

8 (6-inch) corn tortillas

2 cups shredded Slow-Cooker Beer Brisket (page 178)

½ cup Simple Tomato Salsa (page 217)

½ cup shredded romaine lettuce

½ cup reduced-fat shredded Mexican cheese blend

1. Heat a small skillet over medium-low heat. Spray the skillet with the cooking spray. Warm the tortillas, one at a time, for 30 seconds on each side.

2. Coat a medium skillet with the cooking spray and place it over medium heat. When the oil is shimmering, add the shredded brisket and cook until heated through, about 5 minutes. Alternatively, the brisket can be reheated in the microwave for 2 minutes.

3. Place 2 tortillas on each of four plates. Spoon ¼ cup of brisket onto each warmed tortilla. Top each with 1 tablespoon each of salsa, lettuce, and cheese.

REFRIGERATE: The ingredients should be stored in separate resealable containers for up to 1 week. Assemble right before eating.

TOBY'S TIP: Brisket isn't the only thing you can put in these tacos. Try the Slow-Cooker Barbecue Pulled Pork (page 185) or Poached Salmon with Chimichurri Sauce (page 133).

Per Serving (2 tacos): Calories: 360; Fat: 11g; Saturated Fat: 5g; Protein: 36g; Total Carbs: 27g; Fiber: 3g; Sodium: 269mg

DAIRY-FREE   GLUTEN-FREE   PALEO

SHAWARMA STEAK

MAKES 4 SERVINGS

PREP TIME: 15 minutes, plus 30 minutes to marinate   COOK TIME: 20 minutes

During my summers as a young girl living in Israel, I ate shawarma regularly. There would be a huge leg of lamb rotating on a heated skewer, and the chef would shave off pieces and put it in a gyro for me to eat. Needless to say, it's a lot of work to get that done. Luckily, I am still able to enjoy the same flavors at home using this quick-and-easy marinade.

1 tablespoon olive oil

Juice of ½ lemon (about 1 tablespoon)

½ teaspoon ground coriander

½ teaspoon ground cumin

¼ teaspoon ground ginger

¼ teaspoon salt

⅛ teaspoon ground black pepper

⅛ teaspoon turmeric

⅛ teaspoon allspice

⅛ teaspoon ground cinnamon

1½ pounds London broil or top round steak

Cooking spray

1. In a medium bowl, whisk together the olive oil, lemon juice, coriander, cumin, ginger, salt, black pepper, turmeric, allspice, and cinnamon. Add the meat to the bowl and coat it all over with the marinade. Cover the bowl and refrigerate for at least 30 minutes up to overnight.

2. Preheat the barbecue or coat a grill pan with the cooking spray and place it over medium-high heat. When hot, put the meat on the grill. Discard the marinade. Grill the meat, turning it halfway through, until a thermometer inserted in the thickest portion reads 145°F, about 20 minutes. Remove the meat from the heat and let it rest for 10 minutes. Slice into 4 equal portions.

REFRIGERATE: Store the cooled beef in a resealable container for up to 1 week. To reheat, place one or two portions in the microwave for 1 to 1½ minutes.

FREEZE: Store the cooled beef in a freezer-safe container for up to 2 months. Thaw in the refrigerator overnight. To reheat, place one or two portions in the microwave for 1 to 1½ minutes.

> **TOBY'S TIP:** Over the past few decades, many new beef cuts have been introduced to your butcher's counter, some of which you might not be familiar with. Ask your butcher to help you find the cut you want and give it a whirl! If you go through the experience once, it will be much easier the next time around.

Per Serving (1 slice): Calories: 350; Fat: 21g; Saturated Fat: 6g; Protein: 37g; Total Carbs: 1g; Fiber: 0g; Sodium: 245mg

DAIRY-FREE **GLUTEN-FREE**

EASY TRICOLORED PEPPER STEAK

MAKES 4 SERVINGS

PREP TIME: 15 minutes COOK TIME: 45 minutes

This dish is more than just the gorgeous bright colors of the peppers. Bell peppers are packed with phytochemicals (natural plant chemicals) that have been linked to cancer prevention. They also contain the antioxidant lycopene, which has been shown to help lower the risk of heart disease, prostate cancer, and macular degeneration.

- 2 tablespoons olive oil, divided
- ½ teaspoon garlic powder
- ½ teaspoon onion powder
- ¼ teaspoon salt
- ⅛ teaspoon freshly ground black pepper
- 1 pound beef sirloin steak, cut into 1-inch strips
- 1½ cups low-sodium beef broth, divided
- 1 medium yellow onion, thinly sliced
- 1 red bell pepper, cut into 1-inch strips
- 1 green bell pepper, cut into 1-inch strips
- 2 tablespoons cornstarch

1. In a medium bowl, whisk together 1 tablespoon of olive oil with the garlic powder, onion powder, salt, and black pepper. Add the steak strips and toss to evenly coat.

2. In a large skillet over medium heat, heat the remaining 1 tablespoon of olive oil until it shimmers. Add the steak strips in a single layer and cook until brown on all sides, about 6 minutes. Add 1¼ cups of the beef broth and bring it to a boil. Reduce the heat to low and simmer, covered, until the steak is softened and cooked through, about 30 minutes. Add the onion and bell pepper and continue simmering, covered, for 5 minutes more.

3. In a small bowl, whisk together the cornstarch and remaining ¼ cup of beef broth. Stir this into the beef mixture and cook on a medium-low heat, stirring continuously, until the broth thickens, about 3 minutes.

REFRIGERATE: Store the cooled pepper steak and sauce in a resealable container for up to 1 week. Reheat in a saucepan over medium heat until heated through, about 5 minutes. Individual portions can be heated in the microwave for 2 to 2½ minutes.

FREEZE: Store the cooled pepper steak and sauce in a freezer-safe container for up to 2 months. Thaw in the refrigerator overnight. Reheat in a saucepan over medium heat until heated through, about 5 minutes. Individual portions can be heated in the microwave for 2 to 2½ minutes.

Per Serving (1½ cups): Calories: 274; Fat: 12g; Saturated Fat: 3g; Protein: 28g; Total Carbs: 14g; Fiber: 2g; Sodium: 382mg

GLUTEN-FREE

LAMB CHOPS WITH MINT-YOGURT SAUCE

MAKES 4 SERVINGS

PREP TIME: 15 minutes, plus 1 hour to marinate **COOK TIME:** 10 minutes

Lamb delivers, on average, 23 grams of protein along with 175 calories per each 3-ounce portion. It's also an excellent source of vitamin B_{12}, niacin, zinc, and selenium, and a good source of iron and riboflavin.

¾ cup chopped fresh mint leaves, divided

4 garlic cloves, minced, divided

1 cup reduced-fat plain Greek yogurt, divided

2 tablespoons dry white wine

¼ teaspoon salt, divided

¼ teaspoon freshly ground black pepper, divided

8 lamb chops (about 2½ pounds), fat trimmed

Cooking spray

1. In a medium bowl, whisk together ½ cup of mint, 3 minced garlic cloves, ½ cup of yogurt, the wine, ⅛ teaspoon of salt, and ⅛ teaspoon of black pepper. Add the lamb chops and toss to coat evenly. Cover the bowl and refrigerate for exactly 1 hour.

2. Preheat the barbecue or coat a grill pan with the cooking spray and place it over medium-high heat.

3. While the lamb marinates, make the yogurt sauce. In a small bowl, whisk together the remaining ¼ cup of mint, the remaining minced garlic clove, the remaining ½ cup of yogurt, and the remaining ⅛ teaspoon each of salt and black pepper.

4. Remove the lamb from the marinade, allowing the excess to drip off. Discard the extra marinade. Grill the lamb chops, flipping them once, until a thermometer inserted in the thickest part of a chop reads 145°F, about 10 to 12 minutes. Remove the chops from the heat and let them rest for 10 minutes.

5. To serve, place 2 lamb chops on a plate and 2 tablespoons of the yogurt sauce on the side.

REFRIGERATE: Store the cooled lamb chops in a resealable container for up to 1 week. Store the yogurt sauce in a resealable container for up to 5 days. Reheat several lamb chops at a time in the microwave for 1 to 2 minutes. Sprinkle them with water before heating to prevent them from drying. Serve with the yogurt sauce.

Per Serving: Calories: 300; Fat: 10g; Saturated Fat: 4g; Protein: 46g; Total Carbs: 3g; Fiber: 0g; Sodium: 275mg

DAIRY-FREE   GLUTEN-FREE   PALEO

HERBED PORK LOIN

MAKES 8 SERVINGS

PREP TIME: 15 minutes, plus 30 minutes to marinate   COOK TIME: 40 minutes

Several pork cuts, called the "Slim 7," meet USDA guidelines for "lean" or "extra lean." An easy way to remember lean cuts is to look for the word "loin" on the label, such as loin chop or pork tenderloin.

¼ cup olive oil

Juice of 2 lemons (about ¼ cup)

4 garlic cloves, minced

2 teaspoons dried basil

2 teaspoons dried rosemary

2 teaspoons dried thyme

½ teaspoon salt

¼ teaspoon freshly ground black pepper

2 pounds pork loin, fat trimmed

Cooking spray

1. In a medium bowl, whisk together the olive oil, lemon juice, garlic, basil, rosemary, thyme, salt, and black pepper. Add the pork to the bowl and toss to coat evenly. Cover the bowl and refrigerate for at least 30 minutes or up to overnight.

2. Preheat the oven to 400°F. Coat a shallow baking pan with the cooking spray.

3. Transfer the pork to the baking pan and discard the marinade. Cook until a thermometer inserted into the thickest part of the loin reads 145°F, about 40 to 50 minutes. Let the pork rest for 10 minutes before slicing.

REFRIGERATE: Store the cooled pork slices in a resealable container for up to 1 week. Reheat several slices in the microwave for 1 to 2 minutes.

FREEZE: Store the cooled pork slices in a freezer-safe container for up to 3 months. Thaw in the refrigerator overnight. Reheat several slices in the microwave for 1 to 2 minutes.

> **TOBY'S TIP:** Pork loins are typically sold with or without the bone and are between 2 and 4 pounds. I prefer boneless, as it's easier to slice into even portions.

Per Serving (3 ounces): Calories: 194; Fat: 9g; Saturated Fat: 2g; Protein: 25g; Total Carbs: 1g; Fiber: 0g; Sodium: 177mg

DAIRY-FREE   **GLUTEN-FREE**

ROASTED THAI PORK TENDERLOIN

MAKES 4 SERVINGS

PREP TIME: 15 minutes, plus 30 minutes to marinate   COOK TIME: 30 minutes

Many cuts of fresh pork are leaner today than they were two decades ago—on average, about 16 percent lower in total fat and 27 percent lower in saturated fat. In February 2012, pork tenderloin was certified to carry the American Heart Association's heart checkmark, indicating that it is a heart-healthy choice in the meat aisle. It's no surprise—pork tenderloin packs nutrients in every lean serving and, ounce for ounce, is as lean as skinless chicken breast.

Zest of 1 lime

Juice of 1 lime

1 teaspoon freshly grated ginger

1 garlic clove, minced

1 teaspoon Dijon mustard

1 teaspoon fish sauce

1 teaspoon granulated sugar

½ teaspoon sriracha

½ cup canola or safflower oil

1 pound pork tenderloin

Cooking spray

1. In a medium bowl, whisk together the lime zest and juice, ginger, garlic, mustard, fish sauce, sugar, and sriracha until the sugar has dissolved. Whisk in the oil. Add the tenderloin to the bowl and toss to coat it in the marinade. Cover and refrigerate for at least 30 minutes or up to 24 hours.

2. Preheat the oven to 400°F. Coat a shallow baking pan with the cooking spray.

3. Transfer the tenderloin to the baking pan. Discard the marinade. Roast until a thermometer inserted into the thickest part of the meat reads at least 145°F, about 30 minutes. Let the tenderloin rest for 10 minutes before slicing.

REFRIGERATE: Store the cooled pork slices in a resealable container for up to 1 week. Reheat several slices in the microwave for 1 to 2 minutes.

FREEZE: Store the cooled pork slices in a freezer-safe container for up to 3 months. Thaw in the refrigerator overnight. Reheat several slices in the microwave for 1 to 2 minutes.

> **TOBY'S TIP:** When purchasing pork, it should have a pinkish-red color, while any fat should be white in color, with no dark spots. Avoid choosing meat that is pale in color.

Per Serving (3 ounces): Calories: 309; Fat: 23g; Saturated Fat: 2g; Protein: 23g; Total Carbs: 2g; Fiber: 0g; Sodium: 397mg

DAIRY-FREE   GLUTEN-FREE

SLOW-COOKER BARBECUE PULLED PORK

MAKES 6 SERVINGS

PREP TIME: 10 minutes   COOK TIME: 6 hours

If you haven't guessed it by now, I love anything that's super easy to cook. Pulled meat, like pork and chicken, is one of my favorites to flavor and toss in the slow cooker; the meat comes out meltingly tender and deliciously flavorful. Easy, tasty, and healthy equals the perfect prep-ahead meal.

- 1 tablespoon smoked paprika
- 1 tablespoon brown sugar
- ½ teaspoon cayenne
- ½ teaspoon garlic powder
- ½ teaspoon onion powder
- ½ teaspoon salt
- ¼ teaspoon freshly ground black pepper
- 6 pounds bone-in pork shoulder
- 2 tablespoons apple cider vinegar
- ½ cup water

1. In a small bowl, combine the paprika, brown sugar, cayenne, garlic powder, onion powder, salt, and black pepper. Rub the spice mixture onto the outside of the pork.

2. Add the vinegar and water to the slow cooker and then put the pork in. Cover and cook on high for 6 hours.

3. Transfer the pork to a large bowl. Add half of the liquid from the slow cooker to the bowl, discarding the rest. Shred the meat using two forks, discarding any fat and bones.

REFRIGERATE: Store the cooled pork in a resealable container for up to 1 week. Reheat in a saucepan over medium heat until the pork and sauce are warmed through, about 5 minutes. Individual portions can be reheated in the microwave for 1 to 1½ minutes.

FREEZE: Store the cooled pork in a freezer-safe container for up to 2 months. Thaw in the refrigerator overnight. Reheat in a saucepan over medium heat until the pork and sauce are warmed through, about 5 minutes. Individual portions can be reheated in the microwave for 1 to 1½ minutes.

> **TOBY'S TIP:** Use the shredded pork in place of the meats in the Barbecue Chicken Pizza (page 165) or Beer Brisket Tacos (page 179).

Per Serving (about 1¼ cups): Calories: 444; Fat: 26g; Saturated Fat: 9g; Protein: 48g; Total Carbs: 2g; Fiber: 0g; Sodium: 291mg

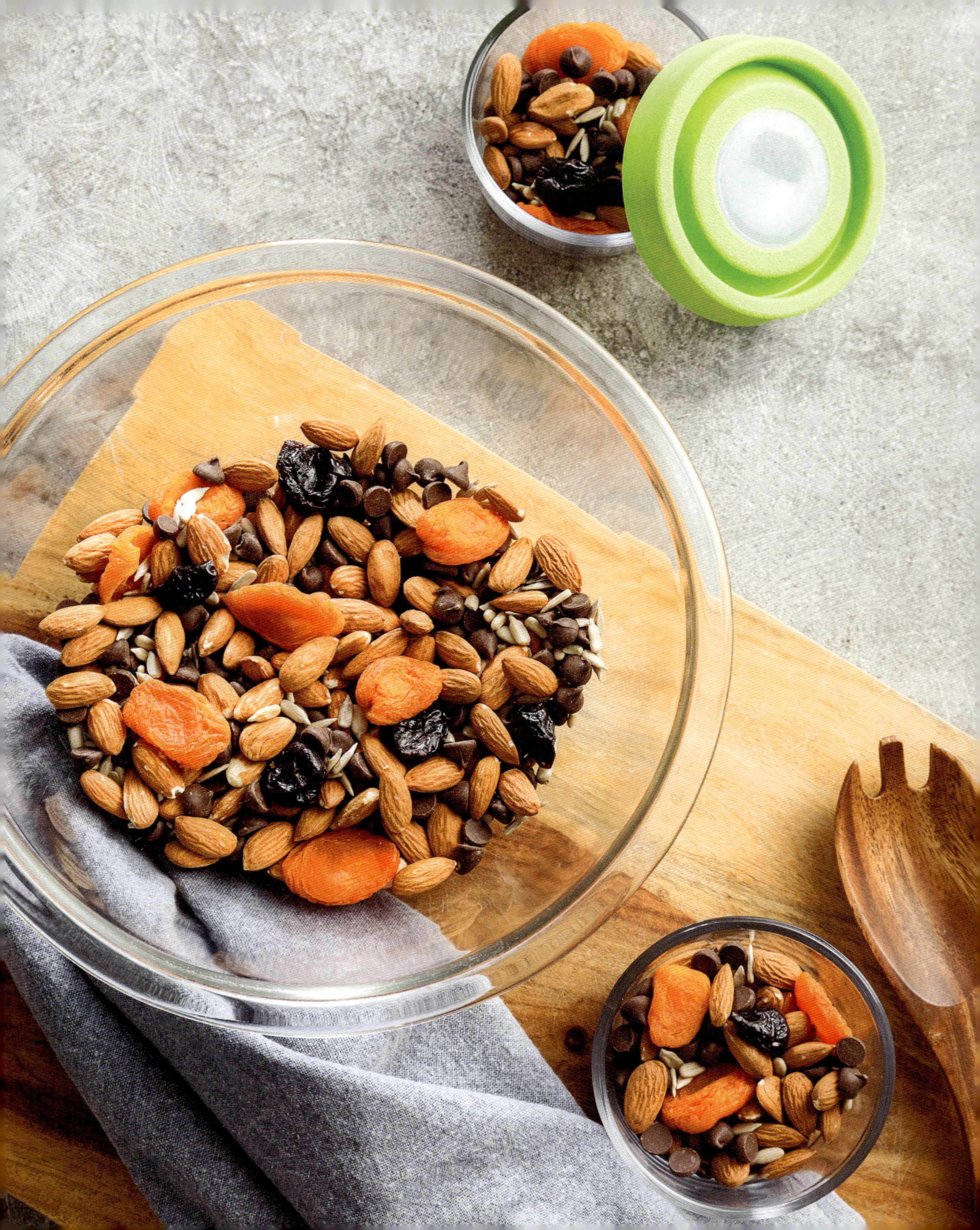

9 READY-TO-GO SNACKS

188 Peanut Butter Banana Energy Cookies
189 Apricot-Orange Oat Bites
190 Chocolate Energy Balls
191 No-Bake Maple Cinnamon Bars
192 Honey Ricotta with Strawberries
193 Homemade Trail Mix
194 Crudité with Herbed Yogurt Dip
195 Chili-Roasted Chickpeas
196 Thyme-Roasted Almonds
197 Cinnamon Cocoa Popcorn
198 Fruit Salad with Mint
199 Mason Jar Key Lime Parfaits
200 To-Go Snack Boxes
201 Sriracha Hummus
202 Rosemary Beet Chips
203 Sriracha-Lime Kale Chips

« Homemade Trail Mix (page 193)

VEGETARIAN

PEANUT BUTTER BANANA ENERGY COOKIES

MAKES 21 COOKIES

PREP TIME: 15 minutes, plus 30 minutes to chill   **COOK TIME:** 15 minutes

Every afternoon, I hit a slump where I would crave chocolate or something sweet. Vending machines or unhealthy fare at the bodega across the street were my closest choices so I made my own snacks. These energy cookies were the perfect answer to satisfy my afternoon craving, while giving me a boost of energy.

1 cup unbleached all-purpose flour

¼ cup unsweetened cocoa powder

1 teaspoon baking soda

⅛ teaspoon salt

½ cup creamy peanut butter, at room temperature

1 banana, mashed (about 1 cup)

¼ cup nonfat plain Greek yogurt

½ cup nonfat milk

½ packed cup dark brown sugar

2 eggs, beaten

1 teaspoon vanilla extract

2 cups rolled oats

½ cup dry roasted unsalted peanuts, roughly chopped

Cooking spray

1. In a medium bowl, sift together the flour, cocoa powder, baking soda, and salt.

2. In a large bowl, stir together the peanut butter, banana, Greek yogurt, and milk until smooth and creamy. Add the brown sugar and stir to combine. Then stir in the eggs and vanilla extract until well combined.

3. Add the flour mixture to the peanut butter mixture and mix until just combined. Then add the oats and peanuts and mix carefully until the dry ingredients are just moistened, taking care not to overmix. Cover the bowl and refrigerate the dough for 30 minutes.

4. Preheat the oven to 350°F. Coat two baking sheets with the cooking spray.

5. For each cookie, drop 1 heaping tablespoon of batter onto the baking sheets, leaving about 2 inches between each cookie. Using clean fingers, gently press down on the top of each cookie to slightly flatten it.

6. Bake until a toothpick inserted into the center of 1 or 2 cookies comes out clean, about 15 minutes. Let the cookies cool for 5 minutes, then transfer them to a wire rack to cool.

STORAGE: Keep the cookies in a resealable plastic container at room temperature for up to 1 week.

Per Serving (1 cookie): Calories: 143; Fat: 6g; Saturated Fat: 1g; Protein: 5g; Total Carbs: 19g; Fiber: 2g; Sodium: 108mg

DAIRY-FREE   **GLUTEN-FREE**   **VEGAN**

APRICOT-ORANGE OAT BITES

MAKES 20 BITES

PREP TIME: 10 minutes, plus 15 minutes to chill   COOK TIME: 5 minutes

When I was a girl, I would always find my dad snacking on dark chocolate–covered orange peels. I don't know why, but he devours anything with orange peels (or zest). So instead of him munching on hundreds, or even thousands of chocolate-filled calories, I make him these bites filled with better-for-you, delicious ingredients.

1 cup rolled oats

1½ cups pitted dates

½ cup dried apricots

½ cup almond butter

⅔ cup shredded coconut

Zest of 1 orange (about 1 tablespoon)

Juice of 1 orange (about 3 tablespoons)

1 teaspoon vanilla extract

1. Preheat the oven to 350°F. Line a baking sheet with parchment paper.

2. Place the oats on the baking sheet and toast them until they are browned, about 5 minutes. Let them cool for 10 minutes.

3. While the oats are toasting, put the dates in a food processor or blender and pulse until smooth.

4. Add the toasted oats, apricots, almond butter, coconut, orange zest and juice, and vanilla extract to the processor. Continue pulsing until the mixture is smooth and forms a ball. Transfer it to a medium bowl.

5. Using clean hands, form 1 tablespoon of batter into a 2-inch ball and place in a resealable container. Repeat for remaining of the batter, making a total of 20 balls. Cover the container and refrigerate to allow the balls to set, at least 15 minutes.

REFRIGERATE: Store the bites in a resealable container for up to 1 week.

TOBY'S TIP: Although oats are gluten-free, many brands manufacture them in a facility where gluten-containing products are processed. The package will indicate whether they were processed in a gluten-free facility.

Per Serving (1 ball): Calories: 117; Fat: 5g; Saturated Fat: 2g; Protein: 3g; Total Carbs: 17g; Fiber: 3g; Sodium: 1mg

DAIRY-FREE   **GLUTEN-FREE**   **VEGAN**

CHOCOLATE ENERGY BALLS

MAKES 12 ENERGY BALLS

PREP TIME: 15 minutes, plus 15 minutes to chill   **COOK TIME:** 0 minutes

Most people need between one to three snacks per day. Snacks are mini meals that provide good-for-you nutrients you may not be able to get during regular meals. I tend to eat two snacks per day, one in the morning and one in the late afternoon. These are the times I find I'm at my hungriest. I aim for 150-200 calories per snack and want to make sure they fill me up until my next meal. Made with protein, healthy fat, and fiber, these energy balls do just that.

½ cup rolled oats

½ cup unsalted sunflower seeds

8 pitted dates

⅓ cup natural smooth peanut butter

1 tablespoon unsweetened cocoa powder

1. Line a medium container with parchment paper.

2. In a food processor or blender, add the oats, sunflower seeds, dates, peanut butter, and cocoa powder. Pulse until the batter has a crumbly consistency. Transfer it to a medium bowl.

3. Using clean hands, form 1 tablespoon of batter into a 2-inch ball and place it in the container. Repeat for remaining of the batter, making a total of 12 balls. Cover the container and refrigerate to allow the balls to set, at least 15 minutes.

REFRIGERATE: Store the energy balls in a resealable container for up to 1 week.

TOBY'S TIP: When rolling balls, wet your hands with water. This will help prevent the batter from sticking to your hands.

Per Serving (1 ball): Calories: 173; Fat: 10g; Saturated Fat: 2g; Protein: 5g; Total Carbs: 19g; Fiber: 3g; Sodium: 68mg

DAIRY-FREE   GLUTEN-FREE   VEGAN

NO-BAKE MAPLE CINNAMON BARS

MAKES 16 BARS

PREP TIME: 15 minutes, plus 1 hour to chill   COOK TIME: 0 minutes

The combination of nuts and fruit in these bars is reminiscent of some of my favorites at the market. Except instead of paying an average of $2 per bar, I can make a whole batch for a lot less. A little work in the kitchen (all of 15 minutes' worth) has never paid off so well.

1 cup pitted dates
1 cup raw unsalted cashews
¼ cup 100% maple syrup
1 teaspoon ground cinnamon
3 tablespoons dried cranberries
Cooking spray

1. Line an 8-by-8-inch baking dish with parchment paper.

2. In a food processor or blender, add the dates, cashews, maple syrup, and cinnamon. Blend until the mixture reaches a paste-like consistency. Transfer to a medium bowl.

3. Add the cranberries to the mixture and gently fold until they are incorporated.

4. Add the mixture to the baking dish and evenly spread it. Using clean hands, press down on the mixture. Cover and refrigerate until the bars set, about 1 hour. Slice into 2-inch bars.

REFRIGERATE: Store the bars in a resealable container for up to 1 week. Line the container with parchment paper and put it between the layers to prevent the bars from sticking.

TOBY'S TIP: Swap the dried cranberries for raisins or dried tart cherries.

Per Serving (1 bar): Calories: 97; Fat: 4g; Saturated Fat: 1g; Protein: 2g; Total Carbs: 15g; Fiber: 1g; Sodium: 2mg

`GLUTEN-FREE` `VEGETARIAN`

HONEY RICOTTA WITH STRAWBERRIES

MAKES 4 SERVINGS

PREP TIME: 10 minutes   COOK TIME: 0 minutes

When I was in high school my parents owned a cheese store on Chambers Street in New York City. I would go in during the holidays to help wrap cheese-filled gift boxes and make the nut-covered cheese balls. I even had the opportunity to taste many of the 400 cheeses offered. Ricotta is still one of my favorites, dressed up here for a luscious snack.

- 1 cup part-skim ricotta cheese
- 2 tablespoons honey
- ¼ cup unsalted cashews, chopped
- 3 cups strawberries, halved

1. In a small bowl, combine the ricotta, honey, and cashews.
2. Place ¼ cup of the ricotta mixture and ¾ cup strawberries in each of four resealable containers.

REFRIGERATE: Store the honey ricotta in the same or separate resealable containers for up to 5 days.

TOBY'S TIP: Swap out the strawberries for blueberries, peaches, apricots, or pears. Go with whatever is in season and cheapest throughout the year.

Per Serving: Calories: 201; Fat: 9g; Saturated Fat: 4g; Protein 9g; Total Carbs 23g; Fiber 2g; Sodium 64mg

DAIRY-FREE **GLUTEN-FREE** **VEGAN**

HOMEMADE TRAIL MIX

MAKES 4 SERVINGS

PREP TIME: 5 minutes   COOK TIME: 0 minutes

Before I became the nutrition expert and blogger at FoodNetwork.com, I worked with my registered dietitian and good friend Dana Angelo White at an online start-up. We were both trying to watch our food dollars and brought in snacks to share. One of our favorites was homemade trail mix, and we would take turns surprising each other with new combinations.

- ½ cup raw almonds
- 10 dried apricots
- 3 tablespoons dried tart cherries
- 3 tablespoons dark chocolate chips
- 2 tablespoons unsalted sunflower seeds

In a medium bowl, add the almonds, apricots, cherries, chocolate chips, and sunflower seeds. Toss to combine.

STORAGE: Keep the trail mix in a resealable container at room temperature for up to 1 month.

TOBY'S TIP: Double or triple the recipe and portion it into small resealable containers or plastic bags so you can grab and go. You can also play with the combination of nuts and dried fruit and customize it for your taste buds.

Per Serving (5 tablespoons): Calories: 216; Fat: 15g; Saturated Fat: 3g; Protein: 6g; Total Carbs: 18g; Fiber: 4g; Sodium: 1mg

`GLUTEN-FREE` `VEGETARIAN`

CRUDITÉ WITH HERBED YOGURT DIP

MAKES 4 SERVINGS

PREP TIME: 15 minutes   COOK TIME: 0 minutes

Ranch dressing is one of my favorite dips for veggies, but I don't like the calories that come with it. I created this flavorful Greek yogurt–based dip instead, which also adds a healthy dose of protein to keep me feeling satisfied after this snack. If I have extra veggies from the week lying around, I'll use those instead of what is listed below to help minimize food waste.

- 1 cup nonfat plain Greek yogurt
- ¼ cup chopped fresh basil
- ¼ cup chopped fresh parsley
- Juice of ½ lemon (about 1 tablespoon)
- 1 garlic clove, minced
- ¼ teaspoon salt
- ⅛ teaspoon freshly ground black pepper
- 2 cups baby carrots
- 2 celery stalks, sliced into 3-inch-long matchsticks
- 1 cup cherry tomatoes
- 1 red or yellow bell pepper, sliced into 2-inch-thick pieces (1 cup)

1. In a small bowl, add the Greek yogurt, basil, parsley, lemon juice, garlic, salt, and black pepper. Stir to combine.

2. Spoon ¼ cup of the dip into small resealable containers and serve with the vegetables on the side.

REFRIGERATE: Store the dip and vegetables in separate resealable containers for up to 5 days.

TOBY'S TIP: If you have extra fresh herbs lying around, like chives, mint or cilantro, use them instead of the basil and parsley. Use whatever combination you like.

Per Serving: Calories: 80; Fat: 1g; Saturated Fat: 0g; Protein: 7g; Total Carbs: 13g; Fiber: 4g; Sodium: 247mg

DAIRY-FREE   **GLUTEN-FREE**   **PALEO**   **VEGAN**

CHILI-ROASTED CHICKPEAS

MAKES 2 CUPS

PREP TIME: 10 minutes   COOK TIME: 45 minutes

Roasted chickpeas have become very popular, and for good reason. A half cup of cooked chickpeas includes 7 grams of protein and is a rich source of fiber and iron. Make them savory, like in this recipe, or if you have a sweeter palate like me, sprinkle them with cinnamon and honey.

Cooking spray

2 (15-ounce) cans reduced-sodium chickpeas, drained and rinsed

1 tablespoon coconut oil

1 tablespoon chili powder

2 teaspoons cumin

½ teaspoon salt

1. Preheat the oven to 400°F. Coat a baking sheet with the cooking spray.

2. In a medium bowl, add the chickpeas, coconut oil, chili powder, cumin, and salt. Toss to combine.

3. Spread the chickpeas in a single layer on the baking sheet. Roast until the chickpeas appear to split apart, 40 to 45 minutes. Let the chickpeas cool for 10 minutes.

STORAGE: Keep the cooled chickpeas in a resealable container at room temperature for up to 1 week.

TOBY'S TIP: Coconut oil adds an additional level of flavor in this recipe. If you don't have any on hand, you can use the same amount of olive or canola oil instead.

Per Serving (¼ cup): Calories: 113; Fat: 4g; Saturated Fat: 2g; Protein: 5g; Total Carbs: 15g; Fiber: 5g; Sodium: 298mg

DAIRY-FREE **GLUTEN-FREE** **PALEO** **VEGAN**

THYME-ROASTED ALMONDS

MAKES 2 CUPS

PREP TIME: 5 minutes   COOK TIME: 8 minutes

Nuts are a healthy snack, but it's important to keep calories under control. A quarter cup of raw almonds, the size of a small handful, has 206 calories. If you mindlessly eat out of large bags, you could be downing thousands of calories and not even realize it! I always recommend portioning out your nuts before sitting down to eat them.

1½ cups raw almonds
2 tablespoons olive oil
1 tablespoon dried thyme
½ teaspoon kosher salt

1. Preheat the oven to 400°F.

2. In a small bowl, add the almonds, olive oil, thyme, and salt. Toss to evenly coat almonds.

3. Spread the almonds in a single layer on the baking sheet. Bake until the almonds are slightly browned and fragrant, about 8 minutes. Let the almonds cool for 10 minutes.

STORAGE: Keep the cooled almonds in a resealable container at room temperature for up to 2 weeks.

TOBY'S TIP: Substitute dried rosemary or chili powder for the thyme to shake things up.

Per Serving (¼ cup): Calories: 238; Fat: 21g; Saturated Fat: 2g; Protein: 8g; Total Carbs: 8g; Fiber: 5g; Sodium: 107mg

DAIRY-FREE   GLUTEN-FREE   VEGAN

CINNAMON COCOA POPCORN | MAKES 4 SERVINGS

PREP TIME: 5 minutes   COOK TIME: 5 minutes

My kids are so crazy about popcorn that I had to teach them how to pop their own in my air popper. After they mastered popping it, I taught them different ways to flavor it. Although they tend to like it with sea salt, we started experimenting with different sweet and savory toppings. Of course, the chocolate version is one of our household favorites.

3 tablespoons coconut oil

½ cup popcorn kernels

Cooking spray

1 tablespoon unsweetened cocoa powder

1 teaspoon ground cinnamon

1 tablespoon granulated sugar

1 teaspoon sea salt

1. In a medium pot over medium-low heat, heat the coconut oil. Add 3 popcorn kernels, and when one of the kernels pops, add the rest of them. Cover and shake the pot occasionally to prevent burning. Once the popcorn is popped, transfer the popcorn to a large mixing bowl.

2. Spray the popcorn with the cooking spray. Using clean hands, toss the popcorn to mix it thoroughly. Sprinkle it with the cocoa powder, cinnamon, sugar, and salt, and mix until the popcorn is thoroughly coated.

STORAGE: Keep the popcorn in a resealable plastic container for up to 1 week.

> **TOBY'S TIP:** Dust off your air popper to pop the kernels. Then toss the popcorn in melted coconut oil before adding the flavors.

Per Serving (4 cups): Calories: 188; Fat: 12g; Saturated Fat: 1g; Protein: 3g; Total Carbs: 24g; Fiber: 5g; Sodium: 533mg

DAIRY-FREE **GLUTEN-FREE** **VEGAN**

FRUIT SALAD WITH MINT

MAKES 4 SERVINGS

PREP TIME: 15 minutes   COOK TIME: 0 minutes

Growing up, my dad had a nice-size garden he took pride in. My brother and I would help him weed, plant, and pick the bounty. He grew carrots, radishes, sunflowers, cucumbers, corn, and lots of herbs, including mint. My mom, the chef of the house, used it in iced tea and fruit salad. To this day, I still love my fruit salad with the refreshing flavor of fresh mint.

½ cantaloupe, cubed

2 cups strawberries, hulled and sliced lengthwise

1 cup blueberries, blackberries, or raspberries

1 cup seedless green or red grapes

¼ cup freshly squeezed orange juice

2 tablespoons chopped fresh mint

1 teaspoon vanilla extract

1. In a large bowl, combine the cantaloupe, strawberries, blueberries, and grapes.

2. In a small bowl, whisk together the orange juice, mint, and vanilla extract. Pour this over the fruit and toss to evenly coat.

REFRIGERATE: Store the fruit salad in a resealable container for up to 5 days.

> **TOBY'S TIP:** The orange juice is used to add acid to the fruit salad. It helps preserve the fruit to make it last longer and prevent it from browning.

Per Serving (2 cups): Calories: 93; Fat: 1g; Saturated Fat: 0g; Protein: 2g; Total Carbs: 22g; Fiber: 3g; Sodium: 13mg

GLUTEN-FREE   VEGETARIAN

MASON JAR KEY LIME PARFAITS

MAKES 2 SERVINGS

PREP TIME: 10 minutes   COOK TIME: 0 minutes

I like to use my homemade goodies among many of my recipes. This helps make sure I'm using all my leftovers, plus I know I carefully selected the ingredients I use. My Homemade Granola (page 84) is a perfect example of a recipe that can be used in parfaits (like here), over oatmeal, or tossed on a salad.

1¼ cups nonfat plain Greek yogurt, divided

Juice of 1 lime (about 2 tablespoons)

Zest of 1 lime

1 tablespoon 100% maple syrup

½ cup Homemade Granola (page 84)

1. In a small bowl, whisk together the Greek yogurt, lime juice and zest, and maple syrup.

2. In each of two Mason jars, layer 5 tablespoons of the Greek yogurt followed by 2 tablespoons of the Homemade Granola. Repeat for a second layer. Cover and refrigerate.

REFRIGERATE: Store the sealed jars for up to 5 days.

TOBY'S TIP: Change up the citrus flavor. Substitute the lime for lemon or orange or get creative with lesser known varieties like Cara Cara oranges, blood oranges, or Meyer lemons.

Per Serving: Calories: 246; Fat: 4g; Saturated Fat: 1g; Protein: 18g; Total Carbs: 35g; Fiber: 2g; Sodium: 223mg

TO-GO SNACK BOXES

MAKES 3 BOXES

PREP TIME: 5 minutes per box   COOK TIME: 0 minutes

I love those bento-type boxes Starbucks now serves, but they don't come cheap. Luckily, I can easily whip these snack boxes up at home and have a few stored for the week. Here are some of my favorite combinations.

BOX 1: CHEESE AND GRAPES

1 ounce Cheddar cheese, cubed

1 cup seedless grapes

6 whole-grain crackers

GLUTEN-FREE

VEGETARIAN

BOX 2: EGG AND CHEESE

1 hardboiled egg, sliced

1 part-skim mozzarella cheese stick

1 cucumber, thinly sliced

DAIRY-FREE

GLUTEN-FREE

VEGETARIAN

BOX 3: PEANUT BUTTER AND CELERY

2 celery stalks, cut into 3-inch sticks

1 tablespoon natural peanut butter

1 medium apple or pear, sliced

PALEO

VEGETARIAN

REFRIGERATE: Store each box in separate resealable containers for up to 1 week. Boxes with sliced apples or pears should be eaten within 3 days.

> **TOBY'S TIP:** Adding a few drops of freshly squeezed lemon, lime, or orange juice to the apples or pears after slicing helps prevent browning. These boxes should be eaten first.

BOX 1 CHEESE AND GRAPES Per Serving: Calories: 270; Fat: 14g; Saturated Fat: 7g; Protein: 10g; Total Carbs: 32g; Fiber: 3g; Sodium: 334mg

BOX 2 EGG AND CHEESE Per Serving: Calories: 182; Fat: 10g; Saturated Fat: 5g; Protein: 15g; Total Carbs: 6g; Fiber: 1g; Sodium: 286mg

BOX 3 PEANUT BUTTER AND CELERY Per Serving Calories: 202; Fat: 8g; Saturated Fat: 2g; Protein: 5g; Total Carbs: 31g; Fiber: 7g; Sodium: 142mg

DAIRY-FREE   GLUTEN-FREE   VEGAN

SRIRACHA HUMMUS

MAKES 1½ CUPS

PREP TIME: 10 minutes   COOK TIME: 0 minutes

Hummus is more than just a dip; it's my condiment of choice. I use it to spread on turkey, roast beef, chicken, and cheese sandwiches, and on burgers and barbecue chicken and lamb. I also dip my eggs, fries, and vegetables in it. The possibilities are truly endless, and the spicy kick of this version adds a little extra pizazz to the meal or snack.

- 1 (15-ounce) can reduced-sodium chickpeas, drained and rinsed
- 1 garlic clove, minced
- 3 tablespoons tahini
- Juice of 1½ lemons (about 3 tablespoons)
- ½ to 1 teaspoon sriracha
- ½ teaspoon salt
- ¼ teaspoon freshly ground black pepper
- ¼ cup extra-virgin olive oil
- 2 tablespoons water

In a food processor or blender, add the chickpeas, garlic, tahini, lemon juice, desired amount of sriracha, salt, and black pepper, and process until well combined. With the machine running, slowly drizzle in the olive oil and water and continue processing until well incorporated, and the hummus is creamy.

REFRIGERATE: Store the hummus in a resealable container for up to 5 days.

TOBY'S TIP: Try different add-ins to your hummus. Substitute the sriracha for roasted red peppers, garlic, parsley, or cilantro.

Per Serving (¼ cup): Calories: 107; Fat: 5g; Saturated Fat: 1g; Protein: 5g; Total Carbs: 12g; Fiber: 4g; Sodium: 304mg

DAIRY-FREE **GLUTEN-FREE** **PALEO** **VEGAN**

ROSEMARY BEET CHIPS

MAKES 4 CUPS

PREP TIME: 10 minutes   **COOK TIME:** 20 minutes

I like to cheat on my go-to Sriracha-Lime Kale Chips (page 203) with these purple-hued bad boys. The color of the beets brings with it an array of vitamins, minerals, and phytochemicals (plant compounds that help fight and prevent disease) that aren't in kale. I like to include both types of chips in my snack repertoire, that way I can take in a wide array of important nutrients.

Cooking spray
2 pounds beets, peeled
1 tablespoon olive oil
2 teaspoons dried rosemary
½ teaspoon salt
⅛ teaspoon freshly ground black pepper

1. Preheat the oven to 375°F. Coat a baking sheet with the cooking spray.

2. Using a mandolin or a chef's knife, slice the beets as thin as possible and in uniform size. The slices should almost curl up.

3. Put the beet slices in a large bowl and drizzle them with the olive oil, rosemary, salt, and black pepper. Toss gently to combine.

4. Place the beets in a single layer on the baking sheet. Bake until the beets are crispy, about 15 to 20 minutes.

STORAGE: Keep the beet chips in a resealable container at room temperature for up to 10 days.

> **TOBY'S TIP:** The purple-red from the beets can be difficult to get off your hands and can stain, too. I recommend wearing food-grade plastic gloves when slicing them.

Per Serving (1 cup): Calories: 130; Fat: 4g; Saturated Fat: 1g; Protein: 4g; Total Carbs: 22g; Fiber: 7g; Sodium: 472mg

DAIRY-FREE **GLUTEN-FREE** **PALEO** **VEGAN**

SRIRACHA-LIME KALE CHIPS

MAKES 3 CUPS

PREP TIME: 15 minutes   COOK TIME: 10 minutes

Because I am in the media, I get a ton of samples from companies that want to introduce me to their products. When kale chips became popular, I had the opportunity to try all kinds of flavors. One that I loved was the combination of lime and hot sauce. But instead of buying pricey bags, I like to make them myself.

Cooking spray

¼ cup olive oil

1 teaspoon sriracha

Zest of 1 lime

Juice of 1 lime (about 2 tablespoons)

1 teaspoon kosher salt

½ teaspoon freshly ground black pepper

1 (10-ounce) bag torn kale

1. Preheat the oven to 400°F. Coat two baking sheets with the cooking spray.

2. In a large bowl, whisk together the olive oil, sriracha, lime juice and zest, salt, and black pepper.

3. Add the kale to the bowl and toss until it is well coated with the dressing. Spread the kale in single, even layers on the baking sheets.

4. Bake until the kale is crisp, about 10 minutes. Let cool for 10 minutes.

STORAGE: Keep the cooled kale chips in a resealable container at room temperature for up to 1 week.

> **TOBY'S TIP:** I find buying the pre-torn bags a huge time saver. You can find them at reasonably priced stores like Trader Joe's and Target. You can also buy a head of kale and tear it yourself.

Per Serving (½ cup): Calories: 102; Fat: 9g; Saturated Fat: 1g; Protein: 1g; Total Carbs: 5g; Fiber: 1g; Sodium: 405mg

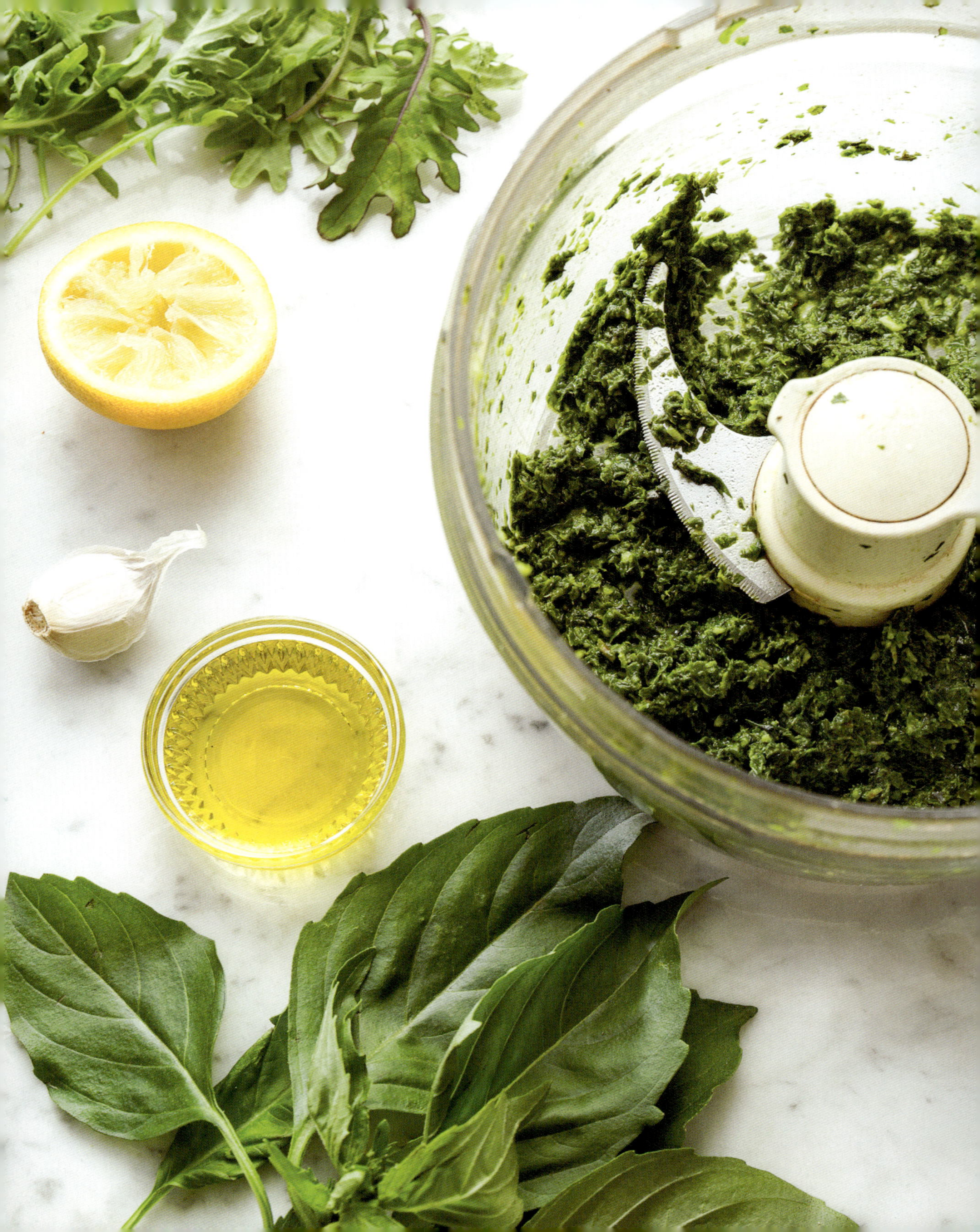

10 SAUCES, DRESSINGS & STAPLES

- **206** Kale Pesto
- **207** White Balsamic Vinaigrette
- **208** Herbed Vinaigrette
- **209** Lighter Blue Cheese Dressing
- **210** Soy-Sesame Dressing
- **211** Asian Peanut Sauce
- **212** Chimichurri Sauce
- **213** Speedy Tomato Sauce
- **214** Thai Marinade
- **215** Avocado Lime Mayonnaise
- **216** Green Olive Tapenade
- **217** Simple Tomato Salsa

« Kale Pesto (page 206)

DAIRY-FREE   GLUTEN-FREE   PALEO   VEGAN

KALE PESTO

MAKES ¾ CUP

PREP TIME: 10 minutes   COOK TIME: 0 minutes

I love pesto, but I don't love the calories of traditional store-brought brands. One cup of traditional pesto has about 1,200 calories! Why so much? It's the oil. Each tablespoon of olive or other oil contains 120 calories, which can rack up calories quickly. In my pesto, the thick pesto consistency comes from the combo of basil and kale, with only a touch of oil. The flavor is there, but the calories are under control.

2 cups baby kale

4 cups basil leaves

¼ cup extra-virgin olive oil

1 garlic clove, chopped

Juice of 1 lemon (about 2 tablespoons)

½ teaspoon salt

In a food processor or blender, add the kale, basil, olive oil, garlic, lemon juice, and salt. Purée until it forms a paste.

REFRIGERATE: Store in a resealable plastic container for up to 1 week.

> **TOBY'S TIP:** Use this pesto over whole-grain pasta, with Baked Turkey Meatballs (page 148), as a sauce for fish, or as a condiment for sandwiches.

Per Serving (2 tablespoons): Calories: 96; Fat: 9g; Saturated Fat: 1g; Protein: 2g; Total Carbs: 3g; Fiber: 1g; Sodium: 206mg

DAIRY-FREE   GLUTEN-FREE   PALEO   VEGAN

WHITE BALSAMIC VINAIGRETTE

MAKES 6 TABLESPOONS

PREP TIME: 5 minutes   COOK TIME: 0 minutes

White balsamic vinegar is made from white grapes, giving it a clear color, instead of the red grapes that make the darker balsamic vinegar. The flavor is the same, but it makes for a prettier dressing, especially when mixed into salads stored in Mason jars.

- 1 garlic clove, minced
- 2 tablespoons white balsamic vinegar
- ½ teaspoon Dijon mustard
- ¼ teaspoon salt
- ¼ teaspoon freshly ground black pepper
- ¼ cup extra-virgin olive oil

In a small bowl, whisk together the garlic, vinegar, mustard, salt, and black pepper. Slowly drizzle in the olive oil while whisking vigorously to emulsify the dressing.

REFRIGERATE: Store the dressing in a resealable container for up to 1 month.

> **TOBY'S TIP:** If you want to make a traditional balsamic vinaigrette, swap the white balsamic vinegar for a traditional dark brown-red balsamic vinegar.

Per Serving (1½ tablespoons): Calories: 155; Fat: 17g; Saturated Fat: 2g; Protein: 0g; Total Carbs: 1g; Fiber: 0g; Sodium: 166mg

DAIRY-FREE **GLUTEN-FREE** **VEGAN**

HERBED VINAIGRETTE

MAKES 6 TABLESPOONS

PREP TIME: 10 minutes **COOK TIME:** 0 minutes

When it comes to dressings, I'm a simple gal. I find many restaurants drown salads in dressings, masking the flavor of the delicious veggies. I want the vegetables to be the star, with any dressing enhancing their flavors. A splash of dressing with a mild flavor, like this vinaigrette, complements the vegetables.

- ¼ cup extra-virgin olive oil
- 2 tablespoons freshly squeezed orange juice
- ½ teaspoon 100% maple syrup
- 2 teaspoons chopped fresh parsley
- 1 teaspoon chopped fresh rosemary
- ¼ teaspoon salt

In a small bowl, whisk together the olive oil, orange juice, maple syrup, parsley, rosemary, and salt until well combined.

REFRIGERATE: Store the dressing in a resealable container for up to 1 week.

> **TOBY'S TIP:** When shopping for fresh rosemary, choose the bunch that is bright in color. To store, wrap in a damp cloth and place in a plastic bag in the refrigerator for up to 5 days.

Per Serving (1½ tablespoons): Calories: 123; Fat: 14g; Saturated Fat: 2g; Protein: 0g; Total Carbs: 1g; Fiber: 0g; Sodium: 148mg

GLUTEN-FREE   VEGETARIAN

LIGHTER BLUE CHEESE DRESSING

MAKES ½ CUP

PREP TIME: 5 minutes   COOK TIME: 0 minutes

A little bit of flavorful whole-fat cheese goes a long way as you can see in this Greek yogurt-based dressing. The recipe only calls for ½ ounce of blue cheese, but once you drizzle and toss over a salad you can taste it in every tangy, delicious bite.

- ½ cup nonfat plain Greek yogurt
- ½ ounce crumbled blue cheese (about 1 heaping tablespoon)
- 1 teaspoon white balsamic vinegar
- 1 teaspoon freshly squeezed lemon juice
- 1 garlic clove, smashed
- ¼ teaspoon salt
- ⅛ teaspoon freshly ground black pepper

In a blender or food processor, add the Greek yogurt, blue cheese, vinegar, lemon juice, garlic, salt, and black pepper. Blend until smooth and creamy.

REFRIGERATE: Store the dressing in a resealable container for up to 1 week.

> **TOBY'S TIP:** The clear color of the white balsamic vinegar complements the light colors of the cheese and yogurt. It is more for eye appeal than anything else.

Per Serving (2 tablespoons): Calories: 45; Fat: 2g; Saturated Fat: 1g; Protein: 4g; Total Carbs: 2g; Fiber: 0g; Sodium: 254mg

DAIRY-FREE   **VEGETARIAN**

SOY-SESAME DRESSING

MAKES ABOUT ½ CUP

PREP TIME: 5 minutes   COOK TIME: 0 minutes

One of my favorite combinations is steak with a soy-based marinade. You can easily find bottled varieties, but most have hidden amounts of added sugar. The honey in my recipe balances the umami flavor of the soy sauce, but you only use 1 teaspoon for 6 servings. The flavor is even better than store-bought, if I do say so myself.

- 2 tablespoons reduced-sodium soy sauce
- 2 tablespoons seasoned rice vinegar
- 1 garlic clove, minced
- 1 teaspoon toasted sesame oil
- 1 teaspoon honey
- ⅓ cup canola oil

In a small bowl, whisk together the soy sauce, vinegar, garlic, sesame oil, and honey. Slowly drizzle in the canola oil, while whisking vigorously to combine.

REFRIGERATE: Store the dressing in a resealable container for up to 2 weeks.

> **TOBY'S TIP:** Use as a dressing or as a marinade for steak or a fatty fish like tuna or salmon. Always throw away the extra marinade used on raw meat and fish after use.

Per Serving (1½ tablespoons): Calories: 122; Fat: 3g; Saturated Fat: 1g; Protein: 0g; Total Carbs: 2g; Fiber: 0g; Sodium: 145mg

DAIRY-FREE · VEGAN

ASIAN PEANUT SAUCE

MAKES 1¼ CUPS

PREP TIME: 15 minutes   COOK TIME: 0 minutes

When I was 18 years old, I was vacationing in Mexico while studying to get my scuba-diving certification. The night before I was set to take the written part of the exam, I had the most amazing chicken with peanut sauce. Ever since then, I love peanut sauce on anything—chicken, tofu, and beef. Needless to say, it's a staple in my refrigerator.

- ½ cup light coconut milk
- ¾ cup creamy peanut butter
- 3 tablespoons reduced-sodium soy sauce
- Juice of 1½ limes (about 3 tablespoons)
- 2 tablespoons chopped shallots
- 1 garlic clove, chopped
- 1 tablespoon brown sugar
- 2 tablespoons water, or more if needed

In a blender or food processor add the coconut milk, peanut butter, soy sauce, lime juice, shallots, garlic, and brown sugar. Blend until smooth. Add the water to achieve your desired thickness.

REFRIGERATE: Store the sauce in a resealable container for up to 1 week.

TOBY'S TIP: Opt for natural peanut butter over reduced-fat peanut butter, which has more sugar over its full-fat counterpart.

Per Serving (2 tablespoons): Calories: 130; Fat: 10g; Saturated Fat: 2g; Protein: 5g; Total Carbs: 7g; Fiber: 1g; Sodium: 225mg

DAIRY-FREE   **GLUTEN-FREE**   **PALEO**   **VEGAN**

CHIMICHURRI SAUCE

MAKES ¾ CUP

PREP TIME: 10 minutes   **COOK TIME:** 0 minutes

This green sauce is popular in Argentina and used as frequently as ketchup is in the United States. I will grill up a lean cut of lamb, beef, chicken, or fish and serve it with 1 to 2 tablespoons of this sauce. It also works fabulously on poached or baked fish. In other words, it pairs well with any protein, no matter how it's prepared.

- 1 packed cup parsley
- 1 shallot, cut into large chunks
- ¼ cup red wine vinegar
- 2 small garlic cloves, smashed
- ½ teaspoon dried oregano
- ¼ teaspoon ground cumin
- ¼ teaspoon salt
- ½ cup extra-virgin olive oil

In a food processor or blender, combine the parsley, shallot, vinegar, garlic, oregano, cumin, and salt. Pulse until the ingredients are combined. Add the olive oil and pulse until coarsely puréed. Let sit for 1 to 2 minutes to allow the flavors to combine.

REFRIGERATE: Store the sauce in a resealable container for up to 5 days.

> **TOBY'S TIP:** Chimichurri is an oil-based sauce, which makes it higher in calories. If you're trying to lose weight, reduce portions to 1 tablespoon per serving.

Per Serving (2 tablespoons): Calories: 172; Fat: 18g; Saturated Fat: 3g; Protein: 1g; Total Carbs: 2g; Fiber: 1g; Sodium: 106mg

DAIRY-FREE   **GLUTEN-FREE**   **PALEO**   **VEGAN**

SPEEDY TOMATO SAUCE

MAKES 7 CUPS

PREP TIME: 15 minutes   COOK TIME: 20 minutes

Most store-bought tomato sauces may have additives and preservatives you don't want in your food. Making your own puts you in the driver's seat for controlling the ingredients. This sauce is quick because it uses canned tomatoes, which should only list "tomatoes" under the ingredients. Canned tomatoes also have more of the antioxidant lycopene compared with their fresh counterpart. Lycopene is associated with a lower risk of heart disease, prostate cancer, and macular degeneration.

- 2 tablespoons olive oil
- 2 medium yellow onions, chopped
- 4 garlic cloves, minced
- 2 (28-ounce) cans crushed tomatoes
- 1 (6-ounce) can tomato paste
- 1 tablespoon dried basil
- 1 teaspoon dried oregano
- 3 bay leaves
- ½ teaspoon dried thyme
- ½ teaspoon salt
- ¼ teaspoon freshly ground black pepper

1. In a medium pot over medium heat, heat the olive oil until it shimmers. Add the onions and cook until they are translucent, about 3 minutes. Add the garlic and cook until fragrant, about 30 seconds.

2. Add the tomatoes, tomato paste, basil, oregano, bay leaves, thyme, salt, and black pepper, and stir to combine. Bring the mixture to a boil, then reduce the heat to medium-low. Cover the pot and simmer the sauce until the flavors combine, about 15 minutes. Remove the bay leaves before eating.

REFRIGERATE: Store the cooled tomato sauce in a resealable container in the refrigerator for up to 1 week. Reheat individual portions in the microwave for about 1 minute. A larger batch can be reheated in a medium saucepan over medium heat for 10 to 15 minutes.

FREEZE: Stored the cooled tomato sauce in a freezer-safe container for up to 3 months. Thaw in the refrigerator overnight. Reheat individual portions in the microwave for about 1 minute. A larger batch can be reheated in a medium saucepan over medium heat for 10 to 15 minutes.

> **TOBY'S TIP:** Old or worn can openers can leave shards of the can in the food. If you find the can opener is having a tough time getting around the can, it's time to invest in a new one. You don't have to spend a lot of money, but you do need to replace it if it's worn.

Per Serving (½ cup): Calories: 26; Fat: 2g; Saturated Fat: 0g; Protein: 0g; Total Carbs: 2g; Fiber: 0g; Sodium: 85mg

DAIRY-FREE **VEGAN**

THAI MARINADE

MAKES 1⅓ CUPS

PREP TIME: 10 minutes   COOK TIME: 0 minutes

I like to be prepared with sauces and marinades that go with everything. You'll find this marinade used in my Thai Chicken Stir-Fry (page 154) and Thai Chicken Thighs (page 151). Besides chicken, you can also use it on fish, turkey, beef, tofu, and pasta or potato salad.

- 1¼ cups light coconut milk
- 2 tablespoons reduced-sodium soy sauce
- 2 tablespoons brown sugar
- Juice of 1 lime
- Zest of 1 lime
- 1 tablespoon curry powder
- 1 teaspoon ground coriander
- 1 garlic clove, minced
- 1 teaspoon minced fresh ginger
- ¼ teaspoon salt
- ⅛ teaspoon freshly ground black pepper

In a large bowl, whisk together the coconut milk, soy sauce, brown sugar, lime juice and zest, curry powder, coriander, garlic, ginger, salt, and black pepper until the sugar has dissolved.

REFRIGERATE: Store the marinade in a resealable container for up to 1 week.

> **TOBY'S TIP:** Looking to swap out the brown sugar? Sweetness is needed to complement the umami flavor from the soy sauce. You can use 1⅛ tablespoons of agave instead.

Per Serving (⅓ cup): Calories: 78; Fat: 4g; Saturated Fat: 4g; Protein: 2g; Total Carbs: 11g; Fiber: 1g; Sodium: 386mg

DAIRY-FREE   GLUTEN-FREE   PALEO   VEGAN

AVOCADO LIME MAYONNAISE

MAKES ¾ CUP

PREP TIME: 10 minutes   COOK TIME: 0 minutes

One cup of regular mayonnaise has a whopping 1,600 calories, much of which is artery-clogging saturated fat. Instead, you can make a saturated fat–free condiment out of heart-healthy avocados. This delicious fruit (yes, avocado is a fruit) is packed with 20 vitamins, minerals, and unsaturated fat. It's the perfect solution for sandwiches or for topping fish or chicken.

- 1 ripe avocado
- 2 tablespoons extra-virgin olive oil
- Juice of 1 lime (about 2 tablespoons)
- Zest of 1 lime
- ¼ teaspoon salt
- 2 tablespoons water (optional)

In a food processor or blender, add the avocado, olive oil, lime juice and zest, and salt. Blend until smooth, adding the water, if needed, to make a creamy texture.

REFRIGERATE: Store the mayonnaise in a resealable container for up to 1 week.

> **TOBY'S TIP:** To speed the ripening of your firm avocado, place it and an apple or a banana in a brown paper bag for several days. The ethylene gas emitted from the fruit will speed up the ripening process.

Per Serving (2 tablespoons): Calories: 55; Fat: 5g; Saturated Fat: 1g; Protein: 1g; Total Carbs: 3g; Fiber: 2g; Sodium: 101mg

Sauces, Dressings & Staples

DAIRY-FREE **GLUTEN-FREE** **PALEO** **VEGAN**

GREEN OLIVE TAPENADE

MAKES 1½ CUPS

PREP TIME: 10 minutes   COOK TIME: 0 minutes

This thick paste originates from France's Provence region. Use it as a condiment for sandwiches, as a dip for vegetable crudités, or spooned over fish, meat, or chicken. It's great to serve at parties or take to a summer barbecue.

- 1 (6-ounce) can pitted green olives
- 1 cup parsley, coarsely chopped
- ½ cup extra-virgin olive oil
- ¼ cup drained capers
- Juice of 2 lemons (about ¼ cup)
- ¼ teaspoon freshly ground black pepper

In a food processor or blender, add the olives, parsley, olive oil, capers, lemon juice, and black pepper. Pulse until mixture is coarsely puréed. Let the mixture sit for 1 to 2 minutes to allow the flavors to combine.

REFRIGERATE: Store the tapenade in a resealable container for up to 5 days.

TOBY'S TIP: Want to make a more authentic version of tapenade? Add 1 to 2 canned anchovies.

Per Serving (2 tablespoons): Calories: 106; Fat: 11g; Saturated Fat: 1g; Protein: 0g; Total Carbs: 2g; Fiber: 0g; Sodium: 197mg

DAIRY-FREE   **GLUTEN-FREE**   **PALEO**   **VEGAN**

SIMPLE TOMATO SALSA

MAKES 3 CUPS

PREP TIME: 10 minutes   COOK TIME: 0 minutes

It's easy to buy jarred salsa, but I love to make my own so I can play with the ingredients. If I want a spicier version, I add more jalapeños. If I want a "fancier" version, I'll add finely diced avocado. This is the best way I can control the ingredients and minimize my intake of additives. Plus, the flavors of fresh salsa blow jarred salsa out of the water every time.

- 1 pound plum tomatoes, chopped
- ½ green bell pepper, chopped
- ½ onion, chopped (about ½ cup)
- ½ jalapeño, seeded and chopped
- ¼ cup chopped cilantro
- Juice of 1 lime (about 2 tablespoons)
- 1 tablespoon extra-virgin olive oil
- ¼ teaspoon salt
- ⅛ teaspoon freshly ground black pepper

In a medium bowl, combine the tomatoes, bell pepper, onion, jalapeño, and cilantro. Add the lime juice, olive oil, salt, and black pepper, and mix to evenly coat.

REFRIGERATE: Store the salsa in the resealable container for up to 1 week.

> **TOBY'S TIP:** Plum tomatoes are oblong in shape and do not have many seeds. They are easier to use for chopped salads, salsas, and other dishes where you don't want it to get too watery or have many seeds. If you use regular tomatoes, I recommend you scoop out the seeds and pulp before chopping them.

Per Serving (½ cup): Calories: 41; Fat: 2g; Saturated Fat: 0g; Protein: 1g; Total Carbs: 5g; Fiber: 1g; Sodium: 103mg

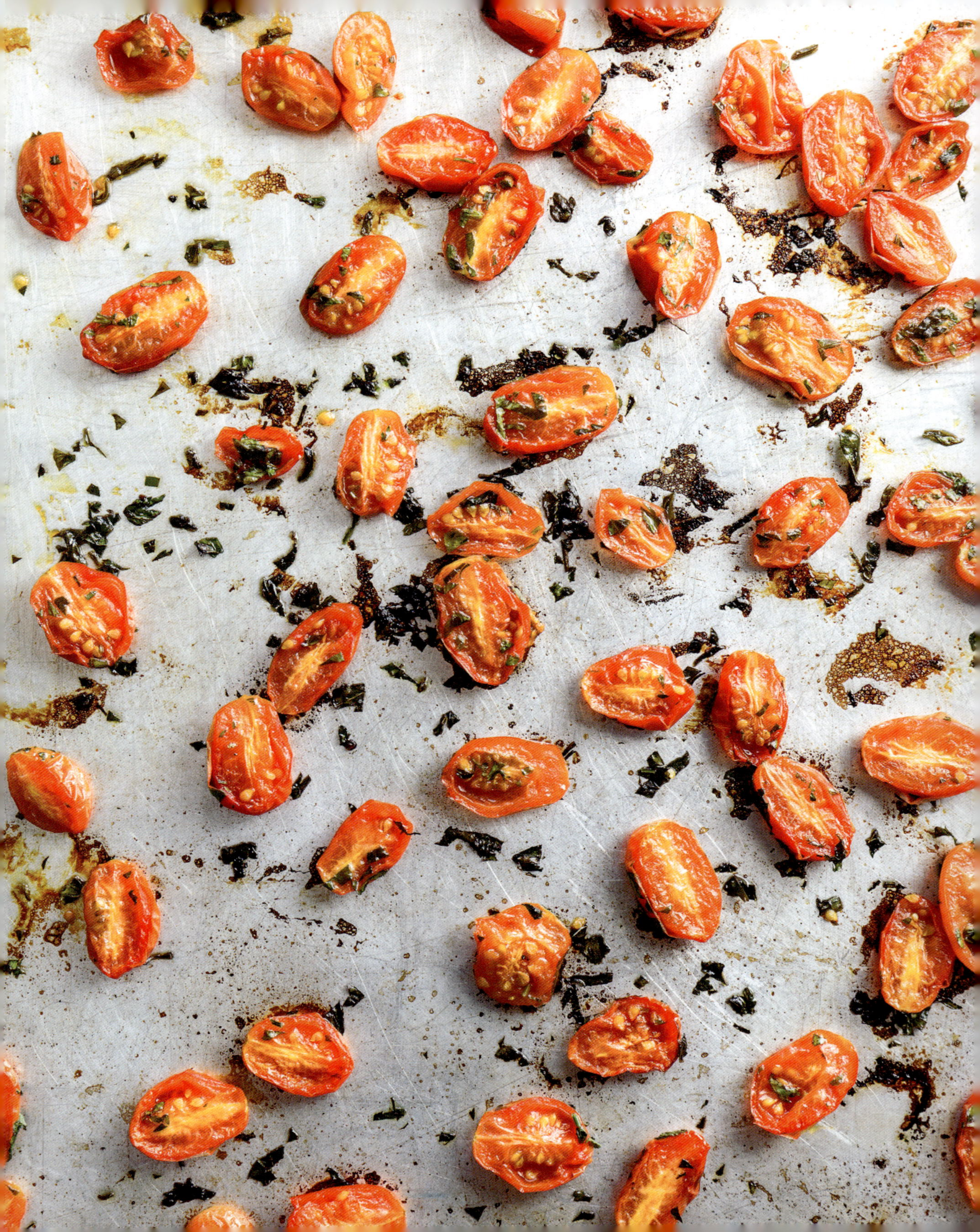

Conversion Tables

Volume Equivalents (Liquid)

US STANDARD	US STANDARD (OUNCES)	METRIC (APPROXIMATE)
2 TABLESPOONS	1 FL. OZ.	30 ML
¼ CUP	2 FL. OZ.	60 ML
½ CUP	4 FL. OZ.	120 ML
1 CUP	8 FL. OZ.	240 ML
1½ CUPS	12 FL. OZ.	355 ML
2 CUPS OR 1 PINT	16 FL. OZ.	475 ML
4 CUPS OR 1 QUART	32 FL. OZ.	1 L
1 GALLON	128 FL. OZ.	4 L

Oven Temperatures

FAHRENHEIT (F)	CELSIUS (C) (APPROXIMATE)
250°F	120°C
300°F	150°C
325°F	165°C
350°F	180°C
375°F	190°C
400°F	200°C
425°F	220°C
450°F	230°C

Volume Equivalents (Dry)

US STANDARD	METRIC (APPROXIMATE)
⅛ TEASPOON	0.5 ML
¼ TEASPOON	1 ML
½ TEASPOON	2 ML
¾ TEASPOON	4 ML
1 TEASPOON	5 ML
1 TABLESPOON	15 ML
¼ CUP	59 ML
⅓ CUP	79 ML
½ CUP	118 ML
⅔ CUP	156 ML
¾ CUP	177 ML
1 CUP	235 ML
2 CUPS OR 1 PINT	475 ML
3 CUPS	700 ML
4 CUPS OR 1 QUART	1 L
½ GALLON	2 L
1 GALLON	4 L

Weight Equivalents

US STANDARD	METRIC (APPROXIMATE)
½ OUNCE	15 GRAMS
1 OUNCE	30 GRAMS
2 OUNCES	60 GRAMS
4 OUNCES	115 GRAMS
8 OUNCES	225 GRAMS
12 OUNCES	340 GRAMS
16 OUNCES OR 1 POUND	455 GRAMS

Recipe Index

A

Apple Walnut Loaf, 81
Apricot Chicken Drumsticks, 157–158
Apricot-Orange Oat Bites, 189
Artichoke and White Bean Salad, 120
Arugula Salad with Salmon, 111
Asian "Fried" Brown Rice, 105
Asian Peanut Sauce, 211
Avocado Lime Mayonnaise, 215
Avo-Egg Scramble Wrap, 70

B

Baked Turkey Meatballs, 148–149
Balsamic Brussels Sprouts, 128
Balsamic Onion and Mango Quinoa, 99
Barbecue Chicken Pizza, 165
Beef Kebobs with Chimichurri Sauce, 175–176
Beef-Mushroom Meatballs, 170
Beef Stir-Fry with Asian Peanut Sauce, 174
Beer Brisket Tacos, 179
Blackberry-Lemon Overnight Oats, 77
Brooklyn Breakfast, 76
Bulgur-Stuffed Tomatoes, 106

C

Cacao-Date Oatmeal, 78
Carrot-Cabbage Slaw, 121
Cauliflower-Rice Mushroom Risotto, 123
Chili-Roasted Chickpeas, 195
Chimichurri Sauce, 212
Chocolate Energy Balls, 190
Chopped Salad with Feta and Lentils, 119
Cinnamon Cocoa Popcorn, 197
Citrus Broccoli Slaw, 118
Coconut Lime Flounder in Parchment Paper, 137
Corn and Tomato Couscous, 103
Crab-Stuffed Flounder, 142
Crudité with Herbed Yogurt Dip, 194

E

Easy Tricolored Pepper Steak, 181
Eggplant Zucchini Provençal, 122

F

Farro, Sardines, and Greens, 138
Farro Tabbouleh, 100
Fruit Salad with Mint, 198
Fruit Salsa and Yogurt Crêpes, 92–93

G

Ginger Soy Tuna Packets with Snap Peas and Bok Choy, 135–136
Green Olive Tapenade, 216
Grilled Asian Steak Salad, 114
Grilled Halibut with Anchovy-Caper Dressing, 143

H

Hawaiian Chicken Skewers, 155–156
Herbed Pork Loin, 183
Herbed Vinaigrette, 208
Homemade Granola, 84
Homemade Trail Mix, 193
Honey Ricotta with Strawberries, 192

I

Indian-Style Sautéed Chickpeas, 104

K

Kale Pesto, 206

L

Lamb Chops with Mint-Yogurt Sauce, 182
Lemony Chicken Breasts, 159
Lemony Green Beans with Almonds, 124
Lentil-Beef Meatloaf, 171
Lighter Blue Cheese Dressing, 209
Lighter Creamed Spinach, 129
Lighter Fish Cakes, 140–141
Lighter Panzanella Salad, 117
Lime Shrimp with Tomato Salsa, 139

M

Maple Orange Glazed Baby Carrots, 125
Mason Jar Cobb Salad, 112–113

Mason Jar Key Lime Parfaits, 199
Mediterranean Stuffed Peppers, 172–173
Mediterranean Turkey Burgers, 147
Meyer Lemon Cranberry-Ricotta Muffins, 87–88
Mini Vegetable Quiches, 71
Mushroom-Kale Brown Rice, 101

N

No-Bake Maple Cinnamon Bars, 191

O

One-Pot Mediterranean Chicken and Quinoa, 152–153
Onion-Parsley Quinoa, 102
Oven-Roasted Tomato Quinoa, 98

P

Peanut Butter Banana Energy Cookies, 188
Pear-Cinnamon Oat Muffins, 85–86
Pesto Chicken, 150
Poached Salmon with Chimichurri Sauce, 133

Q

Quinoa-Kale Salad Bowl, 116
Quinoa Power Breakfast Jar, 91

R

Roasted Root Vegetable Salad with Kale, 110
Roasted Thai Pork Tenderloin, 184
Roasted Trout with Green Olive Tapenade, 134
Root Vegetable and Bean Soup, 96
Rosemary Beet Chips, 202
Rosemary Chicken Breasts, 160

S

Shawarma Steak, 180
Simple Tomato Salsa, 217
Skirt Steak with Asian Peanut Sauce, 168
Slow-Cooker Barbecue Chicken, 164
Slow-Cooker Barbecue Pulled Pork, 185
Slow-Cooker Beef Stew, 177
Slow-Cooker Beer Brisket, 178
Slow-Cooker Three-Bean Chili, 107
Slow-Cooker Tuscan Chicken, 161
Slow-Cooker White Chicken Chili, 162
Soy-Sesame Dressing, 210
Speedy Tomato Sauce, 213
Spicy Tuna with Edamame, 132
Sriracha Hummus, 201
Sriracha-Lime Kale Chips, 203
Steamed Asparagus with Bacon, 126–127
Strawberry-Chocolate-Almond Smoothie Jar, 90
Sweet Potato Protein Pancakes, 73

T

Tart Cherry–Almond Breakfast Cookies, 79–80
Tex-Mex Burgers, 169
Thai Chicken Stir-Fry, 154
Thai Chicken Thighs, 151
Thai Marinade, 214
Thyme-Roasted Almonds, 196
To-Go Snack Boxes, 200
Tropical Green Smoothie, 89
Tuna Niçoise Salad, 115
Turkey-Walnut Salad with Cranberries, 146
Turmeric Wild Rice and Black Beans, 97

W

White Balsamic Vinaigrette, 207
White Chicken Chili and Spinach Quesadillas, 163
Whole-Grain Pancakes with Spiced Greek Yogurt Sauce, 74–75
Wild Blueberry Whole-Grain Scones, 82–83

Z

Zippy's Shakshuka, 72

Index

A

Almond butter
    Apricot-Orange
        Oat Bites, 189
    Quinoa Power
        Breakfast Jar, 91
    Strawberry-Chocolate-
        Almond Smoothie Jar, 90

Almond milk
    Apple Walnut Loaf, 81
    Quinoa Power
        Breakfast Jar, 91
    Tropical Green Smoothie, 89

Almonds
    Homemade Granola, 84
    Homemade Trail Mix, 193
    Lemony Green Beans
        with Almonds, 124
    Roasted Root Vegetable
        Salad with Kale, 110
    Strawberry-Chocolate-
        Almond Smoothie Jar, 90
    Tart Cherry–Almond
        Breakfast Cookies, 79–80
    Thyme-Roasted
        Almonds, 196

American Heart
    Association, 184

Apples
    Apple Walnut Loaf, 81
    Homemade Granola, 84
    To-Go Snack Boxes, 200

Applesauce
    Apple Walnut Loaf, 81
    Meyer Lemon Cranberry-
        Ricotta Muffins, 87–88
    Tart Cherry–Almond
        Breakfast Cookies, 79–80

Apricots, dried
    Apricot-Orange Oat
        Bites, 189
    Homemade Trail Mix, 193

Artichoke hearts
    Artichoke and White
        Bean Salad, 120

Asparagus
    Steamed Asparagus with
        Bacon, 126–127

Avocados
    Avocado Lime
        Mayonnaise, 215
    Avo-Egg Scramble Wrap, 70
    Mason Jar Cobb
        Salad, 112–113

B

Bacon. *See* Turkey bacon

Bananas
    Peanut Butter Banana
        Energy Cookies, 188
    Quinoa Power
        Breakfast Jar, 91
    Tropical Green Smoothie, 89

Basil
    Coconut Lime Flounder in
        Parchment Paper, 137
    Crudité with Herbed
        Yogurt Dip, 194
    Fruit Salsa and Yogurt
        Crêpes, 92–93
    Kale Pesto, 206
    Lighter Panzanella
        Salad, 117
    Slow-Cooker Tuscan
        Chicken, 161

batch cooking, 17

Beans and legumes. *See also*
    Chickpeas; Lentils
    Artichoke and White
        Bean Salad, 120
    as a freezer staple, 28
    Lime Shrimp with
        Tomato Salsa, 139
    Root Vegetable and
        Bean Soup, 96
    Slow-Cooker Three-
        Bean Chili, 107
    Slow-Cooker White
        Chicken Chili, 162
    Turmeric Wild Rice and
        Black Beans, 97

Beef
    Beef Kebobs with
        Chimichurri Sauce,
        175–176
    Beef-Mushroom
        Meatballs, 170
    Beef Stir-Fry with Asian
        Peanut Sauce, 174
    Beer Brisket Tacos, 179
    Easy Tricolored Pepper
        Steak, 181
    Grilled Asian Steak
        Salad, 114
    Lentil-Beef Meatloaf, 171
    Mediterranean Stuffed
        Peppers, 172–173
    Shawarma Steak, 180
    Skirt Steak with Asian
        Peanut Sauce, 168
    Slow-Cooker Beef Stew, 177
    Slow-Cooker Beer
        Brisket, 178
    Tex-Mex Burgers, 169

Beets
    Rosemary Beet Chips, 202
Bell peppers
    Beef Kebobs with
        Chimichurri Sauce,
        175–176
    Beef Stir-Fry with Asian
        Peanut Sauce, 174
    Chopped Salad with
        Feta and Lentils, 119
    Crudité with Herbed
        Yogurt Dip, 194
    Easy Tricolored Pepper
        Steak, 181
    Eggplant Zucchini
        Provençal, 122
    Indian-Style Sautéed
        Chickpeas, 104
    Lighter Panzanella
        Salad, 117
    Mediterranean Stuffed
        Peppers, 172–173
    Simple Tomato Salsa, 217
    Tex-Mex Burgers, 169
    Thai Chicken Stir-Fry, 154
Berries. See also
        Cranberries, dried
    as a freezer staple, 28
    Blackberry-Lemon
        Overnight Oats, 77
    Fruit Salad with Mint, 198
    Fruit Salsa and Yogurt
        Crêpes, 92–93
    Honey Ricotta with
        Strawberries, 192
    Quinoa Power
        Breakfast Jar, 91
    Strawberry-Chocolate-
        Almond Smoothie Jar, 90
    Wild Blueberry Whole-
        Grain Scones, 82–83
Bisphenol A (BPA), 19, 21
Blue cheese
    Lighter Blue Cheese
        Dressing, 209

Bok choy
    Ginger Soy Tuna Packets
        with Snap Peas and
        Bok Choy, 135–136
Bread crumbs, 141
Broccoli
    Beef Stir-Fry with Asian
        Peanut Sauce, 174
    Citrus Broccoli Slaw, 118
    Thai Chicken Stir-Fry, 154
Brussels sprouts
    Balsamic Brussels
        Sprouts, 128

C

Cabbage
    Carrot-Cabbage Slaw, 121
Cantaloupe
    Fruit Salad with Mint, 198
Capers
    Green Olive Tapenade, 216
    Grilled Halibut with
        Anchovy-Caper
        Dressing, 143
Carrots
    Carrot-Cabbage Slaw, 121
    Citrus Broccoli Slaw, 118
    Crudité with Herbed
        Yogurt Dip, 194
    Grilled Asian Steak
        Salad, 114
    Maple Orange Glazed
        Baby Carrots, 125
    Root Vegetable and
        Bean Soup, 96
    Slow-Cooker Beef Stew, 177
Cashews
    Honey Ricotta with
        Strawberries, 192
    No-Bake Maple
        Cinnamon Bars, 191
Cast iron, 21
Cauliflower
    Cauliflower-Rice Mushroom
        Risotto, 123

Celery
    Crab-Stuffed Flounder, 142
    Crudité with Herbed
        Yogurt Dip, 194
    Root Vegetable and
        Bean Soup, 96
    Slow-Cooker Beef Stew, 177
    Spicy Tuna with
        Edamame, 132
    To-Go Snack Boxes, 200
    Turkey-Walnut Salad with
        Cranberries, 146
Cheddar cheese
    To-Go Snack Boxes, 200
    White Chicken Chili and
        Spinach Quesadillas, 163
Cheese. See also specific
    Beer Brisket Tacos, 179
Cherries, dried
    Homemade Trail Mix, 193
    Tart Cherry–Almond
        Breakfast Cookies, 79–80
Chicken
    Apricot Chicken
        Drumsticks, 157–158
    Barbecue Chicken Pizza, 165
    Hawaiian Chicken
        Skewers, 155–156
    Lemony Chicken
        Breasts, 159
    One-Pot Mediterranean
        Chicken and Quinoa,
        152–153
    Pesto Chicken, 150
    Rosemary Chicken
        Breasts, 160
    Slow-Cooker Barbecue
        Chicken, 164
    Slow-Cooker Tuscan
        Chicken, 161
    Slow-Cooker White
        Chicken Chili, 162
    Thai Chicken Stir-Fry, 154
    Thai Chicken Thighs, 151

White Chicken Chili and
    Spinach Quesadillas, 163
Chickpeas
    Baked Turkey Meatballs,
        148–149
    Chili-Roasted
        Chickpeas, 195
    Farro Tabbouleh, 100
    Indian-Style Sautéed
        Chickpeas, 104
    Mediterranean Stuffed
        Peppers, 172–173
    Slow-Cooker Beef Stew, 177
    Sriracha Hummus, 201
Chile peppers. *See also* Bell
        peppers; Jalapeño
        peppers; Serrano chiles
    Slow-Cooker White
        Chicken Chili, 162
Chives
    Hawaiian Chicken
        Skewers, 155–156
Chocolate. *See also*
        Cocoa powder
    Cacao-Date Oatmeal, 78
    Homemade Trail Mix, 193
    Strawberry-Chocolate-
        Almond Smoothie Jar, 90
Cilantro
    Indian-Style Sautéed
        Chickpeas, 104
    Lentil-Beef Meatloaf, 171
    Simple Tomato Salsa, 217
    Tex-Mex Burgers, 169
Clean eating
    about, 13, 31, 34
    foods to avoid, 16
    foods to enjoy, 13
    foods to minimize, 16
    meal plan #1, 36–39
    meal plan #2, 40–44
    pantry staples, 35
Cocoa powder
    Chocolate Energy Balls, 190

Cinnamon Cocoa
    Popcorn, 197
Peanut Butter Banana
    Energy Cookies, 188
Strawberry-Chocolate-
    Almond Smoothie Jar, 90
Coconut
    Coconut Lime Flounder in
        Parchment Paper, 137
Coconut milk
    Asian Peanut Sauce, 211
    Hawaiian Chicken
        Skewers, 155–156
    Skirt Steak with Asian
        Peanut Sauce, 168
    Thai Marinade, 214
Coconut oil, 15
Condiments. *See also*
        Dressings; Sauces
    Avocado Lime
        Mayonnaise, 215
    Green Olive Tapenade, 216
    Kale Pesto, 206
Containers, 19–21
Cooking en papillote, 135–136
Cook Pro, 21
Corn
    Corn and Tomato
        Couscous, 103
    Mason Jar Cobb
        Salad, 112–113
    Slow-Cooker White
        Chicken Chili, 162
Cottage cheese
    Sweet Potato Protein
        Pancakes, 73
Crab
    Crab-Stuffed Flounder, 142
Cranberries, dried
    Meyer Lemon Cranberry-
        Ricotta Muffins, 87–88
    Turkey-Walnut Salad with
        Cranberries, 146
    No-Bake Maple
        Cinnamon Bars, 191

Cream cheese
    Brooklyn Breakfast, 76
Cucumbers
    Chopped Salad with
        Feta and Lentils, 119
    Farro Tabbouleh, 100
    Grilled Asian Steak
        Salad, 114
    Lighter Panzanella
        Salad, 117
    Mason Jar Cobb
        Salad, 112–113
    Quinoa-Kale Salad Bowl, 116
    To-Go Snack Boxes, 200
Cured meats, 113
Cutting boards, 22

D

Dairy-free
    Apricot Chicken
        Drumsticks, 157–158
    Apricot-Orange Oat
        Bites, 189
    Arugula Salad with
        Salmon, 111
    Asian "Fried" Brown
        Rice, 105
    Asian Peanut Sauce, 211
    Avocado Lime
        Mayonnaise, 215
    Balsamic Brussels
        Sprouts, 128
    Balsamic Onion and
        Mango Quinoa, 99
    Barbecue Chicken Pizza, 165
    Beef Kebobs with
        Chimichurri Sauce,
        175–176
    Beef-Mushroom
        Meatballs, 170
    Beef Stir-Fry with Asian
        Peanut Sauce, 174
    Bulgur-Stuffed
        Tomatoes, 106
    Carrot-Cabbage Slaw, 121

Chili-Roasted
    Chickpeas, 195
Chimichurri Sauce, 212
Chocolate Energy Balls, 190
Cinnamon Cocoa
    Popcorn, 197
Coconut Lime Flounder in
    Parchment Paper, 137
Corn and Tomato
    Couscous, 103
Crab-Stuffed Flounder, 142
Easy Tricolored Pepper
    Steak, 181
Eggplant Zucchini
    Provençal, 122
Farro, Sardines, and
    Greens, 138
Farro Tabbouleh, 100
Fruit Salad with Mint, 198
Ginger Soy Tuna Packets
    with Snap Peas and
    Bok Choy, 135–136
Green Olive Tapenade, 216
Grilled Asian Steak
    Salad, 114
Grilled Halibut with
    Anchovy-Caper
    Dressing, 143
Hawaiian Chicken
    Skewers, 155–156
Herbed Pork Loin, 183
Herbed Vinaigrette, 208
Homemade Granola, 84
Homemade Trail Mix, 193
Indian-Style Sautéed
    Chickpeas, 104
Kale Pesto, 206
Lemony Chicken
    Breasts, 159
Lemony Green Beans
    with Almonds, 124
Lentil-Beef Meatloaf, 171
Lighter Fish Cakes, 140–141
Lime Shrimp with
    Tomato Salsa, 139

Maple Orange Glazed
    Baby Carrots, 125
Mushroom-Kale
    Brown Rice, 101
No-Bake Maple
    Cinnamon Bars, 191
One-Pot Mediterranean
    Chicken and Quinoa,
    152–153
Onion-Parsley Quinoa, 102
Pesto Chicken, 150
Poached Salmon with
    Chimichurri Sauce, 133
Quinoa-Kale Salad Bowl, 116
Quinoa Power
    Breakfast Jar, 91
Roasted Thai Pork
    Tenderloin, 184
Roasted Trout with Green
    Olive Tapenade, 134
Root Vegetable and
    Bean Soup, 96
Rosemary Beet Chips, 202
Rosemary Chicken
    Breasts, 160
Shawarma Steak, 180
Simple Tomato Salsa, 217
Skirt Steak with Asian
    Peanut Sauce, 168
Slow-Cooker Barbecue
    Chicken, 164
Slow-Cooker Barbecue
    Pulled Pork, 185
Slow-Cooker Beef Stew, 177
Slow-Cooker Beer
    Brisket, 178
Slow-Cooker Three-
    Bean Chili, 107
Slow-Cooker Tuscan
    Chicken, 161
Soy-Sesame Dressing, 210
Speedy Tomato Sauce, 213
Sriracha Hummus, 201
Sriracha-Lime Kale
    Chips, 203

Steamed Asparagus with
    Bacon, 126–127
Tex-Mex Burgers, 169
Thai Chicken Stir-Fry, 154
Thai Chicken Thighs, 151
Thai Marinade, 214
Thyme-Roasted
    Almonds, 196
To-Go Snack Boxes, 200
Tuna Niçoise Salad, 115
Turmeric Wild Rice and
    Black Beans, 97
White Balsamic
    Vinaigrette, 207
Dairy products. See
    also specific
    recommended servings, 15
Dates
    Apricot-Orange Oat
        Bites, 189
    Cacao-Date Oatmeal, 78
    Chocolate Energy Balls, 190
    No-Bake Maple
        Cinnamon Bars, 191
    Tropical Green Smoothie, 89
Dill
    Mediterranean Turkey
        Burgers, 147
Dressings
    Herbed Vinaigrette, 208
    Lighter Blue Cheese
        Dressing, 209
    Soy-Sesame Dressing, 210
    White Balsamic
        Vinaigrette, 207

E

Edamame
    Asian "Fried" Brown
        Rice, 105
    Spicy Tuna with
        Edamame, 132
Eggplant
    Eggplant Zucchini
        Provençal, 122

Index | 225

Eggs
  Asian "Fried" Brown
    Rice, 105
  Avo-Egg Scramble Wrap, 70
  Brooklyn Breakfast, 76
  Fruit Salsa and Yogurt
    Crêpes, 92–93
  Mason Jar Cobb
    Salad, 112–113
  Mini Vegetable Quiches, 71
  To-Go Snack Boxes, 200
  Tuna Niçoise Salad, 115
  yolks, 73
Equipment, 21–23

F

Fats and oils, recommended
  servings, 15
Feta cheese
  Avo-Egg Scramble Wrap, 70
  Chopped Salad with
    Feta and Lentils, 119
  Mediterranean Stuffed
    Peppers, 172–173
  Mediterranean Turkey
    Burgers, 147
Fish. See also Salmon; Tuna
  as a freezer staple, 29
  Coconut Lime Flounder in
    Parchment Paper, 137
  Crab-Stuffed Flounder, 142
  Farro, Sardines, and
    Greens, 138
  Grilled Halibut with
    Anchovy-Caper
    Dressing, 143
  Roasted Trout with Green
    Olive Tapenade, 134
Flavanoids, 99
Food and Drug Administration
  (FDA), 19
Food safety, 26–27,
  30–31, 133, 134
Freezing foods. See also
  Thawing foods

basics of, 26–27
herbs, 98
safety chart, 30
staples, 28–29
to avoid, 20
Fruits. See also specific
  recommended servings, 14

G

Ginger
  Asian "Fried" Brown
    Rice, 105
  Ginger Soy Tuna Packets
    with Snap Peas and
    Bok Choy, 135–136
  Hawaiian Chicken
    Skewers, 155–156
  Roasted Thai Pork
    Tenderloin, 184
  Thai Marinade, 214
Gluten-free
  Apricot-Orange Oat
    Bites, 189
  Artichoke and White
    Bean Salad, 120
  Arugula Salad with
    Salmon, 111
  Asian "Fried" Brown
    Rice, 105
  Avocado Lime
    Mayonnaise, 215
  Baked Turkey Meatballs,
    148–149
  Balsamic Brussels
    Sprouts, 128
  Balsamic Onion and
    Mango Quinoa, 99
  Beef Kebobs with
    Chimichurri Sauce,
    175–176
  Blackberry-Lemon
    Overnight Oats, 77
  Cacao-Date Oatmeal, 78
  Carrot-Cabbage Slaw, 121

Cauliflower-Rice Mushroom
  Risotto, 123
Chili-Roasted
  Chickpeas, 195
Chimichurri Sauce, 212
Chocolate Energy Balls, 190
Chopped Salad with
  Feta and Lentils, 119
Cinnamon Cocoa
  Popcorn, 197
Citrus Broccoli Slaw, 118
Coconut Lime Flounder in
  Parchment Paper, 137
Crudité with Herbed
  Yogurt Dip, 194
Easy Tricolored Pepper
  Steak, 181
Eggplant Zucchini
  Provençal, 122
Farro, Sardines, and
  Greens, 138
Fruit Salad with Mint, 198
Green Olive Tapenade, 216
Grilled Halibut with
  Anchovy-Caper
  Dressing, 143
Hawaiian Chicken
  Skewers, 155–156
Herbed Pork Loin, 183
Herbed Vinaigrette, 208
Homemade Granola, 84
Homemade Trail Mix, 193
Honey Ricotta with
  Strawberries, 192
Indian-Style Sautéed
  Chickpeas, 104
Kale Pesto, 206
Lamb Chops with Mint-
  Yogurt Sauce, 182
Lemony Chicken
  Breasts, 159
Lemony Green Beans
  with Almonds, 124
Lighter Blue Cheese
  Dressing, 209

Lighter Creamed Spinach, 129
Lime Shrimp with Tomato Salsa, 139
Maple Orange Glazed Baby Carrots, 125
Mason Jar Cobb Salad, 112–113
Mason Jar Key Lime Parfaits, 199
Mediterranean Stuffed Peppers, 172–173
Mediterranean Turkey Burgers, 147
Mini Vegetable Quiches, 71
Mushroom-Kale Brown Rice, 101
No-Bake Maple Cinnamon Bars, 191
One-Pot Mediterranean Chicken and Quinoa, 152–153
Onion-Parsley Quinoa, 102
Oven-Roasted Tomato Quinoa, 98
Pesto Chicken, 150
Poached Salmon with Chimichurri Sauce, 133
Quinoa-Kale Salad Bowl, 116
Quinoa Power Breakfast Jar, 91
Roasted Root Vegetable Salad with Kale, 110
Roasted Thai Pork Tenderloin, 184
Roasted Trout with Green Olive Tapenade, 134
Rosemary Beet Chips, 202
Rosemary Chicken Breasts, 160
Shawarma Steak, 180
Simple Tomato Salsa, 217
Slow-Cooker Barbecue Chicken, 164

Slow-Cooker Barbecue Pulled Pork, 185
Slow-Cooker Three-Bean Chili, 107
Slow-Cooker Tuscan Chicken, 161
Slow-Cooker White Chicken Chili, 162
Speedy Tomato Sauce, 213
Spicy Tuna with Edamame, 132
Sriracha Hummus, 201
Sriracha-Lime Kale Chips, 203
Strawberry-Chocolate-Almond Smoothie Jar, 90
Sweet Potato Protein Pancakes, 73
Tex-Mex Burgers, 169
Thyme-Roasted Almonds, 196
To-Go Snack Boxes, 200
Tropical Green Smoothie, 89
Tuna Niçoise Salad, 115
Turkey-Walnut Salad with Cranberries, 146
Turmeric Wild Rice and Black Beans, 97
White Balsamic Vinaigrette, 207
Grains. *See also* Oats; Quinoa; Rice
Bulgur-Stuffed Tomatoes, 106
Corn and Tomato Couscous, 103
Farro, Sardines, and Greens, 138
Farro Tabbouleh, 100
Mediterranean Stuffed Peppers, 172–173
recommended servings, 14
Grapes
Fruit Salad with Mint, 198
To-Go Snack Boxes, 200

Greek yogurt
Citrus Broccoli Slaw, 118
Crudité with Herbed Yogurt Dip, 194
Fruit Salsa and Yogurt Crêpes, 92–93
Lamb Chops with Mint-Yogurt Sauce, 182
Lighter Blue Cheese Dressing, 209
Lighter Creamed Spinach, 129
Mason Jar Key Lime Parfaits, 199
Mediterranean Turkey Burgers, 147
Peanut Butter Banana Energy Cookies, 188
Pear-Cinnamon Oat Muffins, 85–86
Spicy Tuna with Edamame, 132
Strawberry-Chocolate-Almond Smoothie Jar, 90
Tart Cherry–Almond Breakfast Cookies, 79–80
Tropical Green Smoothie, 89
Turkey-Walnut Salad with Cranberries, 146
Whole-Grain Pancakes with Spiced Greek Yogurt Sauce, 74–75
Wild Blueberry Whole-Grain Scones, 82–83
Green beans
Lemony Green Beans with Almonds, 124
Tuna Niçoise Salad, 115

H

Herbs, fresh. *See also* specific
freezing, 98
storing, 161
Honey
Apple Walnut Loaf, 81

Hawaiian Chicken
  Skewers, 155–156
Honey Ricotta with
  Strawberries, 192
Quinoa-Kale Salad Bowl, 116
Quinoa Power
  Breakfast Jar, 91
Slow-Cooker Barbecue
  Chicken, 164
Soy-Sesame Dressing, 210

I

Ingredients. *See also*
  Pantry staples
  prepping and storing, 24

J

Jalapeño peppers
  Indian-Style Sautéed
    Chickpeas, 104
  Spicy Tuna with
    Edamame, 132

K

Kale
  Kale Pesto, 206
  Mushroom-Kale
    Brown Rice, 101
  Quinoa-Kale Salad Bowl, 116
  Roasted Root Vegetable
    Salad with Kale, 110
  Sriracha-Lime Kale
    Chips, 203
  Tropical Green Smoothie, 89
Kiwis
  Fruit Salsa and Yogurt
    Crêpes, 92–93
Knives, 23

L

Leafy greens. *See also*
  Kale; Spinach
  Arugula Salad with
    Salmon, 111

Beer Brisket Tacos, 179
Grilled Asian Steak
  Salad, 114
Lighter Panzanella
  Salad, 117
Mason Jar Cobb
  Salad, 112–113
Lemons and lemon juice
  Arugula Salad with
    Salmon, 111
  Blackberry-Lemon
    Overnight Oats, 77
  Bulgur-Stuffed
    Tomatoes, 106
  Carrot-Cabbage Slaw, 121
  Chopped Salad with
    Feta and Lentils, 119
  Citrus Broccoli Slaw, 118
  Corn and Tomato
    Couscous, 103
  Crudité with Herbed
    Yogurt Dip, 194
  Farro Tabbouleh, 100
  Fruit Salsa and Yogurt
    Crêpes, 92–93
  Green Olive Tapenade, 216
  Grilled Halibut with
    Anchovy-Caper
    Dressing, 143
  Herbed Pork Loin, 183
  Indian-Style Sautéed
    Chickpeas, 104
  Kale Pesto, 206
  Lemony Chicken
    Breasts, 159
  Lemony Green Beans
    with Almonds, 124
  Lighter Blue Cheese
    Dressing, 209
  Lighter Fish Cakes, 140–141
  Mason Jar Cobb
    Salad, 112–113
  Mediterranean Stuffed
    Peppers, 172–173

Mediterranean Turkey
  Burgers, 147
Meyer Lemon Cranberry-
  Ricotta Muffins, 87–88
Meyer lemons, 88
Rosemary Chicken
  Breasts, 160
Shawarma Steak, 180
Spicy Tuna with
  Edamame, 132
Sriracha Hummus, 201
Steamed Asparagus with
  Bacon, 126–127
Tuna Niçoise Salad, 115
Turkey-Walnut Salad with
  Cranberries, 146
Lentils
  Chopped Salad with
    Feta and Lentils, 119
  Lentil-Beef Meatloaf, 171
Limes and lime juice
  Asian Peanut Sauce, 211
  Avocado Lime
    Mayonnaise, 215
  Coconut Lime Flounder in
    Parchment Paper, 137
  Hawaiian Chicken
    Skewers, 155–156
  Lime Shrimp with
    Tomato Salsa, 139
  Mason Jar Key Lime
    Parfaits, 199
  Roasted Thai Pork
    Tenderloin, 184
  Simple Tomato Salsa, 217
  Sriracha-Lime Kale
    Chips, 203
  Thai Marinade, 214
Lycopene, 181, 213

M

Mangos
  Balsamic Onion and
    Mango Quinoa, 99
  Tropical Green Smoothie, 89

Maple syrup
- Blackberry-Lemon Overnight Oats, 77
- Herbed Vinaigrette, 208
- Homemade Granola, 84
- Maple Orange Glazed Baby Carrots, 125
- Mason Jar Key Lime Parfaits, 199
- No-Bake Maple Cinnamon Bars, 191
- Sweet Potato Protein Pancakes, 73
- Tart Cherry-Almond Breakfast Cookies, 79–80
- Whole-Grain Pancakes with Spiced Greek Yogurt Sauce, 74–75

Mason jars, 20

Meal planning
- about, 23–24
- for clean eating, 34–44
- for muscle building, 57–67
- for weight loss, 45–56

Meal prepping. *See also* meal planning
- benefits of, 12
- defined, 11
- equipment, 21–23
- food storage, 19–21, 25–27
- healthy principles of, 17–21
- ingredients, 24
- meal prep Sunday, 23–25

Meats. *See also* Beef; Pork
- Lamb Chops with Mint-Yogurt Sauce, 182

Milk. *See also* Almond milk; Coconut milk
- Blackberry-Lemon Overnight Oats, 77
- Cacao-Date Oatmeal, 78
- Fruit Salsa and Yogurt Crêpes, 92–93
- Peanut Butter Banana Energy Cookies, 188
- Slow-Cooker White Chicken Chili, 162
- Whole-Grain Pancakes with Spiced Greek Yogurt Sauce, 74–75
- Wild Blueberry Whole-Grain Scones, 82–83

Mint
- Bulgur-Stuffed Tomatoes, 106
- Fruit Salad with Mint, 198
- Lamb Chops with Mint-Yogurt Sauce, 182

Mozzarella cheese
- Barbecue Chicken Pizza, 165
- Lighter Panzanella Salad, 117
- To-Go Snack Boxes, 200

Muscle building
- about, 31, 57
- meal plan #1, 59–63
- meal plan #2, 64–67
- pantry staples, 58

Mushrooms
- Avo-Egg Scramble Wrap, 70
- Beef Kebobs with Chimichurri Sauce, 175–176
- Beef-Mushroom Meatballs, 170
- Cauliflower-Rice Mushroom Risotto, 123
- Lentil-Beef Meatloaf, 171
- Mini Vegetable Quiches, 71
- Mushroom-Kale Brown Rice, 101
- shopping for, 176
- Slow-Cooker Tuscan Chicken, 161
- Thai Chicken Stir-Fry, 154
- Turmeric Wild Rice and Black Beans, 97

N

National Institutes of Health (NIH), 45
Nitrites, 113
Nut butters. *See* Almond butter; Peanut butter
Nuts and seeds. *See* specific

O

Oats
- Apricot-Orange Oat Bites, 189
- Blackberry-Lemon Overnight Oats, 77
- Cacao-Date Oatmeal, 78
- Chocolate Energy Balls, 190
- Homemade Granola, 84
- Peanut Butter Banana Energy Cookies, 188
- Pear-Cinnamon Oat Muffins, 85–86
- Sweet Potato Protein Pancakes, 73
- Tart Cherry–Almond Breakfast Cookies, 79–80

Oils and fats, recommended servings, 15

Olives
- Green Olive Tapenade, 216
- Lime Shrimp with Tomato Salsa, 139
- One-Pot Mediterranean Chicken and Quinoa, 152–153
- Slow-Cooker Tuscan Chicken, 161

Onions
- Balsamic Onion and Mango Quinoa, 99
- Easy Tricolored Pepper Steak, 181
- Eggplant Zucchini Provençal, 122
- Onion-Parsley Quinoa, 102

Simple Tomato Salsa, 217
Speedy Tomato Sauce, 213
Oranges and orange juice
Apricot-Orange Oat Bites, 189
Citrus Broccoli Slaw, 118
Fruit Salad with Mint, 198
Herbed Vinaigrette, 208
Maple Orange Glazed Baby Carrots, 125
OXO LockTop, 21

P

Paleo
Arugula Salad with Salmon, 111
Avocado Lime Mayonnaise, 215
Balsamic Brussels Sprouts, 128
Beef Kebobs with Chimichurri Sauce, 175–176
Chili-Roasted Chickpeas, 195
Chimichurri Sauce, 212
Eggplant Zucchini Provençal, 122
Green Olive Tapenade, 216
Grilled Asian Steak Salad, 114
Grilled Halibut with Anchovy-Caper Dressing, 143
Hawaiian Chicken Skewers, 155–156
Herbed Pork Loin, 183
Indian-Style Sautéed Chickpeas, 104
Kale Pesto, 206
Lemony Chicken Breasts, 159
Lemony Green Beans with Almonds, 124
Pesto Chicken, 150

Poached Salmon with Chimichurri Sauce, 133
Roasted Trout with Green Olive Tapenade, 134
Rosemary Beet Chips, 202
Rosemary Chicken Breasts, 160
Shawarma Steak, 180
Simple Tomato Salsa, 217
Slow-Cooker Tuscan Chicken, 161
Speedy Tomato Sauce, 213
Sriracha-Lime Kale Chips, 203
Steamed Asparagus with Bacon, 126–127
Thyme-Roasted Almonds, 196
To-Go Snack Boxes, 200
Tuna Niçoise Salad, 115
White Balsamic Vinaigrette, 207
Pantry staples
clean eating meal plans, 35
freezer, 28–29
muscle building meal plans, 58
weight loss meal plans, 46
Parmesan cheese
Artichoke and White Bean Salad, 120
Baked Turkey Meatballs, 148–149
Cauliflower-Rice Mushroom Risotto, 123
Lighter Creamed Spinach, 129
Mini Vegetable Quiches, 71
Oven-Roasted Tomato Quinoa, 98
Roasted Root Vegetable Salad with Kale, 110
Parsley
Artichoke and White Bean Salad, 120

Baked Turkey Meatballs, 148–149
Beef-Mushroom Meatballs, 170
Bulgur-Stuffed Tomatoes, 106
Chimichurri Sauce, 212
Chopped Salad with Feta and Lentils, 119
Corn and Tomato Couscous, 103
Crudité with Herbed Yogurt Dip, 194
Farro Tabbouleh, 100
Green Olive Tapenade, 216
Grilled Halibut with Anchovy-Caper Dressing, 143
Herbed Vinaigrette, 208
Lighter Fish Cakes, 140–141
Mediterranean Stuffed Peppers, 172–173
Onion-Parsley Quinoa, 102
Oven-Roasted Tomato Quinoa, 98
Turkey-Walnut Salad with Cranberries, 146
Parsnips
Roasted Root Vegetable Salad with Kale, 110
Root Vegetable and Bean Soup, 96
Peanut butter
Asian Peanut Sauce, 211
Chocolate Energy Balls, 190
Peanut Butter Banana Energy Cookies, 188
To-Go Snack Boxes, 200
Peanuts
Peanut Butter Banana Energy Cookies, 188
Pears
Pear-Cinnamon Oat Muffins, 85–86
To-Go Snack Boxes, 200

Peas
- Beef Stir-Fry with Asian Peanut Sauce, 174
- Ginger Soy Tuna Packets with Snap Peas and Bok Choy, 135–136
- Slow-Cooker Beef Stew, 177

Phytochemicals, 181

Pineapple
- Hawaiian Chicken Skewers, 155–156
- Quinoa-Kale Salad Bowl, 116
- Tropical Green Smoothie, 89

Pomegranate arils
- Citrus Broccoli Slaw, 118

Pork
- cuts, 183
- Herbed Pork Loin, 183
- purchasing, 184
- Roasted Thai Pork Tenderloin, 184
- Slow-Cooker Barbecue Pulled Pork, 185

Portion control, 12, 22

Potatoes. *See also* Sweet potatoes
- Tuna Niçoise Salad, 115

Poultry. *See* Chicken; Turkey

Processed foods, 13, 16, 34

Proteins, recommended servings, 14

Pyrex, 21

Q

Quinoa
- as a freezer staple, 28
- Balsamic Onion and Mango Quinoa, 99
- Beef Stir-Fry with Asian Peanut Sauce, 174
- One-Pot Mediterranean Chicken and Quinoa, 152–153
- Onion-Parsley Quinoa, 102
- Oven-Roasted Tomato Quinoa, 98
- Quinoa-Kale Salad Bowl, 116
- Quinoa Power Breakfast Jar, 91

R

Recommended servings, 14–15

Refrigerating foods, 26–27, 30

Rice
- Asian "Fried" Brown Rice, 105
- Mushroom-Kale Brown Rice, 101
- Thai Chicken Stir-Fry, 154
- Turmeric Wild Rice and Black Beans, 97

Ricotta cheese
- Baked Turkey Meatballs, 148–149
- Honey Ricotta with Strawberries, 192
- Meyer Lemon Cranberry-Ricotta Muffins, 87–88

Rosemary
- Balsamic Onion and Mango Quinoa, 99
- Herbed Vinaigrette, 208
- Mini Vegetable Quiches, 71
- Roasted Trout with Green Olive Tapenade, 134
- Rosemary Chicken Breasts, 160

S

Salmon
- Arugula Salad with Salmon, 111
- Brooklyn Breakfast, 76
- Poached Salmon with Chimichurri Sauce, 133

Saponin, 91

Sauces
- Asian Peanut Sauce, 211
- Chimichurri Sauce, 212
- Thai Marinade, 214

Scallions
- Asian "Fried" Brown Rice, 105
- Balsamic Onion and Mango Quinoa, 99
- Bulgur-Stuffed Tomatoes, 106
- Corn and Tomato Couscous, 103
- Ginger Soy Tuna Packets with Snap Peas and Bok Choy, 135–136
- Lighter Fish Cakes, 140–141
- Onion-Parsley Quinoa, 102
- Spicy Tuna with Edamame, 132

Serrano chiles
- Baked Turkey Meatballs, 148–149

Sesame seeds
- Apricot Chicken Drumsticks, 157–158

Shallots
- Asian Peanut Sauce, 211
- Chimichurri Sauce, 212
- Lemony Green Beans with Almonds, 124

Shopping lists, 19

Shrimp
- Lime Shrimp with Tomato Salsa, 139

Slow cookers, 22

Sour cream
- White Chicken Chili and Spinach Quesadillas, 163

Spinach
- Farro, Sardines, and Greens, 138
- Lighter Creamed Spinach, 129
- Mediterranean Turkey Burgers, 147

Index | 231

Mini Vegetable Quiches, 71
Root Vegetable and Bean Soup, 96
Tropical Green Smoothie, 89
Tuna Niçoise Salad, 115
White Chicken Chili and Spinach Quesadillas, 163

Squash. *See also* Zucchini
Lighter Fish Cakes, 140–141

Storing foods, 19–21, 25–27

Sunflower seeds
Chocolate Energy Balls, 190
Citrus Broccoli Slaw, 118
Homemade Trail Mix, 193

Sweeteners, 16. *See also* Honey; Maple syrup

Sweet potatoes
Roasted Root Vegetable Salad with Kale, 110
Slow-Cooker Beef Stew, 177
Sweet Potato Protein Pancakes, 73

T

Thawing foods, 27, 31

Thermometers, 134

Tomatoes
Artichoke and White Bean Salad, 120
Arugula Salad with Salmon, 111
Avo-Egg Scramble Wrap, 70
Beef Kebobs with Chimichurri Sauce, 175–176
Brooklyn Breakfast, 76
Bulgur-Stuffed Tomatoes, 106
Cauliflower-Rice Mushroom Risotto, 123
Chopped Salad with Feta and Lentils, 119
Corn and Tomato Couscous, 103
Crudité with Herbed Yogurt Dip, 194
Eggplant Zucchini Provençal, 122
Farro Tabbouleh, 100
Grilled Asian Steak Salad, 114
Hawaiian Chicken Skewers, 155–156
Lighter Panzanella Salad, 117
Mason Jar Cobb Salad, 112–113
Mediterranean Stuffed Peppers, 172–173
One-Pot Mediterranean Chicken and Quinoa, 152–153
Oven-Roasted Tomato Quinoa, 98
Quinoa-Kale Salad Bowl, 116
Simple Tomato Salsa, 217
Slow-Cooker Three-Bean Chili, 107
Slow-Cooker Tuscan Chicken, 161
Speedy Tomato Sauce, 213
Tuna Niçoise Salad, 115

Tuna
Ginger Soy Tuna Packets with Snap Peas and Bok Choy, 135–136
Spicy Tuna with Edamame, 132
Tuna Niçoise Salad, 115

Turkey
Baked Turkey Meatballs, 148–149
Mediterranean Turkey Burgers, 147
Turkey-Walnut Salad with Cranberries, 146

Turkey bacon
Mason Jar Cobb Salad, 112–113
Steamed Asparagus with Bacon, 126–127

Turnips
Root Vegetable and Bean Soup, 96

U

USDA Dietary Guidelines for Americans (2015), 14–15, 18

V

Vegan
Apricot-Orange Oat Bites, 189
Asian Peanut Sauce, 211
Avocado Lime Mayonnaise, 215
Balsamic Brussels Sprouts, 128
Balsamic Onion and Mango Quinoa, 99
Bulgur-Stuffed Tomatoes, 106
Carrot-Cabbage Slaw, 121
Chili-Roasted Chickpeas, 195
Chimichurri Sauce, 212
Chocolate Energy Balls, 190
Cinnamon Cocoa Popcorn, 197
Corn and Tomato Couscous, 103
Eggplant Zucchini Provençal, 122
Farro Tabbouleh, 100
Fruit Salad with Mint, 198
Green Olive Tapenade, 216
Herbed Vinaigrette, 208
Homemade Granola, 84
Homemade Trail Mix, 193
Indian-Style Sautéed Chickpeas, 104
Kale Pesto, 206

Lemony Green Beans with Almonds, 124
Maple Orange Glazed Baby Carrots, 125
Mushroom-Kale Brown Rice, 101
No-Bake Maple Cinnamon Bars, 191
Onion-Parsley Quinoa, 102
Root Vegetable and Bean Soup, 96
Rosemary Beet Chips, 202
Simple Tomato Salsa, 217
Slow-Cooker Three-Bean Chili, 107
Speedy Tomato Sauce, 213
Sriracha Hummus, 201
Sriracha-Lime Kale Chips, 203
Thai Marinade, 214
Thyme-Roasted Almonds, 196
Turmeric Wild Rice and Black Beans, 97
White Balsamic Vinaigrette, 207
Vegetables. *See also* specific
  and meal prepping, 18
  as a freezer staple, 29
  recommended servings, 15
Vegetarian
  Apple Walnut Loaf, 81
  Artichoke and White Bean Salad, 120
  Asian "Fried" Brown Rice, 105
  Avo-Egg Scramble Wrap, 70
  Blackberry-Lemon Overnight Oats, 77
  Cacao-Date Oatmeal, 78
  Cauliflower-Rice Mushroom Risotto, 123
  Chopped Salad with Feta and Lentils, 119
  Citrus Broccoli Slaw, 118

Crudité with Herbed Yogurt Dip, 194
Fruit Salsa and Yogurt Crêpes, 92–93
Honey Ricotta with Strawberries, 192
Lighter Blue Cheese Dressing, 209
Lighter Creamed Spinach, 129
Lighter Panzanella Salad, 117
Mason Jar Key Lime Parfaits, 199
Meyer Lemon Cranberry-Ricotta Muffins, 87–88
Mini Vegetable Quiches, 71
Oven-Roasted Tomato Quinoa, 98
Peanut Butter Banana Energy Cookies, 188
Pear-Cinnamon Oat Muffins, 85–86
Quinoa-Kale Salad Bowl, 116
Quinoa Power Breakfast Jar, 91
Roasted Root Vegetable Salad with Kale, 110
Soy-Sesame Dressing, 210
Strawberry-Chocolate-Almond Smoothie Jar, 90
Sweet Potato Protein Pancakes, 73
Tart Cherry–Almond Breakfast Cookies, 79–80
To-Go Snack Boxes, 200
Tropical Green Smoothie, 89
Whole-Grain Pancakes with Spiced Greek Yogurt Sauce, 74–75
Wild Blueberry Whole-Grain Scones, 82–83

W

Walnuts
  Apple Walnut Loaf, 81
  Arugula Salad with Salmon, 111
  Mushroom-Kale Brown Rice, 101
  Quinoa-Kale Salad Bowl, 116
  Turkey-Walnut Salad with Cranberries, 146
Weight loss
  about, 31, 45
  meal plan #1, 47–51
  meal plan #2, 52–56
  pantry staples, 46
White, Dana Angelo, 193

Y

Yogurt. *See* Greek yogurt

Z

Zucchini
  Carrot-Cabbage Slaw, 121
  Eggplant Zucchini Provençal, 122

Acknowledgments

There are many people I want to thank for making this cookbook possible. Thank you to my parents for always supporting me. My dad, Henry Oksman, always taught me that anything is possible if you put your mind to it. I have found this advice true every time I achieve a milestone in my life. My mother, Zipporah Oksman, showed me what it is to truly be passionate for food and cooking. The bond we share in becoming registered dietitians (RDs) together will be cherished forever.

A huge thank you to my literary agents Sally Ekus and Jaimee Constantine from The Lisa Ekus Group for your support and kindness throughout this process. Many thanks to my editors Andrew Yackira and Elizabeth Castoria from Callisto Media for bringing this project to life and being an absolute pleasure to work with.

I am overwhelmed and flattered by the dedication and hard work that each member of my team put into this cookbook. Thank you Gail Watson, MS; Gena Seraita, RD, CDN; Mary Opfer, MS, RD, CDN; Alicia Slusarek, RDN; and Tyler Brown, RYT 200. A big thank you to my assistant Cristiane Camargo for helping me with anything and everything that needed to get done.

Lastly, thank you to my wonderful, amazing children, Schoen, Ellena, and Micah, for your honest taste-testing feedback and for bearing with me through my insane schedule. You are the forces that drive everything I do, and you have taught me the true meaning of life and love.